Contents

Acknowledgments   vii

1 Introduction   1

2 Aging in the Labor Market   5

3 The Structure of the Youth Labor Market   15

4 The Evolution of the Youth Labor Market   51

5 Unemployment and Labor Market Structure   75

6 Racial Differentials in Youth Unemployment   98

7 Conclusion   150

Appendix: The Interviews   161

Notes   171

Index   189

Getting Started
The Youth Labor Market

Paul Osterman

The MIT Press
Cambridge, Massachusetts, and London, England

© 1980 by
The Massachusetts Institute of Technology

All rights reserved. No part of this book may be reproduced in any form or by any means, electronic or mechanical, including photocopying, recording, or by any information storage and retrieval system, without permission in writing from the publisher.

This book was set in Baskerville by A & B Typesetters, Concord, New Hampshire and printed and bound in the United States of America.

Library of Congress Cataloging in Publication Data

Osterman, Paul.
  Getting started.

  Bibliography: p.
  Includes index.
  1. Youth—Employment—United States. I. Title.
HD6273.087   331.3'412'0973   80-18932
ISBN 0-262-15021-2

Acknowledgments

My greatest debt is to Michael Piore. Michael read numerous drafts of this book and suggested many improvements. More important, he always took the book seriously and his continuing interest and enthusiasm helped maintain my energy and, when I needed it, reassured me that the effort was worthwhile.

Several people read the entire book and made many helpful comments. For this I thank Peter Doeringer, Harry Katz, Mike Miller, and Robert Schrank. Peter also provided a comfortable and fruitful research environment.

Numerous friends and colleagues read portions of the book and helped improve it. I am grateful to Richard Freeman, Marcia Freedman, Bennett Harrison, Ned Hill, Edward Kalachek, Robert Lerman, Francis Fox Piven, Mary-Kay Plantes, Marty Rein, Ralph Smith, Bill Spring, Lester Thurow, Michael Useem, Bruce Vermeulen, Sam Bass Warner, and Finis Welch.

I enjoyed the help of quite a few research assistants. I am particularly grateful to Peggy Gallagher, Bob Garrett, Fran Hagopian, Mary Hyde, Tom Moore, John Ost, Russell Williams, and Rand Wilson.

Financial support for various portions of the book was provided by the Department of Labor, the National Commission on Employment Policy, the National Council on Employment Policy, The National Committee for Full Employment, the Ford Foundation, and the Boston University Regional Institute For Employment Policy.

Susan Eckstein, my wife, was both an intellectual companion and a good friend throughout. I am sure that she is as happy as I am that the book is finished.

Getting Started

1 Introduction

In June 1978 electrical and plumbing unions in New York City opened their apprenticeship programs to 550 youth. The weekend before the applications were to be distributed, over a thousand youths camped out for two nights on sidewalks outside the union halls, hoping to be hired.[1] That same summer the city received 110,000 applications for 55,000 federally funded summer jobs.[2] The national unemployment rate for white teenagers in June 1978 was 11.6 percent, for blacks an astounding 37.1 percent.[3]

Events like these and the colder but more informative national data have pushed youth labor market problems to the forefront of national social policy concerns. Youth unemployment has made the cover of national magazines, become a favorite topic of television documentaries, and evoked a plethora of policy suggestions. And the concern is not limited to the United States. A recent OECD report spoke of a youth employment "crisis" growing out of "long-term imbalances" affecting most of the developed world.[4] Part of the response to this crisis in the United States was a $1.5 billion youth employment bill. This piece of legislation, one of President Jimmy Carter's first successful legislative initiatives, proved so popular that in 1980 the President's only major domestic initiative was an expansion of the program.

The youth legislation was called the Youth Employment and Demonstration Projects Act. The key word is "demonstration," for both Congress and analysts were forced to admit that over a decade of experience with training programs for youth had yielded little understanding of youth unemployment or what to do about it. Although the remarkably high black youth unemployment rates seem almost inexplicable, there was no dearth of explanations (shifts of employment outside central cities, the minimum wage, the baby boom, poor education, inappropriate work ethic, discrimination, all of the above, none of the above), but there was no agreement either. In fact, it is possible to argue that youth unemployment in general (though not black youth unemployment) is not much of a problem. Although teenage unemployment rates are high, they seem not to portend later trouble because unemployment rates fall sharply with age. Furthermore, many unemployed teenagers are only looking for part-time work, roughly a third are unemployed due to entry or reentry into the labor market, a transitional stage, and half are in school. Given the disagreement about the causes of youth unemployment, its consequences, and its importance, the lack of agreement about policy is not surprising.

An important portion of this book is devoted to understanding the causes and consequences of youth unemployment; however, my concern is more general. Youth unemployment is only the most visible consequence of the operation of the youth labor market. I shall attempt to analyze this labor market from a variety of perspectives and by employing a variety of data, including historical material on the changing economic functions of youth, results of interviews with youths and their employers, and national surveys containing more conventional economic data.

Social scientists have long made youth a central topic in disparate literatures, and in many of these areas the youth labor market plays an important role. Sociologists concerned with status attainment and the transmission of well-being from one generation to the next have developed complex statistical models relating ability, education, and family characteristics to aspirations and occupational attainment.[5] These models do not explain how the operation of the labor market determines the estimated parameters of the equations, but the labor market plays a central, albeit background role. Sociologists concerned with the revolt of youth against their elders and the emergence of a youth culture have pointed to the secular trend of more years in school and delayed entrance into the labor market.[6] They assert that this trend has led to a growing estrangement between youth and adults. Entrance into the full-time labor market has been delayed, but well over half of 16-19-year-old students hold jobs during the school year.[7] Whatever the merits of the analysis, the youth labor market is important, if only for understanding why labor market entrance has been delayed.

Economists, too, are concerned with the youth labor market. The dominant model in labor economics is human capital theory, which argues that individual choices about schooling, training, and jobs should be modeled as investment decisions. In deciding how much and what kind of schooling to pursue, the individual weighs the stream of present and future costs and benefits of education; in choosing jobs, the individual chooses between differing packages of wages and training provided by different firms. Clearly the operation of the youth labor market shapes the character of the alternatives and access to them.

Other economists have sought to shift the emphasis from individual choice to the ways that economic structures limit and shape observed outcomes. From this perspective schools become mechanisms for sorting and channeling people into jobs largely on the basis of social class. Whatever the merits of this perspective as a generalization, the mechanics depend on how people find jobs, hiring requirements, and the array of opportunities. These issues again bring us back to the youth labor market.

Understanding the youth labor market is thus important not merely because of its immediate relevance to unemployment but because of its general interest to issues in understanding social systems. Every year over 1.5 million young people leave high school and do not enter college. All but two hundred thousand enter the labor market.[8] How they find, choose, are selected for, and are sorted into jobs has a major impact on the shape of the society.

Unemployment is thus one theme of this book. More general problems of occupational and status attainment are another. A third issue is race. In my view racial differences in occupational outcomes remain the nation's most important social problem. Despite the efforts of the past several decades, enormous racial differences in income and unemployment persist from generation to generation, largely as the result of the operation of the labor market.

Some Questions

Despite the strenuous efforts devoted to youth employment problems in the past several decades, we still lack a clear understanding of how the youth labor market works and why we seem to be experiencing a youth employment crisis. Some important questions remain unanswered.

• How does the youth labor market work? When a youth leaves school and enters the job market what happens? How does he or she find a job? What kind of job is it? How important are school guidance and placement services? Is the first job held especially consequential, or does the youth move through a number of different jobs? What are the youth's attitudes toward work, how do these change over time, and how do they affect labor market behavior? In short, how are people and jobs actually matched, and what are the implications of this process?

• Why are youth unemployment rates so high, and why have they seemingly worsened? How much youth unemployment is due to cyclical factors, how much is due to structural shifts in the economy, and how much is due simply to the nature of youth? What, if anything, has changed recently to account for either the existence or the perception of a crisis?

• Why is unemployment so much higher among black youth than whites? Even more puzzling, why the growing unemployment differential when there is some evidence that in other respects the labor market's treatment of black youths has improved modestly in recent years?

• Does unemployment have long-term consequences for the youth, or is it a passing stage requiring at most short-term income maintenance programs? Do the consequences of youth unemployment vary with the group?

•Do the current employment problems of youth represent a new crisis? Has there been a structural change in the youth labor market in recent years? How can we best understand the modern youth labor market from a historical perspective?

The next two chapters describe the normal operation of the youth labor market. Chapter 2 simply shows how labor market outcomes change as young people age, while chapter 3 sets forth a theory of the structure of the youth labor market and explains how that structure leads to the outcomes described in chapter 2. Chapter 4 tries to understand when and how the modern structure emerged. Chapters 5 and 6 both address unemployment. Chapter 5 explains how high youth unemployment emerges from the structure of the youth labor market and also examines the possible long-term consequences of youth unemployment. Chapter 6 takes up racial differentials in youth unemployment. The final chapter pulls the book's arguments together and draws some lessons for policy.

2 Aging in the Labor Market

The young person entering the labor market after leaving high school holds jobs and attitudes quite different from those that he will later hold. Very little is known about what happens during this transition from marginal participant in the labor market to adult worker, or how the transformation occurs. The literature speaks of the "school-to-work transition," but this phrase is misleading because it implies that the transition occurs shortly after leaving school and that leaving is the key event. Rather, the transition from marginal status occurs over a number of years and is associated with both psychological maturation and the pattern of demand for youth labor.

In this chapter I will describe this process with national survey data and in the next chapter I will employ interviews with youth and firms. It should be understood at the outset that the material in both chapters is constrained in two important ways. First, it is limited to youth who have not attended college. Unemployment rates are highest among this group and it is to this group that most public policy is directed. These young people cannot rely on educational credentials to open doors, and less is known about how they make their way in the labor market.

Second, this material is limited to men. The labor markets for men and women, despite some progress in equal employment opportunity, continue to differ considerably, both because of occupational discrimination and segregation and because of differences in life-cycle attachment to the labor force. Although many of the concepts developed here also apply to women, the structure and the behavior of the labor market for women are sufficiently different that a separate analysis is necessary. Chapters 4-7 deal with both men and women.

The survey data in this chapter are drawn from the National Longitudinal Survey of Young Men (NLS).[1] The survey interviewed young men aged 14-24 in 1966 and annually thereafter through 1971. In this chapter I use a subset of data on young men who in 1971 had a high school degree or less and who were interviewed every year between 1966 and 1971.

Because these data are longitudinal, they make it possible to observe the evolution of labor market outcomes for the young men. The data also contain considerable information on their personal characteristics, an advantage for studying individual unemployment experiences. However, the survey contains little information on the characteristics of the firms employing these men, and this omission is one of the reasons for conducting the interviews reported in the next chapter.

The Basic Patterns

Table 2.1 summarizes the basic pattern of labor market adjustments for blacks and whites with respect to wages and unemployment. Two facts stand out: as youths age, their situations improve, and while this holds true for both races, blacks lag consistently behind whites.

Wage rates increase sharply with age, partly because of promotions and improved skill levels, and partly because of the movement from low-wage to high-wage firms. Modern labor economists have devoted much energy to understanding this pattern of wage increases. The common explanation, which goes under the rubric of human capital theory, is that wage increases result from the early investment by youth in education and on-the-job training. This investment certainly plays a role, but so does the simple process of aging and maturation.

The improvement in the employment experience of youth also reflects the effect of aging. As youths age, they quit jobs less frequently and get jobs in firms with lower layoff rates. In addition, they obviously also gain seniority and hence are less likely to be laid off. Thus the improvement in their employment experience is due to maturation, to penetration into different sectors of the labor market, and to seniority.

Young workers move in a systematic way among firms. They tend not to simply stay in one firm from the period of entry onward. Some evidence of this is provided in tables 2.2 and 2.3 which report the industrial distribution by age and by race of the youths in the sample. Early employment for both races is concentrated in three industries—construction, manufacturing, and wholesale and retail trade. These three industries account for 79 percent of white and 65 percent of black employment among 17-year-olds. With aging, however, come some important shifts in the industrial distribution. Construction and manufacturing remain important, but wholesale and retail diminish for both groups. Since these trade jobs are typically casual and unskilled work, the movement out of these categories represents a shift toward more stable employment. For blacks there is an additional, and comparable, movement out of agriculture into other fields.

These figures are, of course, highly aggregate and hence may mask important distinctions. For example, the manufacturing category may include General Motors and a local candy factory. The employment structures of these two firms are likely to be quite different, and lumping them into a single category may obscure as much as it reveals. I shall attempt to deal with this in the next chapter, which employs considerably more tex-

Table 2.1
Wages and Weeks of Unemployment by Age

Age	Hourly Wage Whites	Hourly Wage Blacks	Annual Weeks of Unemployment Whites	Annual Weeks of Unemployment Blacks
17	$2.18	$1.83	1.32	3.89
18	2.23	2.01	2.66	4.79
19	2.46	2.19	3.27	4.50
20	2.68	2.16	2.53	4.14
21	2.82	2.13	2.05	3.09
22	2.86	2.18	1.79	3.14
23	2.95	2.16	1.12	2.30
24	3.17	2.34	1.12	2.76
25	3.41	2.44	0.85	2.10
26	3.60	2.67	1.03	1.53
27	3.84	2.71	1.20	2.93
28	3.99	2.97	1.57	3.03
29	4.38	3.03	1.43	1.36

Note: These data are for out-of-school youth and are from the National Longitudinal Survey of Young Men (NLS). The figures are averages for all youths during the sample period (1966–1971). Thus, for example, the data in the cells for 24-year-olds are the average of 1966 wage rates of 24-year-olds in 1966, the 1967 wage rates for 23-year-olds in 1966, the 1968 wage rates for 22-year-olds in 1966, the 1969 wage rates for 21-year-olds in 1966, the 1970 wage rates for 20-year-olds in 1966, and the 1971 wage rate for 19-year-olds in 1966 (assuming that during the specified year the youth was out of school). Cells with an N less than 30 are not reported. The NLS weights employed here and throughout the book are adjusted to maintain the original sample size of whites and blacks. Thus, in effect, the data are weighted for all factors other than race. Of course, elsewhere when separate racial breakdowns are not presented, the NLS weights are used without adjustment. The figures for annual weeks of unemployment may seem low given the high youth unemployment rates. This is because unemployment reported in the NLS is considerably below that reported in the census, for reasons that are not well understood.

Table 2.2
Industry Distribution of Whites by Age (in percentages)

Industry	17	19	21	23	25	27	29
Agriculture	7.7	6.5	6.1	4.5	4.6	4.9	9.3
Mining	0.7	1.1	1.0	1.0	1.6	1.7	2.7
Construction	9.7	12.4	14.4	11.9	12.4	12.6	14.2
Durable manufacturing	22.9	25.2	30.8	27.0	25.9	25.5	21.5
Nondurable manufacturing	13.8	10.8	11.8	12.5	13.6	12.5	15.7
Transportation	1.7	5.8	5.7	10.1	9.4	11.0	6.3
Wholesale and retail	32.8	25.0	16.4	19.6	19.3	16.7	15.7
Finance	2.5	1.7	1.7	2.4	1.7	2.0	1.8
Business services	2.6	3.9	4.5	3.8	3.9	3.1	4.4
Personal services	2.5	1.7	1.2	1.2	0.9	0.9	0.0
Entertainment	0.7	0.5	0.1	0.2	0.2	0.3	0.0
Professional services	1.4	3.3	4.6	2.2	1.9	2.0	3.2
Public administration	0.9	2.1	1.5	3.7	4.6	6.8	5.3

tured data, but for now we must be content with the observation that aging brings with it shifts in the industrial distribution.

Stability

The basic data show that as young people age their wages increase, unemployment falls, and the kinds of jobs they hold change. Aging thus appears to bring important changes. The next step is to get a better grip on this process by examining career patterns.

There is considerable evidence that as youth age their behavior changes. Quit rates, for example, fall with age. The National Longitudinal Survey records for 1969-1970 every job held and the causes of all job changes. For out-of-school 18-year-olds the annual quit rate was 0.65. Thus more than one of every two youths quit a job during a year. By the age of 27 the rate was more than halved, to 0.29.

These rates imply that at the younger ages there is considerable movement while older youth tend to settle down. Quits are an imperfect measure of career patterns, however, since a person may leave one firm to take a bet-

Table 2.3
Industry Distribution of Blacks by Age (in percentages)

Industry	19	21	23	25	27
Agriculture	9.3	8.8	8.3	7.7	9.0
Mining	0.4	—	—	0.4	0.6
Construction	12.5	8.7	12.0	11.2	14.5
Durable manufacturing	24.2	24.8	25.3	27.5	24.8
Nondurable manufacturing	10.7	13.6	15.8	19.2	17.3
Transportation	6.8	8.4	10.7	6.1	6.7
Wholesale and retail	20.4	19.7	12.8	15.3	18.3
Finance	1.1	1.5	3.8	1.3	0.7
Business services	2.0	2.7	1.0	2.3	0.0
Personal services	1.8	1.7	2.1	0.8	0.6
Entertainment	2.0	1.2	0.9	1.5	0.6
Professional services	6.9	4.6	4.0	4.2	4.8
Public Administration	1.8	4.1	3.3	2.7	2.2

Note: See note to table 2.2

ter job with stronger prospects elsewhere. What is needed is a measure of job movement that incorporates a test for career building in the sense of an articulated and consistent pattern of job holding. To this end I have constructed an index of year-to-year job stability. The NLS provides for each survey year the industry of the job held at the time of the survey and whether the job was in the same firm as the previous year. The measure of stability is defined as follows:

$$\text{STABILITY} = \begin{cases} 1 & \text{if the job held in year } t \text{ is in the same firm as the job held in year } t\text{-1 or if it is the same three-digit industry.}[3] \\ 0 & \text{otherwise.} \end{cases}$$

Obviously if the job is in the same firm, a stable career pattern is presumed. An individual can also build a career by moving among firms. This is captured by categorizing as stable individuals who change jobs but remain in the same industry.

This measure is obviously imperfect in a number of respects. It does not distinguish between voluntary and involuntary changes. Furthermore, there is no guarantee that a job change even within a three-digit industry is career building, nor does staying in the same firm necessarily lead to a career. Nevertheless, the measure goes some way toward capturing the notion of stable career pattern, and the movement of the measure is consistent with expectations.

Table 2.4 shows that the relationship of the stability measure to age for blacks and whites is strong and unambiguous. At the ages of 16, 17, and 18, less than half of the sample for both races are stable; by the ages of 26–28 nearly 80 percent are stable. The stability measure does not capture wage rates, a key indicator of labor market success. Still, the pattern strongly suggests that we should be most concerned not with the unstable teenagers but rather with the 20 percent of youth in their late twenties who still have not settled down.

The age pattern for whites indicates that the key transition period occurs at about age 20, when there is a major jump in the fraction of youth who are stable. The pattern is somewhat different for blacks. Their rates are consistently below those of whites until age 26. Furthermore, there is no sharp jump as there is for whites.

The pattern of the stability variable clearly suggests that as young men

Table 2.4
Stability Rates for Out-of-School Youth

Age	Whites	Blacks
16	.342	—
17	.419	.311
18	.484	.345
19	.582	.437
20	.707	.555
21	.700	.585
22	.701	.652
23	.755	.610
24	.770	.742
25	.777	.723
26	.802	.741
27	.768	.795
28	.803	.857

Note: See note to table 2.1.

age, they are more likely to begin a career pattern. Furthermore, at least for whites there is a key transition age. However, the majority of the youth are unstable at early ages, and even in the later twenties roughly 20 percent are still unstable. If unstable behavior is simply a stage, then instability at an early age should have few long-term consequences. By the same reasoning, youth who are unstable at later ages should have more difficulty later than their stable brethren. The next two tables examine these hypotheses.

Tables 2.5 and 2.6 show the proportion of youth who are stable in years $t+1$, $t+2$, $t+3$, and $t+4$, given that they were unstable in year t. For example, of the whites who were unstable at age 21, 0.448 were stable at age 22, 0.712 at 23, and 0.594 at 24. These tables strongly confirm the notion that early instability has few lasting consequences while unstability at later ages can be serious. For example, whites who were unstable at ages 17–19 are only slightly less likely than the group as a whole to be stable (see table 2.4). Expressed in the notation of probability,

$$P(\text{stable}_{t+1} | \text{unstable}_t) \approx P(\text{stable}_{t+1})$$

for younger ages.

On the other hand, instability in a later year portends serious consequences. For example, 0.499 of the unstable 24-year-old whites were stable at age 25, compared with an overall average of 25-year-olds of 0.777. The pattern for blacks is the same. Once again, the transition occurs at about age 20.

Table 2.5
The Impact of Prior Instability on Later Stability, Whites

Unstable at Age	Probability of Being Stable at			
	$t+1$	$t+2$	$t+3$	$t+4$
17	.336	.515	.690	.673
18	.426	.578	.579	.623
19	.590	.290	.479	.673
20	.506	.576	.596	.797
21	.448	.712	.594	
22	.523	.666	.678	
23	.510	.655	.640	
24	.499	.632		
25	.550	.699	.766	
26	.457			

Note: See note to table 2.1. Cells with N less than 30 are left blank.

Table 2.6
The Impact of Prior Instability on Later Stability, Blacks

Unstable at Age	Probability of Being Stable at			
	$t+1$	$t+2$	$t+3$	$t+4$
17	.313	.408	.590	.718
18	.422	.567	.545	.758
19	.352	.570	.528	.495
20	.394	.398	.517	.628
21	.481	.459	.567	
22	.304	.487		
23	.402	.592	.662	
24	.529	.648		
25	.517	.617		

Note: See note to table 2.1. Cells with N less than 30 are left blank.

The other side of this analysis is what happens year in $t+1$ to those who were stable in year t. The data in tables 2.7 and 2.8 show a clear pattern: early stability is very likely to be maintained. That is,

$$P(\text{stable}_{t+1} \mid \text{stable}_t) > P(\text{stable}_{t+1}).$$

This is true for both races, although blacks have generally lower probabilities of being stable.

In short, most young people under 20 are likely to be unstable, but after 20 stability becomes the dominant pattern. Instability at early ages does not imply special difficulties later, although those who fail to make the transition at 20 are more likely to experience later difficulty. Once stable behavior occurs, it is likely to be maintained regardless of the age (although this likelihood increases with age).

Industrial Mobility

Parallel to the analysis of stability is the relationship between the first job after school and later jobs. If, as the stability analysis implies, early experience bears a weak relationship to later experience, then much industrial mobility should be observed. Table 2.9 shows the probability that a job held in 1971 is in the same industry as the first job after high school.[4] The results are ordered by the number of years elapsed since leaving school and are presented for three-digit and one-digit industry classifications.

The more recent the departure from school, the more likely that the two

Table 2.7
The Impact of Prior Stability on Later Stability, Out-of-School Whites

Stable at Age	Probability of Being Stable at			
	t+1	t+2	t+3	t+4
17	.621	.771		
18	.755	.841	.819	
19	.809	.762	.762	.777
20	.766	.705	.783	.805
21	.747	.738	.815	.763
22	.838	.803	.837	.737
23	.831	.828	.783	.805
24	.851	.841	.781	.853
25	.863	.764	.820	
26	.813	.834		

Note: See note to table 2.1. Cells with N less than 30 are left blank.

Table 2.8
The Impact of Prior Stability on Later Stability, Out-of-School Blacks

Stable at Age	Probability of Being Stable at			
	t+1	t+2	t+3	t+4
17	.589			
18	.596	.654		
19	.705	.649	.784	
20	.681	.759	.632	.730
21	.744	.714	.801	.693
22	.823	.805	.863	
23	.898	.855	.780	
24	.796	.778	.804	.865
25	.833	.871	.852	
26	.932	.902		

Note: See note to table 2.1. Cells with N less than 30 are left blank.

Table 2.9
Industrial Mobility (Probability that 1971 Industry Is the Same as the Industry of the First Job Held after School)

Year Left School	Three-Digit Industry		One-Digit Industry	
	Whites	Blacks	Whites	Blacks
Prior to 1966	.186	.185	.289	.276
1966 or 1967	.170	.201	.305	.291
1968 or 1969	.196	.323	.440	.395
1970 or 1971	.327	.323	.475	.434

industries are the same. Greater aggregation (one-digit industries) also increases the chances that the two industries match. However, the strongest implication is the very weak overall relationship between current and first-job industries. The odds that the 1971 industry is the same as the first job never reach 0.5 and are generally much less. Once again, early experience has a very uncertain impact on later outcomes.

3 The Structure of the Youth Labor Market

The statistical patterns discerned from the data in the previous chapter are, of course, highly simplified versions of reality. Because of the data's lack of institutional detail, I was not able to characterize the firms in which young people of different ages work nor could I describe their behavior. The purpose of this chapter is to get behind the statistical patterns and provide a more detailed description of the process. The statistical patterns now become the phenomena to be explained.

The Interviews

In order to obtain a better sense of the youth labor market, I interviewed youths, firms, and other important actors in the youth labor market. The interviews were conducted in two stages. Twenty-seven interviews held with young men found in arbitrary locations—at work, at the unemployment office, and on the street—were intended simply to provide a preliminary sense of important patterns. In the spring and summer of 1977 I then conducted 112 more formal interviews in two Boston communities, East Boston and Roxbury, with nonstudent men who were between the ages of 16 and 26 and had completed 12 or fewer years of education. Names were chosen randomly from the city census of 1976. Roxbury was chosen because it is Boston's largest and most important black community, East Boston because research and conversations with people knowledgeable about Boston led me to believe that it is representative of white working-class communities. A copy of the questionnaire and a more detailed discussion of the sampling procedure appear in the appendix.

I also conducted interviews with 35 firms in Boston and in Worcester, Massachusetts. Worcester was included because prior contacts with the local Chamber of Commerce provided entree and cooperation. These firms represented a wide variety of industries.[1] In all firms I interviewed the person responsible for hiring new entrants, and in many cases I also interviewed other personnel officers and supervisors. The interviews were open ended, although I always sought information on hiring criteria and rules of thumb used in hiring, on recruitment patterns and practices, on training and promotion procedures, on turnover patterns, and on wages.

Finally, I also conducted over 50 interviews with school officials, manpower program staff, youth workers, and others with an active interest and knowledge of the youth labor market. These interviews were all open ended and were intended to elicit the respondent's experience with and ideas about the youth labor market.

The Behavior of Youth

In the first several years after leaving school young people are frequently in what might be termed a *moratorium* period, a period in which adventure seeking, sex, and peer group activities are all more important than work. Some years later comes *settling down,* a stage characterized by a very different set of attitudes about work. This movement from moratorium to settling down is largely responsible for the stability patterns observed in chapter 2.

A similar progression has been observed elsewhere in the attitudes of young people toward work. In their 1937 study of occupational mobility in California, Davidson and Anderson characterized the first period after school as the "floundering period."[2] A few years later Hollingshead observed that "the typical worker passes through a two-phase cycle in his adjustment to the work world. The first normally lasts from a year to a year and a half after he leaves school. The average boy holds five jobs in this phase. . . . this phase of the work cycle is a period of adjustment to the demands of the job, of accumulation of some experience, and of learning how to get and keep a job. . . . Once the experience and age requirements are met, a youth generally enters the second phase of his work career. This phase is marked by better performance on the job, higher pay, and a steady job by local standards."[3]

Perhaps the best way to understand this process is to describe the work histories of representative youths in the sample who have passed through the entire process.

Jim is 22. He left high school after tenth grade in 1972 and held a series of unskilled jobs. For the first year he was a shipper, a job he got by walking in off the street. He quit and worked in a chemical company for two months, a job he got through his wife's uncle. He then worked as general help in a paperbox company where his father works, quit that job after four months, got a truck-driving job through an ad in a newspaper, was laid off. For three months he worked at odd jobs and then took the first formal job he was offered, a laborer in a shipyard. He found this job through a friend. A year and a half later he quit to go to work as a machine operator for a large electronics firm, a job he got through his brother-in-law who is employed there. He has been working at this job for over a year and plans to stay. He says that when he left high school all he wanted was jobs "to put money in my pocket," but that now he has "a sense of responsibility."

Mark, 25, left school in 1968 after the twelfth grade. He wanted to do construction work, although he saw it not as permanent but as something to do until something better came along. A friend who worked in a construction company helped him get a job, and he worked as a laborer for eight months, until he was laid off. He was unemployed for six months and said he mostly loafed. He said that he looked an average of eight hours a week but could recall only one place where he applied for work. Finally, his girl friend's brother got him a job in the telephone company, and he has been there for the past seven years.

Mario, 25, was born in Sicily and has lived in East Boston since he was 11. He left school after the twelfth grade in 1969. For nine months he neither worked nor looked for work. His first job, which he held for two months until being laid off, was as a trucker's helper. He got the job by walking in off the street. He got his next job, as a rigger in a steel mill, the same way, and he remained on it until he was laid off seven months later. He was unemployed for two months, and this time he seriously looked for work, searching fifteen hours a week. He finally found a job repairing refrigerators, a job he held for five years until he quit to take a similar job in another firm. He found both jobs by walking in off the street. He says that after high school he was "lost" for a year or two but then started looking for a trade.

These three young men are representative of the sample. Their stories capture the importance of families and friendship networks in finding jobs, the progression from casual to more serious work environments, and the general absence of career patterns in the sense of continuity of occupation or skill, all issues I will take up later.

It is difficult to give precise definitions of stages that unambiguously categorize a youth's behavior into one stage or the other. Observed behavior is partly a manifestation of a state of mind, and it can be difficult to infer the state of mind from behavior. In addition, the same state of mind can lead to very different behavior. Nonetheless, the notion of stages does seem to capture an important aspect of the problem.[4]

Many youths in the moratorium period explicitly indicate that they are interested only in short-term jobs to get money for traveling, buying a car, or recreation. The point is not that they are not planning for a career — virtually none of the men in the sample consciously chose a line of work. Rather a long-term, stable job is not very important to them. Unemployed moratorium youth largely "hang out"; they participate in sports, go to the beach, drink, and travel. Those who are working tend to say that they would be in no hurry to find another job if they found themselves out of work.

Youth workers are well aware of the nature of this moratorium behavior. Most manpower program staff with whom I spoke regard 17- and 18-year-old out-of-school youths as unreliable and are reluctant to expend resources on what seem to be very uncertain investments.

The settling-down stage is characterized by the understanding that a steady job is important and desirable. As one youth said, "When I left school I wasn't interested in the kind of work I did. Now I'm getting older and have to look out for myself." A young welder for Amtrak said, "After high school I didn't know what I wanted to do. I just looked for any job. Now I would like to start my own business, probably involving welding. What's changed is that I need the money. When I got out of school if I had $20 or $30 I was flying." Young people settle down for a variety of reasons. Often it's simply to look out for themselves, to plan for the future. In other instances marriage and children are the precipitating factors. In yet other cases peer pressures seem to play a role because as friends settle down the pressure builds to follow suit in order to maintain a comparable lifestyle.

Settling-down behavior is characterized by steadier commitment to a job and to the labor force. There is less quitting, and average job tenure increases. When unemployed, young men in the settling-down period search more intensively for a job and show much less tendency to drop out of the labor force.

These stages have several implications for interpreting labor market outcomes. Unemployment clearly has different meanings for different groups. For many in the moratorium stage unemployment is the result of the unstable behavior characteristic of this stage.[5] Furthermore, the welfare interpretation of unemployment varies with the stage. Unemployment is a greater hardship for a 24-year-old trying to raise a family than it is for a 17-year-old living at home who would rather be on the beach.

This pattern is the dominant one, but it is not universal. Two important exceptions are those who settle down easily and those who fail to settle. In the East Boston sample 15 youths settled down without passing through the moratorium stage. A typology of jobs is developed later but it is worth noting here that these early settlers do not seem to have notably better jobs than others in the sample. For example, 4 hold stock jobs in large retail stores, and 1 is a handyman for a small contractor. Another possibility is that these youths are unusually mature, but this was not evident in the interviews. Two characteristics do stand out. Three of the youths were born in Italy; they represent 60 percent of the youths born there. Eight of the remaining 12 youths got their jobs directly through a parent or a sibling who worked in the firm. The percentage of jobs found through immediate family is higher for this group than for the entire sample. It seems likely that young people who find jobs through family are less likely to quit or to be fired. The presence of immediate family serves as a behavioral control.

This, of course, is a reason that many firms prefer to recruit through family networks.

The other significant deviation from the standard pattern is failure to settle. Nine of the youths over the age of 20 in the sample fall into this category. Failure to settle can be due to continued moratorium behavior or to lack of opportunity. Two of the cases seem to be of the former variety. A 21-year-old youth with a ninth-grade education spent time in the Army but went AWOL, was heavily involved with drugs, held dishwashing and landscaping jobs, and has been out of work for over a year. During this latter period he has traveled and turned down several jobs. This young man is clearly not ready or willing to settle down.

The other case is more ambiguous. The young man was 21 and had graduated from high school. He worked as a security guard, an usher at baseball games, as a mail clerk in an insurance company, and in a sausage-making factory. He quit all of these jobs. At the time of the interview he had just started work as a delivery boy in a bakery owned by his father. Although this youth seemed committed to working, he did not seem committed to staying in one job. However, all the job changes may simply have been preparatory to settling into the family business; indeed, his comments indicate that he planned to stay in the bakery.

In the other seven cases the problem seems to be lack of opportunity. This "identification problem" — the difficulty of disentangling personal readiness, which is what the stages are about, and opportunity, which is a question of demand, is a persistent difficulty in the analysis. One of the young men had just left the army and was unemployed while awaiting the results of Civil Service Tests. Another held a series of casual jobs but was on the waiting list for the job he had long wanted, a toll collector on the turnpike. Another is a trained auto mechanic and held a series of jobs in that field but could not find work. Yet another held a series of jobs driving trucks and delivery vehicles but was getting married and trying to find a steadier job. In each of these cases it seems that the desire to settle exists, or is emerging, and what is lacking is opportunity.

The great number and variety of jobs that these youths, and indeed all the youths in the sample, have held indicates that there seems to be no lack of jobs. Rather the problem, where there is one, is more the nature of the jobs: low pay, boring work, no future, and so forth. Very few youths said they could not find work, but there were frequent complaints about the kind of work available.

Jobs

The behavioral patterns of young men obviously form only half of the picture of the youth labor market; the other half is the nature of the jobs. In their early years in the labor market youths generally work in firms that provide unskilled and casual work. These jobs, which some economists characterize as secondary jobs, are typically held in the moratorium period. Settling down frequently occurs in firms offering jobs that involve greater skill, better long-term prospects for advancement, and greater job security. These jobs can be characterized as primary labor market jobs.

The changing industrial and occupational distribution of youths as they age is apparent from the following table, a list of the first jobs held after high school and the current job of youths over 20 in the East Boston sample. Although the pattern is not uniform, three conclusions can be drawn. First, there is considerable mobility. Very few youths hold jobs in the same firm in which they started. Second, there is generally little relationship between the two jobs in terms of task. Third, and most important for this discussion, the first jobs are clearly of a lower level than the later jobs. The occupational title seems less advanced, the work is less skilled, and the firm is more likely to be retail and service oriented.

First Job	Current Job
construction laborer	repairman, telephone company
quality control, electronics firm	same
general help, department store	proofreader, securities firm
clerk, candy store	machine operator, paint company
various odd jobs	medical worker, city hospital
laborer, gum factory	laborer, cleaning company
guard, security company	guard, security company
stockboy, shoe company	laborer, gum factory
tire changer, tire company	draftsman, computer firm
cleaner, hotel	cleaner, cleaning company
sandblaster, shipyard	janitor, realty company
laborer, construction company	mechanic, auto dealer
laborer, steel mill	salesman, computer firm
machinist, bellows company	same
cook, sandwich shop	deleader, city hospital

The Structure of the Youth Labor Market

busboy, hotel
production worker, electronics firm
machine operator, box company

trucker's helper, motel
dye maker, bookbinding company
stockboy, department store
trainee, CETA
laborer, produce market
tire changer, tire company
dishwasher, restaurant
clerk, hospital
clerk, restaurant
bouncer, nightclub
warehouseman, photo company
odd jobs

baker's helper, bakery
clerk, grocery store
sandblaster, shipyard
laborer, chemical firm
parts manager, auto company
general help, car wash
general help, auto rental
claims adjuster, insurance
cleaner, cleaning company
help, department store
clerk, insurance company
laborer, carpet company
forklift driver, airport
laborer, construction firm
attendant, gas station
busboy, racetrack
cleaner, cleaning company

repairman, auto body firm
production worker, computer firm
warehouse worker, picture frame company
refrigerator engineer, hotel
same

machine operator, tool firm
auto salesman, car dealer
carpenter, door company
clerk, supermarket
laborer, landscaping firm
supply clerk, federal government
same
manager, car rental firm
welder, Amtrak
production worker, clothing factory
warehouseman, department store
same
laborer, steel company
machinist, photo company
same
general help, parking lot
clerk, machine tool firm
same
delivery, bakery
same
same
truck driver, airport
guard, bank
supervisor, insurance company
driver, bank
clerk, carpet company
machinist, machine parts company

The observation that youths start off in a narrow sector of the labor market is not new. For example, Hugh Folk wrote:

The average youth enters the labor market initially as a part-time or summer job seeker. He is not available for "career" jobs, rather he seeks a "youth" job. The distinction is not precise, only useful. Youth jobs do not necessarily lead to career jobs, but are open to young workers. They include babysitting, farm labor, sales clerks in a variety of food stores, and the like.[6]

This observation is essentially correct, but it is limited. First, youths typically work in these jobs not simply in school or during the summer but also during the first several years after leaving school. In addition, the range of jobs is broader than babysitting, farm labor, and retail sales, and the jobs are more closely linked to the regular economy. For example, unskilled factory jobs fall into the category of first jobs. Finally, the term *youth job* is not quite appropriate. The jobs held by young people during this period are also held by older workers, particularly older women, and in urban areas by adult blacks and Spanish-speaking people. There is no youth segment of the labor market.

It is most useful to think of these jobs in terms of primary and secondary jobs, terms that grow out of dual labor market theory.[7] Secondary jobs can be defined either descriptively or in the context of a broad theory about the nature and operation of the labor market. In descriptive terms secondary jobs can best be understood by contrasting them with primary jobs. Piore has made the distinction in these terms:

The primary market offers jobs which possess several of the following traits: high wages, good working conditions, employment stability and job security, equity and due process in the administration of work rules, and chances for advancement. The secondary market has jobs which, relative to those in the primary sector, are decidedly less attractive. They tend to involve low wages, poor working conditions, considerable variability in employment, harsh and often arbitrary discipline, little opportunity to advance.[8]

Primary jobs thus tend to have strong internal labor markets and offer opportunities for training and for stable employment. They are the jobs into which most young men settle. By contrast, secondary jobs require few skills and offer few opportunities for skill acquisition. Since workers make few investments in acquiring specific skills in secondary jobs and firms make few investments in workers, there is little incentive on either side to encourage job stability. In a sense, from workers' viewpoints all secondary jobs are alike, since there is little basis for choosing among them.

Proponents of duel or segmented labor market theory offer several competing explanations for the differentiation between secondary and primary jobs. Some theorists argue that divergent technological development in different sectors, growing out of differences in the stability, predictability, and extent of product demand, accounts for the existence of stable employment and strong internal labor markets in the primary sector and for their absence in the secondary sector.[9] Other theorists argue that the development of the two sectors resulted from attempts by capitalists to develop and employ technology and labor market structure to divide the working class against itself.[10] It is difficult to choose between these theories since many of the events are collinear and because the choice seems to rest ultimately on assumptions about the dynamics of technological change and the relationship of such change to labor market institutions. It is not necessary for my argument to make such a choice, since I am merely arguing that young people at a certain stage of their careers tend to work in secondary jobs.

In the course of the debate about the theory two different arguments have become confused. Dual labor market theory originally developed from studies of low-income labor markets. Early proponents of the theory argued that low-income workers, particularly urban minority groups, tended to become trapped in secondary jobs because primary employers preferred not to hire secondary workers. Thus the debate about dual labor market theory became a debate about intragenerational mobility. This seems to miss the point. The central theoretical issue of dual labor market theory is whether there exist segments of the labor market that operate according to different behavioral rules with respect to issues such as wage setting, labor recruitment, and training and advancement. The answer to this question in turn has implications for the dynamics of labor markets and for structural problems in the economy. Such a segmentation could exist in the presence of mobility between the segments. In fact for most young men such mobility is common. It thus seems important to distinguish mobility from behavioral differences between segments.[11]

Many, and probably most, youths spend their initial years after school in secondary jobs. It is difficult to be exact about this proposition since the literature contains considerable disagreement about identifying primary and secondary jobs in large data sets. The previous list of jobs is certainly suggestive and a more precise classification will be provided. In addition, other studies using national data sets have found that substantial numbers of youths start in secondary jobs.[12]

Moratorium youths work in secondary firms because these firms find youth to be a satisfactory source of labor while primary firms do not. The unstable behavior of youths in moratorium makes them a risky investment for firms that put resources into training. Secondary firms do not have this problem since they usually provide little training. Nor are they overly concerned if their employees do not stay very long on the job. These firms are interested primarily in an assured supply of low-wage, unskilled labor, and they prefer to employ individuals, or groups, who are passive and unlikely, for example, to unionize in the face of unstable employment. Youths fit these requirements well. They are plentiful and thus provide an elastic source of labor. They view their employment as temporary and are thus unlikely to be "troublesome" employees. In fact, youths provide such a satisfactory source of labor that some secondary firms organize their production schedules to recruit them. For example, one candy factory I visited, which employs large numbers of Spanish-speaking adults, also runs a special after-school production shift in order to employ youth. Large retail establishments also organized work shifts to attract youth.

These secondary jobs meet the requirements of young people in the moratorium period. The jobs are casual and unskilled. Little penalty is attached to unstable behavior, since all jobs are similar and none lead to careers. The jobs provide spending money with very little responsibility or long-term commitment.

The interviews suggest that there are three major types of secondary employment—large firms, "mom and pop" stores, and "under the table work." The major examples of large secondary firms are security firms, grocery stores, cleaning companies, and a gum products company. All of these firms are large, employing well over one hundred workers each. They all paid the minimum wage or very close to it and hired youths for unskilled jobs. The youths who worked in these jobs reported either that the job required only common sense or that it took one week or less to learn the job. These firms also hired more frequently than other firms through walk-ins, applicants who came in and asked for work. This is indicative of the unimportance of stable work behavior to the firms. These firms were known to have casual low-paid jobs; many unemployed youths indicated that they could always find a job in one of these firms. A remarkably high percentage of youths in the sample (29 percent) at one time or another, usually in the first two years after school, worked in these firms, but a considerably smaller fraction of youths older than 20 worked in them. These firms provided standby secondary labor jobs for youths in the community.

Examples of small family operations are bakers, small construction contractors, newsstands, unskilled and some skilled jobs at gas stations and auto service operations, and restaurant help. These firms are small, located in the neighborhood, and family owned. Like the larger employers, they also provide low-paid casual unskilled work without a future, but their atmosphere is quite different from that of the large secondary employers. Although many of the youths who worked in these jobs characterized the work as boring, there was very little of the bitterness about personal relationships, supervision, and working conditions that occurred repeatedly in the descriptions of large secondary employers. The conditions in the small firms, as might be expected, are much more paternalistic and relaxed. Finally, these jobs are virtually always found through personal contacts. Because the firms are small and family run, the few available jobs go to relatives and friends. Except for the occasional son destined to take over the business, most youths soon leave these moratorium jobs in search of better-paying work with a possiblity of advancement.

The third category of jobs, described as "under the table" and "off the books" work, consisted of jobs that are not reported to tax, unemployment insurance, and welfare authorities. Youths who characterized themselves as unemployed often indicated that they received some income from occasional jobs such as painting houses, repairing cars, or construction. Except for the "off the books" aspect, these jobs are similar in structure to the second category; they are neighborhood based and found almost exclusively through family and friends. However, they are very unstable since they are one-time opportunities. Casual criminal activity, which several youths in the sample hinted at, also fall in this category.

Primary Firms

For young men who are successful the end of moratorium comes with the acquisition of a job in a primary firm, a firm that is large, stable, and likely to provide long-term jobs, security, and reasonable opportunities for promotion and advancement. These firms are typically large enterprises with well-articulated internal labor markets.[13] Jobs in these firms are generally high-paid, and the firms provide a strong measure of job security since, whether or not the firm is unionized, seniority is respected and layoffs occur in the reverse order of seniority. Most of these firms also have reasonably extensive benefit packages. It is for these reasons that I term finding a job in a primary firm "successful" settling down.[14]

The hiring practices of these primary firms are probably the most important determinant of the structure and operation of the youth labor market.

These firms provide the best-paid, most sought-after jobs, and their decisions about whom and when to hire determine the availability of labor to the other kinds of firms and also strongly influence the job-holding and search patterns of young workers.

These firms generally prefer not to hire young men just out of high school who are engaged in moratorium behavior. Obviously this preference is modified by business conditions, and as we shall see patterns of settling vary with the business cycle. However, on average, the firms prefer to hire youths who have already had some experience in the labor market.

A person who is hired by a primary firm (and passes a probationary period, if there is one) is likely to stay with the firm for a long time. Because the firm invests in training and because the individual has also invested time and resources, both parties have an incentive to maintain a stable employment relationship. Internal labor markets promote this stability and the worker moves up through the internal labor market as he acquires more skills and as openings become available. It is expensive and disruptive for a firm to train an individual (either formally or through on-the-job training), promote that person to an important place in the production process, and then have him leave.

Because of the importance of stability, the key issue in understanding the hiring process is how firms judge who will and who will not become a stable worker. This concern is often more important to the firm than prior skills or relevant experience. Essentially, the firms seek to evaluate an individual's reliability and maturity.[15] The other important factor is the applicant's ability to learn future jobs, not necessarily the job they are being hired for, since that job is simply the first rung on the bottom of the internal ladder.[16]

These considerations explain why a rather nebulous attribute of job applicants, their attitude, was cited consistently by firms as the most important consideration in the hiring decision. This term seems to encompass several attributes: a neat appearance and respectful manner during the interview, a clear interest in the proferred work, willingness to learn the job, and a general alertness. Virtually every firm interviewed cited "attitude" as the main criterion in hiring.[17]

Because firms have to judge the potential stability of the applicant and their ability to mesh well with the work group, it is not surprising that attitude is such an important criterion. In effect, attitude is a proxy for maturity and is a way of screening out moratorium-stage applicants and those who, for other reasons, are judged unlikely to be stable and reliable. Proper attitude is likely to be related to age, and its importance implies that moratorium-stage workers are less likely to be hired by primary fi_. inference is supported by the findings of other studies of industr... ..i.ing practices.

Managements generally have a definite conception of the type of worker they prefer to hire from among their applicants. That is particularly true of well established firms with a sizeable investment in plant and equipment. Such firms would, for the most part, prefer to hire men twenty-five to thirty years of age, who are married and ready to settle down, after they have, so to speak, sowed their industrial wild oats in other plants.[18]

Similarly, Malm found in his study of hiring in San Francisco that smaller firms, construction firms, and firms hiring large numbers of clerical workers tended to hire younger workers, while large manufacturing firms with skilled blue-collar jobs preferred to hire older workers.[19]

The reluctance of primary firms to hire young workers forces youth into the secondary sector where their natural tendencies toward unstable behavior are reinforced. Thus it is the hiring pattern of primary firms that is the central structural characteristic of the youth labor market rather than, as is frequently argued in the popular literature, the youngsters' lack of entry level skills.

Most of the firms whom I interviewed did not place much emphasis on hiring youths who already knew how to do the job. These firms shared the views of an employer interviewed by Lester: "We would rather hire a young man with no moulding experience and train him ourselves, than to hire a man with moulding experience from another firm and have to break him of acquired habits and really retrain him."[20]

There are two explanations for this attitude. First, much production has firm-specific technology. Two firms may produce the same product with machinery that looks identical. However, the layout of the machines, the organization of the steps, and myriad details make the process quite different for the workers. Thus the advantage of previous experience is diminished. In addition, firms with internal labor markets generally cannot hire from the outside into skilled jobs. Rather they hire people for unskilled entry positions and train and promote from within. This greatly reduces the advantage of previous skills.

Since skills are thus not of central importance to most firms, inadequate experience cannot explain the inability of young people to find jobs. Most youths in the sample did not already know how to do their primary jobs. At the same time, firms do not generally consider previous skills a disadvantage, as the preceding quotation implies; on balance, it probably helps.

Although previous job-related experience is not as important as attitude or "trainability," some firms do look for relevant previous experience. A history of stable work in a related firm shows maturity and interest in the field. Thus previous experience is another proxy for maturity and stability. Relevant work experience in a similar job helps the firm acquire and evaluate references. In addition, some skills are industry-specific general skills. For example, in the machine tool industry being able to read a blueprint might be an industry-specific general skill. Since firms do not want to teach these skills if they can avoid it, larger firms try to shift the costs of this training to the school system and to other firms by giving preference to applicants with some previous work experience and by supporting vocational programs in the public schools.

The extent of the preference for skills depends on the importance of the skill and the local industrial structure. A firm in an industry with a number of similar firms and subcontractors in the area can more easily insist on previous experience than can a more isolated operation. Firms that are isolated in this sense may still seek to identify other industries that require similar skills; a number of firms that I talked to identified different industries that had similar job patterns and hence provided helpful training.

Many of the manufacturing firms I interviewed were active in supporting public school vocational education programs. At the minimum, they stayed in touch with the schools and instructors, and in some instances provided equipment and initiated new programs, even though they rarely hired people directly out of high school.[21] These firms want the schools to teach general skills, and they hope that young workers will sharpen their skills in other firms before coming to work in the larger firms. Thus the firms that require previous experience require industry-specific general skills. They do not expect the new hire to have the skills necessary to step into a high-level production job.

The behavior of these primary firms toward the vocational schools raises an interesting question. Although they support vocational programs, firms rarely hire people directly from vocational schools, and a growing body of evidence suggests that graduates of vocational high schools do no better than graduates of general high school programs, either in terms of wages or in terms of jobs placement.[22] Why then do firms support vocational programs? Many firms seem to do so in order to enlarge their general labor pool. A number of firms that I spoke with felt that good young workers were going into other fields. Firms complained that construction, for example, is more attractive to young workers despite its lower expected annual earnings because it offers more flexible hours (new workers did not have to work on the night shift), greater variety, more opportunity for conviviality on the job, and so forth. Industrial employers seem to support vocational programs in order to encourage high school students to apply later to these firms. By providing some equipment and advice to the schools and by appearing at career days, the firms are making a modest investment in their future labor pool. The firms' interest in vocational programs is thus less a concern for skill training (which most observers would agree the schools cannot adequately provide) than an attempt to orient young workers toward these firms.

This point implies that many firms do not take their labor pool to be exogenous but rather attempt, with varying degrees of seriousness and of effectiveness, to influence their supply. A more extreme example in Worcester is the "More Machinists for Massachusetts" campaign, which seeks to encourage high school students to become machine tool workers. This effort is well funded and seems to be vigorously supported by local machine tool firms. Obviously the campaign is not an attempt to turn out skilled machinists, since it takes years of experience to learn the trade, but an effort to enlarge the pool of applicants for training and to drive down wages.[23]

Classifying the Jobs

The interviews in East Boston and Roxbury provided some quantitative information on the characteristics of the jobs held by the youths. In fact, a special effort was made to elicit information on the firms because most national surveys tend to focus heavily on individual characteristics and ignore the nature of jobs.

A first step toward quantifying the relationship of primary and secondary jobs to labor market adjustment is to classify the jobs held by the youth as primary or secondary. The criterion for making this decision is not self-evident. Pay level at first seems to be the obvious candidate, since the dual labor market argument implies that primary jobs pay well while secondary jobs do not. This criterion may be useful for adults but is clearly inadequate for young people. An entry position in a firm that provides training and a future may pay no better than some casual labor jobs, yet one would not want to classify the former as secondary. Employment stability is another criterion, yet some skilled jobs, such as those in construction, are frequently unstable. The best criterion seems to be the presence or absence of career lines or internal labor markets on the job. Firms with progression paths, either in the craft or industrial sense, provide the sheltered employment that is intrinsic to the notion of dual labor markets. Employment stability and good wages are generally derivative of industrial-type internal labor markets because the firm-specific training becomes embodied in the worker. Craft labor markets provide less stability, but the skills involved typically provide the worker with a stable career.

The interviews included two questions that sought to measure the presence of internal labor markets. The youths were asked what jobs they could expect to be doing after two, three, and five years in the firm. They were also asked about promotions they had already received. The answers to these questions made it possible, as I had hoped they would, to discern the presence or absence of career lines in the firms. Both questions, however, reveal the worker's perception of the firm and his possibilities rather than an objective appraisal. An overly optimistic or pessimistic worker may convey a misleading impression. This danger is partly mitigated by the objectivity of the past promotion question, but there remains the problem of an unusually good or bad worker or a worker who has not been on the job long enough to receive a promotion. The ideal solution, of course, would be to interview each of the firms which employed the youths but that was beyond our resources.

Even with a criterion and a measurement device it proved difficult to classify all jobs. Most were straightforward: large firms such as Polaroid and Gillette and skilled crafts jobs were primary, while small retail firms, casual labor, and the security and cleaning firms were secondary. However, some difficult decisions remained. Insurance companies in the Boston area typically hire large numbers of high school graduates for short-term, clerical positions that pay poorly, and the youths in them have no future with the company. The companies treat these employees as a secondary work force, hiring them with the expectation that they will not stay long and will remain in the most menial jobs. (This description is based on interviews with young people and with companies.) However, these companies also have well-developed personnel systems, do not engage in the personalistic and arbitrary treatment of employees that is characteristic of many secondary firms, and do have a bidding system that enables some of the youths to move into lower white-collar jobs. Thus for most youths these are secondary employers but for a few they are primary. The company itself operates two tracks. The majority of these jobs were classified as secondary, but for a few of the youths who seemed to be on the career track the jobs were classified as primary.

Another difficulty arose in the case of medium-sized retail stores, such as clothing stores, in which a few youths were employed as salesmen. These firms in some sense were like craft jobs—there was no career ladder, the employment seemed unstable—but skills were required, the youths saw the jobs as a career, and it seemed possible to move from one store to another. On balance these seemed to be primary jobs.

The classifications of the firms, although arbitrary, is generally accurate and meaningful, and the results tend to confirm the classification. Nonetheless, it is sobering to apply a fairly straightforward theory to the enormous and complex array of jobs in the economy.

Table 3.1 provides data on how the jobs were found, and table 3.2 contains a variety of characteristics of primary and secondary jobs in the sample. However, before turning to these tables it is worth noting that in this sample 39.0 percent of the jobs held by youth less than 20 years old were classified as primary while for youth 20 and older the figure was 60.4 percent. Thus these data confirm the earlier discussion about the relationship of aging and firm type.

As table 3.1 shows, most jobs are found through personal contacts. Secondary jobs are much more likely to be found through friends, while primary jobs are more frequently found through parents and relatives. Similarly, table 3.2 shows that secondary jobs average over two friends per job and 0.33 parents or relatives, while the magnitudes are reversed for primary jobs, with fewer friends and more parents and relatives. (The question that elicited these data requested the number of parents, relatives, and friends who were already on the job when the youth arrived.)

The heavy emphasis on friends in secondary jobs confirms that these jobs tend to be either neighborhood small retail or contracting operations,

Table 3.1
Job-Finding Techniques

Source of Referral	Primary Jobs	Secondary Job
Friends	19.7%	36.2%
Parents/relatives	30.8	19.7
Ads/walk-in	24.6	19.7
Institutions[a]	12.3	16.4
Other	12.9	8.0
N	79	85

a. Institutions include private employment agencies, schools, the employment service, and manpower programs.

Table 3.2
Characteristics of Primary and Secondary Jobs

Characteristic	Primary	Secondary
Mean number of friends	0.75	2.05
Mean number of parents/relatives	0.63	0.33
Mean number of promotions	0.55	0.11
Mean months to learn the job	4.3	0.8
Already knew job	41.6%	58.4%
Learned new skills	60.6%	39.4%
Continue to learn	58.7%	31.5%
N	79	85

Note: In this table and in the previous one the unit of observation is jobs. Thus for all primary jobs in the sample the mean number of friends per job was 0.75.

which are likely to have youths from the same area who know each other, or larger firms such as the security and cleaning companies, which have developed reputations for hiring youths and are hence likely already to employ the youth's friends.

Jobs in primary firms are more often found through relatives, and there are more relatives than friends already on the job. This is to be expected, given that these firms are interested primarily in stability. While friends are likely to be poor sources of referrals in this respect, relatives and parents are likely to be good since they can exercise some control.

More striking is that the sample averages well over one previous acquaintance (friend, relative, or parent) per job. The Boston area is very large, yet these youths do not move in an impersonal labor market. Nor is this simply a neighborhood phenomenon; 67 percent of the jobs in the sample were outside the neighborhood. Clearly youths enter this large dense labor market through channels already traveled by people they know.

The remaining characteristics in table 3.2 all refer to the acquisition of jobs skills. The pattern of these variables confirms that a large fraction of holders of secondary jobs already knew the job (implying less complex tasks), fewer learned new skills when they took the job, learning the skills in secondary jobs took less time, and fewer holders of secondary jobs continued to learn new skills.

The main lines of the argument are thus confirmed by these learning patterns. However, the pattern is more complex than the simple version of the theory implies. Secondary jobs can permit on-the-job learning. It is possible to improve even the most straightforward jobs, and it is even possible to learn new skills. Of perhaps greater interest is the pattern in primary jobs. Almost 60 percent of the youths in primary jobs did not already know how to do the work when they were hired. This would not be surprising except for the recurrent arguments in the popular literature, and some professional writing, that a major source of youth unemployment is that entry skill requirements are rising and that the schools are failing to produce competent workers. In fact, most people do not know how to do the job when they are hired; the firm trains them. Hence preexisting skills are not central. These data bear out this earlier observation.

It may be instructive to close this section with an observation made in *Elmtown's Youth:*

The economy has had need for the labor of adolescents; and just as important, the vast majority of the adolescents need the jobs the economy provides to earn the money they have to have in order to participate in the commercialized forms of recreation available to them. . . . There are no union pressures to keep them out of any small business or off the farm. . . . The demand of the retail trades and services for part-time employees synchronizes well with the high school student's needs and desires.[24]

It is remarkable how much the American economy has changed in the 35 years since *Elmtown's Youth* was written, and how little the employment experiences of young workers has changed.

The Impact of the Business Cycle

This picture of the operation of the youth labor market is conventional in its structure if not its content. The supply side is modeled in terms of the stages of youth behavior, and the demand side is described in terms of the kinds of firms, secondary and primary, and their differing preferences for youth labor. However, an important ambiguity remains. In the labor market supply and demand interact; neither force operates in isolation. Because of this, and because the description of young workers' behavior is very qualitative, it is possible that the picture is considerably simpler than painted.

In particular, the stages may well have no life of their own, and youth behavior may be completely demand or opportunity determined. When primary firms refuse to hire them, young people are forced into secondary jobs, which by their nature lead to minimal work commitment and unstable behavior. When the demand for products of primary firms is sufficiently strong to force firms to hire the young, then the moratorium stage is skipped and youth quickly become stable primary workers.

My strategy for examining this possibility is to study differences in outcomes over the business cycle in order to determine whether the pattern of stages and labor demand varies over the cycle. There are historically based reasons to suspect that the stages do not result from immutable psychological processes, but here I am seeking to disentangle supply and demand forces in a purely short-term way.

There is no question that outcomes change over the business cycle. More jobs are available during peaks, and the unemployment rate falls. Patterns of labor force participation change, since good times draw young people out of school and into the labor force. However, these gross changes can reflect either one of two phenomena. Primary firms may be hiring more youths and hence changing the structure of the labor market. On the other hand, more secondary jobs may be available to the young; thus increased availability of secondary jobs shortens the duration of unemployment and makes work more attractive to youths without fundamentally altering labor market structure. I cannot resolve this question definitively, but the evidence strongly suggests that in tight labor markets primary firms tend to hire more youth and youth do settle down more readily but that the fundamental structure of the market does not change.

For the labor force as a whole, peaks in the business cycle draw workers out of secondary jobs into primary work. This upgrading was first identified by Okun as an important distributional consequence of full employment and was empirically documented by Vroom.[25] However, the empirical work was not age specific. Tables 3.3 and 3.4, constructed from the National Longitudinal Survey, show the industry distribution of black and white youths with 12 years of education or less; hence they are comparable to the youths in my interviews. The tables show the industry distribution of youths who were 18 and 19 years old in 1968, a year of full employment, and in 1971, a year of considerable slack in the economy. Because age and education are held constant, differences in industrial distribution can reasonably be attributed to the business cycle. In addition, table 3.5 also shows the industrial distribution of all males in those two years.

The implications of the tables are mixed. The data for 18-19-year-old whites shows that the industries most likely to consist largely of secondary firms — wholesale and retail trade and services — provided 28.5 percent of employment in 1968 and 33.9 percent in 1971. Thus there is some evidence of upgrading in tight labor markets. At the same time the industry most likely to have the highest proportion of primary firms, durable manufacturing, was more likely to provide employment for youths in a tight economy

Table 3.3
Industrial Distribution, 1968 and 1971, Whites (in percentages)

	18–19		20–21		22–24	
Industry	1968	1971	1968	1971	1968	1971
Agriculture, mining	9.9	8.1	6.1	4.7	8.8	7.8
Construction	10.1	13.5	12.8	15.5	10.6	15.7
Durable manufacturing	33.2	20.1	33.1	20.6	28.3	28.4
Nondurable manufacturing	19.2	19.1	17.4	15.2	22.0	20.1
Wholesale	0.7	4.3	2.4	2.8	5.6	2.5
Retail	19.0	20.2	16.1	24.2	9.5	15.8
Services	8.8	9.4	8.5	14.7	10.3	6.6
Entertainment	0.5	1.6	0.7	0.3	0.4	0.4
Public administration	1.2	3.7	2.8	2.0	4.5	2.7
N	188	307	236	318	255	242

Note: The data are for white men out of school with 12 or fewer years of school completed.

Table 3.4
Industrial Distribution, 1968 and 1971, Blacks (in percentages)

	18–19		20–21		22–24	
Industry	1968	1971	1968	1971	1968	1971
Agriculture, mining	4.3	5.6	10.4	4.7	11.4	9.1
Construction	10.1	11.2	8.3	11.7	12.8	7.7
Durable manufacturing	35.5	17.9	21.7	30.5	30.0	23.1
Nondurable manufacturing	17.9	20.2	25.3	19.2	14.7	25.2
Wholesale	3.4	5.2	3.1	3.0	2.3	5.8
Retail	13.5	16.1	17.7	14.1	11.2	13.1
Services	12.4	20.3	10.9	10.7	9.9	13.2
Entertainment	1.1	1.8	0.8	0.4	2.2	0.6
Public administration	1.8	1.9	1.8	5.6	5.5	2.3
N	109	152	118	162	126	126

Note: The data are for black men out of school with 12 or fewer years of school completed.

Table 3.5
Industrial Distribution, 1968 and 1971, All Males (in percentages)

Industry	1968	1971
Agriculture, mining	7.7	7.3
Construction	8.3	9.1
Durable manufacturing	19.5	17.3
Nondurable manufacturing	10.5	9.8
Wholesale	3.5	4.0
Retail	11.5	12.4
Services	15.9	17.4
Entertainment	1.0	1.0
Public administration	6.1	5.7

Source: U.S. Department of Labor, Special Labor Force Report No. 115; table A-2, Special Labor Force Report No. 162; table A-2. These data do not control for educational attainment or school enrollment status and are thus not fully comparable with tables 3.3 and 3.4.

(1968). The young seem drawn into durable manufacturing from wholesale trade, construction, and public administration. The evidence for blacks follows the same pattern, although the upgrading into durable manufacturing is sharper, consistent with the notion that discriminatory barriers tend to break down in periods of strong demand. Finally, the industrial distribution of all males shows a similar cyclical response (more retail employment and less manufacturing employment in a slack economy), but the effect is more muted. This is consistent with the observation that youth are at the bottom of a hiring queue and thus their upgrading is more pronounced in tight labor markets.

This analysis suggests that there is some upgrading over the business cycle as primary firms reach down to hire younger workers. However, the basic pattern—for example, the heavy concentration of youth in wholesale and retail trade—is not dramatically altered.

Another less direct approach is to examine the unemployment rates of youths of different ages. If the stages have some life of their own, then unemployment rates of the younger group should be less responsive than the rates of the older group to a tightening in the labor market. The reason is that a large component of unemployment in the younger group is due to causes other than weak aggregate demand. On the other hand, the older group would be more likely to settle down as jobs become available.

This expectation is confirmed. Table 3.6 shows the elasticity of each age group's unemployment rate with respect to the unemployment rate of prime-age white males (a measure of the tightness of the economy). For all race and sex groups the unemployment rate of 20–24 year olds is more responsive than that of the younger group. This relative lack of responsiveness of the younger group's unemployment rate reflects the stages and the hiring patterns that I have described. Thus even in tight labor markets the essential structural characteristics of the youth labor market seem to prevail.

Occupational Choice

A different way of organizing much of this material is by the topic of occupational choice. In fact, even this label is misleading: it is rarely occupations that are chosen, and it is very unclear to what extent and in what form choice plays a role. Nonetheless, the topic is a useful way of thinking about how young people end up doing what they do.

Table 3.6
Unemployment Regressions, 1948–1976

Age Group	Constant	U35WM	Time	R^2	D.W.
18–19 WM	.3316 (2.13)	.7329 (18.99)	.0108 (3.04)	.953	1.73
20–24 WM	.6765 (3.20)	.9648 (17.29)	.0130 (3.76)	.944	1.76
18–19 BM	−.0865 (0.24)	.5447 (6.19)	.0368 (4.01)	.868	1.95
20–24 BM	.7119 (2.88)	.8229 (12.59)	.0146 (3.77)	.912	1.74
18–19 WF	−.7158 (2.78)	.5066 (9.28)	.0020 (2.58)	.898	2.09
20–24 WF	−.9888 (6.98)	.5732 (15.41)	.0229 (9.42)	.957	1.60
18–19 BF	−.8695 (2.34)	.2792 (2.80)	.0338 (6.67)	.789	1.94
20–24 BF	−.3572 (1.07)	.5251 (5.85)	.0229 (6.03)	.732	1.95

Source: U.S. Department of Labor *Employment and Training Report of the President*, (Washington D.C.: Government Printing Office), 1977, p. 170
Note: The dependent variables are the natural logs of the unemployment rates of each race-age-sex group, and the independent variables are the natural logs of the unemployment rate of 35–44-year-old white males and a time trend. The t-statistics are in parentheses.

Sociologists, psychologists, and economists have all written extensively on the topic. In general, the sociological-psychological perspective focuses on the formation of ambitions, goals, and aspirations and pays less attention to how those goals are mediated in the labor market.[26] I shall focus here on economic theories of occupational choice; I am in sympathy with elements of sociological-psychological approach (the moratorium stage can be viewed as a form of aspirations), but it is not clear that final outcomes are conditioned as much by aspiration as by labor market structure and process.

The economic theory of occupational choice is largely a variant of human capital theory. This set of ideas lies at the heart of much recent research in labor economics, and for this reason I shall attempt to see how well the data from the interviews support or contradict these ideas.

An important limitation of these approaches and of my analysis is the bias toward individualistic explanations. If the topic is formulated in terms of the question, Why did John become a _____? then the individualistic explanation makes sense. However, this may not be the most interesting question. More general questions about social stratification or class reproduction lead to research strategies and answers that focus less on individual decision making than on social and institutional structure. For example, one might ask why children of working-class families tend to remain in the working class while children of professional families maintain their status. Although I touch on some of these issues, the analysis remains largely at the individual level. This focus is necessitated by the nature of the data and can be justified because individual questions are still interesting and because it seems important to come to grips with human capital theory. However, another concern is the operation of the labor market as an institution, and thus the analysis goes beyond purely individualistic considerations.

An economic view of occupational choice more general than human capital theory is simply that, all else constant, people respond to economic incentives in choosing jobs.[27] The results from the interviews cast no doubt on this proposition. A large fraction of the youths, in response to the question "What would you like to be doing in five years?" mentioned a job other than their current one. Most wanted higher-level jobs and attributed their desire to better pay and opportunity. Clearly standard economic incentives appeal to the youths, and given a choice between two jobs these considerations would weigh heavily.

Even at this simple level the relative importance of economic versus other considerations in determining actual outcomes remains a question. For what fraction of young people does the weighing of net occupational advantages actually determine the outcome, and for what fraction is the process different? This question is typically finessed by an appeal to aggregate flows: it does not matter whether the theory is descriptive of most youths; as long as it is descriptive of some, an aggregate supply curve will conform to economic predictions. While this may be satisfactory for forecasters, it is incomplete as social science. Why should we not attempt to understand individuals, and why is it not important to discover which model best describes the experience of most people as opposed to the relatively few on the margin?

Human capital theory specializes the general principle of net advantage into a tighter, more constrained theory of rational maximizing behavior. The theory makes strong claims, for example Becker's assertion that human capital theory can explain why youth change jobs frequently.[28] Even if we accept the loose version of economic occupational choice, it pays to examine the human capital version in more detail.

In general, human capital theory is an effort to model in investment terms the decisions of individuals. Choices about how much and what kind of education to acquire, expenditures on health care, and what kind of jobs to take are put into the familiar maximizing framework of microeconomic theory. The essence of the theory is that these decisions are made in a conscious and rational fashion in which the costs and benefits are carefully weighed.

Most of human capital theory touches only indirectly on occupational choice since the theory focuses primarily on decisions concerning education and training rather than jobs. One of the few efforts to apply the theory to job decisions is Richard Freeman's *Market for College-Trained Manpower*.[29] Freeman concludes that labor supply decisions can be successfully modeled in terms of human capital models of occupational choice. He reaches this conclusion by examining aggregate data on the labor supply to various high-level occupations and by analyzing the results of interviews with college students. By showing that economic considerations play a role in occupational choice, Freeman concludes that the human capital choice model is vindicated for college-educated youth bound for the professions. Nothing I have to say here contradicts this conclusion, but it is important to see how well the model stands up for a considerably different group.

Freeman's model captures the essence of the human capital approach. The individual surveys the range of occupations and forms expectations about the future income streams of these occupations. From these expectations he or she applies a discount rate and determines the present discounted value of each income stream. The individual also calculates the costs of acquiring the human capital necessary to enter the occupation and arrives at the net present value of each occupation. The individual then maximizes a utility function whose arguments are net present value, unearned income, and the nonpecuniary characteristics of each job. The occupation that maximizes the utility function becomes the occupational choice.

This approach seems to imply complete knowledge, lack of uncertainty, access to financing, and other conditions that are unlikely to pertain. These limitations, however, do not vitiate the model in a fundamental way, since they can be incorporated as additional constraints on the decision-making process. The nonpecuniary considerations play a muted role in the model, but this is justified by the academic division of labor. Although these considerations are important (the surge of applications to journalism school following the Watergate case is an example), the human capital theorist would argue that it is sufficient to show that with all else constant the economic calculus plays a role at the margin. Although this is true in a formal sense, it raises the question of human capital theory's importance relative to other considerations in explaining outcomes.

The determination of outcomes is summarized by Freeman: "Characteristically, it [occupational choice] is an 'all or nothing' decision in which one career is selected from a set of mutually exclusive alternatives." Furthermore, "The worker investing in human capital normally limits himself to a single occupation"[30] because of the time it takes to teach skills and because investments are typically made early in order to maximize the period of return. The key assumptions here are that workers have careers, that the careers are in some nontrivial sense selected, and that once selected the careers are followed. How well do the work histories of the youths in the sample match these assumptions?

Several points in the interviews cast doubt on the underlying logic of the human capital model:

1. The sequence of jobs held by the youth does not follow career patterns. More often, the jobs are random with respect to skills and occupations.
2. Because most jobs are found through personal contacts, the range and role of careful search and rational choice seems limited.
3. Unemployed youths generally take the first job offered, and they do so even though they have applied for a wide range of jobs with varying characteristics.

4. The youths when asked how they found their jobs rarely described the process in terms of choice or selection.

The appendix to this chapter shows each out-of-school job held by the youths in the East Boston sample. The vertical lines above jobs or periods of unemployment show other jobs or firms for which the youth applied, either during the period of unemployment or while searching for the job they eventually found. As the chart shows, very few youths have what is conventionally thought of as a career. There is enormous variety in the jobs actually held, both with respect to the nature of the work and with respect to the kind of firm. These youths do not seem to have a "career."

Such a pattern could, of course, result from the structure of opportunities. The young people in this sample may have chosen and felt committed to an occupation but were forced to settle for a job in another area. However, the same wide range of firms and skills is found in the jobs that these youths sought. That is, even when looking for work, they showed little evidence of pursuing a "chosen" occupation or industry. Thus the notion of an occupational choice seems weakened.

However, the human capital approach can be recast in terms of labor market exploration. If youths lack information on the nature of jobs and the structure of opportunities within particular firms, they may move from job to job until they find the optimum setting. Two models that employ this idea are Sherwin Rosen's learning model and William Johnson's job-shopping model.[31]

In Rosen's model individuals seek to purchase learning opportunities (on-the-job training) by finding a firm that will provide training in return for a wage lower than the value of the marginal product of output during the training period. Workers thus invest in themselves and at some point switch to a nonlearning job in order to recoup, via a higher wage, the fruits of their earlier investment. If a job does not provide the desired combination of wages and learning, the worker moves to another firm. Thus the model generates mobility because of the eventual switch from learning to nonlearning jobs (although this is likely to occur within the same firm) and because of the search for the firm that provides the desired sequence of job types.

Johnson's job-shopping model also generates early mobility. The driving force of this model is the worker's uncertainty about his or her ability or productivity on a particular job. Because of this uncertainty, the worker is prepared to switch to another job if the first proves unsatisfactory. The model also predicts that the worker will choose the riskier (higher-quality) job first.

Both models generate search and exploration. However, the observed nature of the process is contrary to the model. First, most of the first jobs held by the youths in the sample are virtually devoid of learning and advancement opportunities. Nor did this come as a surprise to the youths who sought those jobs. There is considerable knowledge in the community about the nature of firms that provide secondary work, and it seems unlikely that the youths would expect very much from these jobs. The early jobs are not the sort predicted by the learning or search models. In addition, unemployed youths generally take the first job they are offered. In the sample in 78 percent of the periods of unemployment that ended by finding a job, that job was the first one offered. This finding has been replicated in other surveys.[32] Thus there is little evidence of search for bundles of learning and earning opportunities.

That most jobs, both primary and secondary, are found through personal contacts also weakens the human capital interpretation. This method of job acquisition implies a considerably narrower range of search and choice than is implied by the model. From the viewpoint of the youth, if not from an observer concerned with social structure, the jobs are available as a result of accident and chance, not active search and evaluation of alternative jobs. One function served by advanced education is to broaden this range of possibilities both by bringing to bear credentials that may substitute for personal contacts and by widening the range of personal contacts to include teachers and colleagues in addition to family and friends. However, for the youths in this sample, and possibly for other youths in similar circumstances, the range of contacts is narrow and jobs are found more by accident than by design.

The youths themselves accurately perceive the nature of the process. When they were asked, "How did you become a _____?" their answers overwhelmingly stressed chance, not design. Thirty percent of the youths said they "lucked into their job," and another 40 percent attributed their occupation to a contact. Only 8 percent indicated they had a previous interest in the field or examined jobs and selected one. The remaining 22 percent mentioned school, the typical answer being a shop course. Thus only 30 percent of the sample (the group who planned plus the school group) seem to fit the human capital model.

What scope is there for the role of choice? The evidence suggests that choice occurs with respect to broad occupational categories. This evidence derives from responses to questions about the jobs that the youths would refuse. Some youths, for example, said they would refuse indoor work; others rejected outdoor labor. Some youths made a distinction between working in a factory and other jobs. Some youths distinguished between jobs "with a future" as opposed to casual labor. These seem to be the categories among which choices are made. However, within these categories, for example, "indoor nonfactory work with a future," there is enormous variety, with respect to occupation, firm, and pay levels. The job that a youth gets from among the great variety is more a function of labor market structure than of individual decision making.

Summary

For many youths the process of entry and adjustment to the labor market is lengthy and involves distinct periods. The behavior of the youths changes over time, moving from a period of casual attachment to an increasing commitment to work and to stable behavior. At the same time the youths hold jobs in firms with quite different characteristics. Secondary firms provide the unskilled casual jobs characteristics of the moratorium stage, while primary firms seek to hire older youth who are prepared to settle down.

This pattern is not invariant over the business cycle because a strong economy leads some primary firms to hire workers they would normally avoid. However, the essential structure does not change. Finally, the youth in this labor market do not appear to have careers or to choose occupations in the manner predicted by conventional models. Although choice and economic considerations are not unimportant, the structure of the labor market, access to contacts, and chance play central roles.

Appendix

Current Status				Initial Status
	meter reader in gas company			
repairman in phone company	— unemployed —	laborer in construction		
proofreader in security firm	— general help in department store —	unemployed —	army	
machine operator in paint co.	— unemployed —	bakery manager —	clerk in candy store	
police department				
service worker in city hospital	— cab driver —	bank teller —	odd jobs	
cleaner in cleaning company	— manager in variety store —	laborer in gum products —	unemployed	
department stores	cleaning company			
security guard in security firm	— security guard in security firm —	clerk in bra factory —	guard in security company —	army
various factories	office work in insurance company	"everywhere"		factories; insurance
operative in gum factory	— unemployed —	laborer in paper factory —	stockboy in shoe company —	unemployed

The Structure of the Youth Labor Market

(rotated text, job history timelines:)

other drafting jobs
draftsman in computer firm — drafting school — tire changer in tire company
cleaner in cleaning company — cleaning in motel — cleaning in cleaning company
shipping & receiving — civil service; shipping & receiving
janitor in building company — unemployed — sand blaster in shipyard — unemployed
unemployed — driver in city government — cleaner in cleaning company
CETA
unemployed — recreation worker in city government
mechanics job — mechanics jobs — mechanics jobs
unemployed — mechanic in car dealership — mechanic in gas station — CETA — janitor in temple — laborer
United Parcel Service; restaurants
computer company
installer in electronics firm — unemployed — laborer in steel mill — unemployed
laborer in tile company — army
machinist in bellows company
supermarket
machinist — general help in electronics company — unemployed

Appendix *(continued)*

Current Status			Initial Status
laborer jobs; shipyards & construction	laborer in construction	maintenance; laborer	
unemployed	deleader in city hospital	unemployed	cook in sandwich shop ——— manager, oil dealer
cleaner in cleaning company	cleaner in cleaning company	laborer in silverware company	
security guard; shuttler in rent-a-car company; toll collector			
unemployed	general help in rent-a-car	stockboy in insurance company	
construction; auto body			
unemployed	repair in auto body	busboy in hotel	repair in bike shop
operative in computer firm	operative in electronics firm		
	taxi driver	driving jobs	parking jobs; driving jobs
unemployed	laborer in picture frame factory	operative in box company	unemployed
stock handler in department store			

The Structure of the Youth Labor Market

refrigerator repair
refrigerator repair in hotel —— refrigerator repair in refrigerator firm —— rigger in steel company —— unemployed —— truckers helper in hotel —— unemployed

dye maker in bookbinding firm —— dye maker in dye firm —— dye maker in dye firm —— dye maker in dye firm

machine operator; tool maker —— attendant in gas station

auto sales
auto sales
unemployed —— auto sales; dealer —— unemployed —— auto sales; dealer —— auto sales; dealer

carpenter in door company —— laborer in produce market —— unemployed

clerk in supermarket —— tire changer; auto dealer

unemployed —— laborer in landscaping firm —— dishwasher in restaurant

security guard   security guard
laborer, CETA —— guard in security firm —— unemployed —— army

clerk in restaurant —— unemployed

clerical jobs   clerical jobs
supply clerk in state government —— file clerk in federal government —— unemployed —— army

general help in department store;
truck loader;
factory laborer

clerk in restaurant —— unemployed

Appendix *(continued)*

Current Status	Initial Status
manager in rent-a-car firm —— unemployed —— car sales; factory work; cooking jobs	carpentry —— unemployed
electric company; steel rigger; telephone company	bouncer in night club
welder, Amtrak —— unemployed —— warehouseman in electronics firm	
laborer in paper factory; laborer in wall paper company; help in department store	
spreader in clothes factory —— unemployed —— odd jobs	
United Postal Service; General Dynamics, shipping yard —— General Dynamics —— unemployed —— temporary office work —— unemployed —— bakery helper	trucking; U.P.S; gum factory
laborer in department store	
stock clerk, grocery store	
unemployed —— laborer in steel company —— unemployed —— sandblaster in shipyard —— unemployed —— laborer in construction —— clerk on fruit stand	janitor; fish pier laborer

The Structure of the Youth Labor Market

machinist in electric company — laborer in shipyard — general help in paper box company — truck driver in oil company — general help in electronics firm

musician

parts salesman; auto dealer — proprietary school — unemployed

parts manager for auto company

groundskeeper in realty company — stockboy in restaurant — laborer in catering service

construction jobs

unemployed — general help in garage — laborer in carpentry — cleaning in cleaning company — tow truck driver, gas station — car wash

Polaroid; Sylvania; United Parcel Service

unemployed — clerk for machine maker — Stop & Shop; office jobs; Hood milk — unemployed — shuttler, rent-a-car company

claims adjuster in insurance company

deliverer for bakery — help in sausage company — mail clerk for Blue Cross — usher in Fenway Park — unemployed — security guard in security company — cleaner in cleaning company

Post Office; police

unemployed — army — unemployed — machine operator in auto parts company — assembler in eye glass company

department manager in department store

Appendix *(continued)*

Current Status		Initial Status
clerk in insurance company		

truck driving;   security;   mechanic;
steel company;   mechanics;   Jordan Marsh   mechanic
air freight   flight attendant

unemployed ——— truck driver at airport ——— unemployed ——— mechanic for auto dealer ——— unemployed

other jobs in same bank

security guard in bank ——— mail handler in post office ——— fork lift driver at airport

supervisor for Blue Cross

big companies and stores

printing press operator; insurance company

airline flight attendant;
gas station;
Coca Cola;
Massport

shuttle driver for bank ——— tow truck driver for gas station

                       gas station;   machinist;   laborer in
                       machinist   gas station   gas station   cook in   fish cutter in
machinist in   machinist in   restaurant ——— fish company ——— cleaner in hotel
machine parts company ——— rubber company ——— unemployed

clerk in carpet company ——— clerk in bank ——— unemployed

4 The Evolution of the Youth Labor Market

Youths today play a marginal role in the economy. They account for a small share of employment and a high share of unemployment; in 1975, 16-19 year olds accounted for 8.5 percent of employment but 22.3 percent of unemployment.[1] More fundamental, their jobs are generally low skilled, casual and consist of informal work such as odd jobs, part-time clerking, and casual construction as well as more formal but equally dead-end employment for example in fast food chains, gas stations, and department stores. These jobs are not merely the low-skilled, bottom rung of a job ladder; they are qualitatively different from most other jobs in the economy. They form a sector reserved for youth and other marginal workers.

The tenuous attachment of youths to the labor force also betrays the marginal nature of their employment. Many teenagers voluntarily work at or look for part-time jobs. Others work for short periods and then drop out of the labor force. Many young people work only in the summers, and most work not to build a career but to earn money for recreation.

Given the marginal nature of the youth labor market, the high rates of unemployment among the young are not surprising. Nor is it surprising that those who need or wish to have more serious or remunerative employment have difficulty finding it. Age has become a convenient label, and individual treatment is dominated by group characteristics. When and how did this marginal status come about?

The Turn of the Century

The crucial elements of the modern institutional structure were put into place at the turn of the century. Youths left the labor market and stayed in school longer. Child labor and compulsory education laws were strengthened and extended, and the high schools became mass institutions. These events were part of broader changes in society's definition and treatment of the young. Prior to this period there was no notion of an adolescent stage; the concept was invented during these years,[2] and the invention was formalized by the publication of G. Stanley Hall's highly influential psychological work, *Adolescence*. Many of the modern institutions serving (or controlling) the young were put into place. The Boy Scouts were founded in England in 1908 and brought to the United States in 1910; the YMCAs developed and extended their youth programs; adolescence became a legal category with the extension of the juvenile court system. Adolescence today is widely accepted as a stage of human development, and the adolescent is frequently segregated from other age groups and treated in ways that, by accident or design, create a sense of separateness and distance from society.

Although young people were not fully integrated economic actors before the turn of the century, the available evidence suggests that the labor market experiences of youth in the mid nineteenth century differed in important ways from the modern pattern. It is, of course, difficult to characterize the youth labor market of the mid nineteenth century. One source of the difficulty is inadequate sources. Another, more substantive, problem is that the experiences of the young were more heterogeneous than they are today. Regardless of class or region, the patterns of adolescence today are essentially the same for all youths. In earlier times pathways into the labor market were more diverse, the children of the farmer, the urban merchant, the immigrant, the brahmin, and the laborer had quite different experiences. Despite the difficulties in characterizing the youth labor market, a key difference was greater economic freedom for the young. From the turn of the century onward, the consistent trend has been a reduced scope of youth labor, forcing them into their marginal work status.

One form of the greater economic autonomy of the mid nineteenth century youth was an ability to find and hold the factory jobs that are closed to today's young person. "The acceleration of demand for cheap boy laborers was particularly intense during the early stages of industrialization, those marked by the concentration of workers into factories and the subdivision of tasks."[3] This autonomy was no blessing; working in those factories was deadly. Nonetheless, working-class children found serious jobs.

The greater autonomy was not simply the greater availability of jobs. Their ability to find work also allowed them some economic independence from their families. Some youths simply left home to seek their fortunes.[4] Those who left home were not only from the comfortable classes; the transiency rate among youth of all social classes was remarkably high in nineteenth-century America.[5]

Another common pattern was to remain in town but find a job and move in with another local family as a boarder. Michael B. Katz characterizes this as a stage of "semi-autonomy, a phase of the life cycle common in times past but since virtually lost. Its loss during modernization reflects the prolongation of dependence of young people upon their families."[6] During this stage youth escaped the scrutiny of their parents and enjoyed the resulting social and economic freedom, but remained under some adult discipline from the family with whom they boarded. Furthermore, it appears that youth were able to find and hold skilled and responsible jobs. In Katz's 1861 sample 79 percent of sons living with their families held either professional, commercial, or artisan jobs.[7]

From the turn of the century on, the social and economic autonomy of the young was under attack. As Katz notes, "A prolonged and increasingly regulated and institutionalized dependency created what we term adolescence [which is not] a perennial biological state but rather the codification of a new and socially determined phase of the life cycle."[8]

The Transformation

The last years of the nineteenth century and the early years of the twentieth century set the pattern for the modern economy. Technological innovation, the advent of mass production and distribution, and the creation of giant corporations transformed the economy. At the same time there was a rapid extension of the length of schooling and a simultaneous reduction of widespread child labor in the nonagricultural sectors. By the second decade of the twentieth century the modern pattern was in place, and by the third decade it was dominant. The transformation was consolidated in later decades as high school attendance and graduation rates rose. The cohort most strongly affected was teenagers in their middle years, those between 14 and 16. At the beginning of the century this group was largely out of school and working; their later age mates were in school and out of the labor market.

As the balance between work and school changed, youth entered high school and high schools grew rapidly.[9] However, many of the youth who remained in school did so in earlier grades.[10] The data underlying these generalizations are presented in table 4.1. There are serious problems with the accuracy of the data and their comparability over time, but the trend is unmistakable.[11] From decade to decade the proportion of each cohort in the labor market declined sharply, over two-thirds between 1900 and 1930. During the same period the fraction of each cohort attending school increased.[12] These trends remain even after controlling for the decline in agricultural employment and migration from rural to urban areas.[13]

A more concrete sense of the change emerges from a study of one community during this period. The Lynds, in their classic *Middletown*, documented the transformation of that community between 1890 and the early 1920s.[14] In 1892, 41 percent of employment in the town's leading glass factory were "boys," and the Lynds report that new firms considering locating in the town always inquired about the availability of child labor.[15] In 1897 the first compulsory education law was passed and led to far-reaching changes. Between 1897 and 1924 Middletown's population in-

Table 4.1
Child Labor and School Enrollment

	1890	1900	1910	1920	1930
Percentage of 10–15-year-olds working					
Males	25	26	21	16	6
Females	10	10	8	5	2
Percentage of 14–15-year-olds working					
Males			43	23	12
Females			18	11	5
Percentage of 14–17-year-olds enrolled in school	7	11	15	32	51

Sources: Rows 1 and 2: A. Dewey Anderson and Percy Davidson, *Occupational Trends in the United States* (Stanford, Calif.: Stanford University Press, 1940), p. 45; rows 3 and 4: 1900 from Twelfth Census, vol. 2, *Population,* pp. clxii, xxxvi; 1920 from Bureau of the Census, *Children in Gainful Occupations at the Fourteenth Census* (Washington, D.C.: U.S. Government Printing Office, 1924), p. 14; 1930 from Fifteenth Census, *Population,* vol. 5, p. 345; row 5 from Robert Bremner et al., *Children and Youth in America,* (Cambridge MA: Harvard University Press), 1970, vol. 2, p. 1392.

creased by 350 percent, but the size of the high school graduating class grew 19-fold. The labor of boys in the factories ended, and "the whole working population tends to start work from two to five years later than in 1890."[16]

The high school quickly became a recognizable modern institution. School became the hub of social life; clubs, athletic teams, and other less formal peer group activities dominated the scene. The extensive and complicated high school social arrangements, segmented along class lines, which were described in the 1940s in *Elmtown's Youth* and in the 1950s by James Coleman, emerged in Middletown in this period.[17] The nature of the curriculum also changed. In 1897 the high school provided only one vocational course; by 1924 eight of the 12 high school courses were vocational, and roughly 20 percent of student time was spent in them. Civics and citizenship courses were also introduced during this period.

In the United States between 1900 and 1930 child labor declined dramatically and the years of school attendance were considerably extended. Schooling had become the dominant pattern for youths of all classes, although middle-class students stayed in school longer.[18] The new pattern signaled the emergence of the modern system, what Tyack has termed the move from the "symbolic" to the bureaucratic stage.[19]

The driving forces behind declining labor market participation and extended school attendance were changes in the structure of the youth labor market. These changes consisted of both supply and demand effects that complemented each other and thus led to dramatic change in the economic status of youth. The "second industrial revolution" sharply reduced the relative demand for unskilled labor, and the flood of immigrants increased the supply of unskilled labor.[20] The consequence was a shift in the labor market for unskilled labor and a shift in the scope of economic activities required of and available to the young.

The Changing Demand for Unskilled Labor

The 1890s in Britain according to David Landes "saw the lusty childhood, if not the birth, of electrical power and motors; organic chemistry and synthesis; the internal combustion engine and automotive devices; precision manufacture and assembly-line production—a cluster of innovations that have earned the name of the second industrial revolution."[21] Development in the United States seems to have followed a similar pattern of a sudden spurt of technological progress. Average annual output per unit of labor input was one third higher between 1900 and 1920 than between 1879 and 1899.[22]

Behind the dramatic changes lay a wide variety of labor-saving inventions, many of which seem to have had the most serious consequences for unskilled labor. Two major new power sources—the internal combustion engine and electrical power—reduced considerably the unskilled labor involved in feeding the small steam engines that had been scattered around factories.[23] Technological developments had similar effects. In textiles the introduction of the Draper loom in the 1890s increased from 6 to 20-24 the number of machines that could be tended by one worker.[24] The output per hour for machines opening bales was 350 lbs in 1900; in 1920 the output rose to 2,000 lbs.[25]

One of the most important technological innovations of this period was the advent of continuous-processing techniques. Machines that turned out products automatically were invented, and plants were organized to assure the continuous flow of materials from one stage to the next. In both cases the demand for labor was severely reduced. Continuous processing signaled the beginning of the era of mass production. The new techniques revolutionized production in industries such as tobacco processing, match making, soap making, film, grain processing, and canning.[26]

Other industries were also deeply affected by the advent of continuous processing, again with the effect of reducing the demand for labor, particularly unskilled labor. In the steel industry, for example, the transition to the twentieth century was marked by widespread adoption of continuous-process rolling mills, which introduced considerable efficiencies.[27] One British observer said, in 1906, "Perhaps the greatest difference between American and English conditions in steel works practice is the very conspicuous absence of laborers in the American mills. The large and growing employment of every kind of both propelling and directing machinery . . . is responsible for this state of things. It is no exaggeration to say that in a mill rolling three thousand tons of rail a day, not a dozen men are to be seen on the mill floor."[28]

In addition to technological change, the relative demand for unskilled labor, particularly young labor, was reduced due to changes in the distribution of labor. In 1880 farmers and farm laborers constituted 51 percent of the labor force; in 1900 they represented 40 percent, and by 1920 the figure had declined to 28 percent.[29] This shift off the farms had the double effect of reducing the demand for youth labor and increasing the supply of unskilled labor available for other employments.

The pattern seems similar to that portrayed by Musgrove for turn-of-the century England: "Advances in technology were . . . displacing the young worker. . . . Steam power in the lace and pottery industry was being substituted for children's energy and dexterity; the dramatic decline in the proportion of young people engaged in agriculture in the second half of the century has been similarly attributed in part to technical development. . . . Young people were no longer central to the economy."[30]

Changing Supply Conditions

At the same time that the relative demand for unskilled labor was falling, the supply of that labor was rapidly increasing. Between 1895 and 1899 the average annual arrival of immigrants was 340,000. Between 1900 and 1904 the average stood at 764,000, and the stream became a flood between 1905 and 1913, when the average rose to 1,160,000 per year.[31] Between 1880 and 1890 immigration accounted for 33.9 percent of the growth in the labor force, 26.4 percent between 1890 and 1900, a remarkable 41.6 percent between 1900 and 1910, and 26.0 percent between 1910 and 1920. By contrast, in the next 30 years the (unweighted) decadal average was less than 6 percent, and between 1950 and 1965, it was 18 percent.[32] Immigrants quickly came to dominate the labor force of many of the central industries in the economy. In 1910 foreign-born workers constituted 57 percent of the labor force in iron and steel, 60 percent in slaughtering and meat packing, 61 percent in bituminous coal, 61 percent in woolen and worsted, 34 percent in silk, 68 percent in cotton goods, and 27 percent in boots and shoes.[33] Since most immigrants occupied low-skill jobs, the main impact of the influx was on the supply conditions in that strata of the labor market.[34]

These changes in the supply of and demand for unskilled labor are evident from wage data for the period. Trends in the ratio of skilled to unskilled wages show that "1896 is a turning point for earnings differentials in much the same fashion that it is a turning point for so many other long-run economic indicators. After two decades of stable or declining pay differentials the skill differential undergoes another 'epic surge.' "[35] The wage differential increased by over 15 percent between 1896 and 1914[36] and then remained relatively stable, except for the World War I period, until the permanent narrowing that occurred as a result of World War II.

Some Examples

Developments in three industries illustrate these changes in the labor market. In retail trade technological change displaced young people, the textile industry felt the impact of immigration, and the glass industry was affected by both forces.

According to Selwyn K. Troen, the young workers of the 1870s were heavily represented in large retail stores such as Macy's and Marshall Fields, where they made up one-third of the labor force.[37] They worked as cash boys and girls, shuttling money and goods between the sales counter, the cashier, and the wrapping desk. By 1902 the introduction of the pneumatic tube and the spread of cash registers had virtually eliminated these jobs. Labor-saving technological progress deprived substantial numbers of youth of low-skilled jobs.

The textile industry illustrates the impact of immigration. New England and the South differed with respect to the importance of children and the availability of immigrants. The South had virtually no immigrant labor and made heavy use of children, while the North, with its ready supply of immigrants, found much less use for children. In New England the number of workers under 16 declined by 46 percent between 1880 and 1905, while the over-16 labor force grew by 32 percent. This period coincided with rapid French-Canadian immigration into the industry.[38] There is also a hint that technology played a role. Of the two technologies for spinning, ring and mule spinning, ring spinning was more "suitable" for children because it involved little heavy work and no mechanical skill. Ring spinning required only "quick and nimble fingers" while "the mule is a very complicated machine and much mechanical skill is required."[39] Mule spinning was unknown in the South, the region where children were most intensively employed.[45]

Events in the glass industry clearly show the interaction of both supply and demand forces. This industry is also representative of the heat- and chemical-based industries which were in the forefront of the shift to continuous processing. The glass industry formed the economic base of Middletown.

In 1880 child laborers constituted 20 percent of the national labor force in the glass industry,[41] yet only twenty-five years later "modern factory requirements [have changed] to such an extent that it can truthfully be said that, as a rule, the glass factory of today which still requires the work of the small boy is operated in the crudest, most primitive, most expensive and antiquated manner."[42]

In 1880 the glassmaking industry was still organized around centuries-old handicraft production techniques. Blowing was done by hand, and skilled blowers had several assistants, usually young boys, who opened and closed molds ("mold boys"), cleaned excess glass off the pipe ("cleaning off boys"), and carried finished and semifinished articles around the shop ("snapping-up boys" and "carrying-in boys").

The glass industry thus looked like several other important U.S. industries just prior to the second industrial revolution. Production was still organized along crafts line, craftsmen exercised a restraining influence on technology, and child labor was important. As in many other industries, the next several decades witnessed a remarkable transformation originating from technological innovations that replaced highly skilled craftsmen and unskilled child laborers with semiskilled machine tenders. The innovations, coming from the Owens and Libby glass factories in Toledo, included paste-mold machines for blowing bulbs, the automatic Owens bottle machine, the Davies tube-drawing machine, and the Colburn window glass machine.

The impact of these innovations is apparent from the following figures: in 1890 all jars and bottles were handcrafted; in 1917, 70 percent were made by machines. In 1895 all light bulbs were made by hand, yet in 1920, 60 percent were machine made.

These developments had predictable effects on the demand for child labor. In fact, machines were dubbed and advertised as the "no-boy." The productivity of the machines was such that between 1903 and 1907 hand factories paid $1.50 in direct labor costs per gross of pint beers produced compared with $0.10 for users of Owens machines.

The glass industry reflects the demand-side developments for the economy as a whole. Technological innovation led to enormous gains in productivity and altered the nature of labor demand, decreasing demand for highly skilled craftsmen and for their unskilled assistants. The supply-side developments will also seem familiar because the new glass workers were increasingly Eastern European immigrants.

According to the 1911 Congressional Report on the Conditions of Women and Child Wage Earners, the major substitute for boys in glass factories was "the recent immigrant from southern or eastern Europe—the Slav, the Italian, the Greek, the Hungarian, etc."[43]

These immigrants were particularly important in large (and presumably more modern) firms, "there not being a single large establishment in Illinois, Indiana, or Ohio in which the immigrant of 18 years and over does not form a large, if not dominant part of the unskilled worker staff."[44] Thus in 16 establishments that made important use of immigrants they constituted 13.9 percent of the under-16 work force, 32 percent of the 16–20-year-old work force, and 60.6 percent of the adult work force.[45] This change had occurred just in the five years prior to the report. These immigrants replaced youth in traditional "boys jobs" and manned the new machines, a task in which they were considered superior to the boys.

Thus the movement of immigrants into the glassmaking industry led to an increase in the supply of unskilled labor, just as occurred elsewhere in the economy. Technological change reduced the demand for unskilled labor, the influx of immigrants provided a growing supply of that labor. It therefore should not be surprising that in Middletown at the end of this period the "boys" were in school. They had been pushed out of industry, and society needed to find new institutions to accommodate them.

The Process of Change

Faced with declining opportunities for unskilled labor and growing opportunities for educated labor (for example, between 1900 and 1930 the number of accountants and auditors in the labor force increased ninefold while the labor force did not quite double)[46] many young people chose to stay in school. However, there is also considerable evidence that coercion was involved in rising school attendance. This period was crucial in the evolution of child labor and compulsory education legislation.[47] Although some states had laws on the books prior to this time, it was in this period that the laggard states passed laws, and throughout the nation legislation was enacted extending age ranges, eliminating exemptions, and installing adequate enforcement machinery. As the 1920 United States Commissioner of Education Report noted, "No field in education, with the possible exception of school revenues, has in recent years been more prolific of progress as regards to legislative provisions than has compulsory school attendance."[48] Great progress was also made on the national level; the Children's Bureau was established in 1912, and national child labor legislation was first enacted in 1916. At both the state and national levels the advocates of extended compulsory schooling and the opponents of child labor had their greatest triumphs during the early twentieth century.

Schools were organized to force attendance. The educational literature of the period discusses truancy programs, school censuses, and other devices aimed at enforcing attendance.[49] Evidently, attendance was a real problem. Edith Abbot's study of truancy in Chicago in 1916 shows that 39 percent of the boys and 40 percent of the girls normally enrolled for a full year in elementary school missed 30 or more half days in the year.[50] Furthermore, the overwhelming bulk of these students were from foreign born and poor families. In New York City in 1910 truancy officers investigated over 130,000 cases, or 21 percent of students registered, and in Pittsburgh 30,000 to 50,000 cases of irregular attendance were investigated annually between 1911 and 1920.[51]

David Tyack wrote: "During the first two decades of the twentieth century compulsory schooling laws became increasingly effective. From 1900 to 1920 educators became less ambivalent about coercion than they had often been during the nineteenth century."[52] Thus this period witnessed a truancy and nonattendance problem and the emergence of bureaucratic structures to force youth into school.

Because of this coercion, individual choice seems to be an incomplete explanation of the link between change in the unskilled labor market and change in the structure of the youth labor market. Also needed is an explanation of the relationship between the labor market changes and the political events that led to the passage of effective child labor and compulsory education laws.

Any major social transformation is the result of a change in the balance of political forces. In the extension of schooling, the changing labor market for unskilled labor shifted the balance in favor of those pressing for the educational transformation. Since firms no longer required the labor of children and adolescents, those pressing for longer compulsory schooling were able to succeed.[53] A subtle shift in the balance of power resulted from diminished industrial opposition to strong child labor and school attendance legislation.

An exception which illustrates this argument is the case of southern textiles. Textiles had traditionally been the major employer of children in the United States; even in 1905 textiles employed more children than the combined total of the next four largest industries. However, children were only 6 percent of the New England work force, compared with 23 percent of the southern textile work force. Of the families interviewed by the congressional researchers, 95 percent in New England were foreign born, while in the south 99 percent were native.[54] Evidently, decreasing reliance on child labor characterized the North's textile industry, but in the South the unavailability of immigrant labor led to continued reliance on children. As one would thus expect, the only major opposition to federal child labor legislation came from southern textile manufacturers,[55] and the public schools expanded less rapidly in the South.

There is other evidence that manufacturers altered their attitude toward child labor legislation during this period. For example, Forest Ensign's description of the struggles over child labor legislation in New York State refers frequently to "manufacturing interests" who were "financially interested in the employment of children [and] were able to offer bitter and resourceful opposition" to reforms. Yet, at the turn of the century this opposition seems to have diminished dramatically. Ensign reports that in the first decade of the new century laws " 'with teeth in them' were enacted, enforcement was stimulated, and employers themselves became to an appreciable extent supporters of the very principles they had so long successfully opposed." John R. Commons and his co-workers reported that "the Pennsylvania Child Labor Association credits the textile manufacturers of that state with 'very active support' of the 1905 bill which raised the minimum age from 13 to 14."[56]

Why did firms not continue to employ children as well as the new immigrant labor? Although the relative demand for unskilled labor had fallen, the economy was expanding and the absolute demand had probably increased. Furthermore, it might seem that firms should prefer as large a labor pool as possible. Part of the answer is that although firms might have preferred to have young people available, they did not truly need them. They had a large and elastic supply of immigrant labor.[57] Firms therefore reduced their opposition to child labor legislation and enforcement, and the shifting balance led to the withdrawal of young people from the market.

The immigrants may also have enjoyed some positive advantages over youth. The immigrants were largely male, between the ages of 14 and 45, and were either single or had left their family in the country of origin. Thus, more than local youth, they were a "mobile, migrating wage earning class . . . free to follow the best industrial inducements."[58] Their mobility and the low wages they would accept made them attractive employees. Another advantage may have been that the new technologies, which emphasized machine tending instead of skilled workers with child helpers, created jobs better suited to adults. The National Industrial Conference Board, a business organization, wrote in 1925:

In most manufacturing industries which have attained any large development . . . there is increasing pressure and tendency toward the use of complex, expensive, and highly productive labor saving machinery and the introduction of highly organized methods of management, training, and selection of personnel. The employment of very young workers under such conditions would increasingly entail larger costs of training, selection, direction, and protection of the work force and expensive equipment, all of which would render such labor costly in the end.[59]

And Joseph Kett wrote:

Industrialization led employers to seek cheap labor, but adult immigrants rather than teenagers were the preferred choice, for the boys were too unsteady in their habits and too prone to switch jobs, get into fights, and grant themselves holidays.[60]

Finally, the reports of migrants picture them as "tractable and uncomplaining."[61] To the extent this was true (and racist attitudes doubtlessly colored this assessment), employers would obviously find these traits desirable. They may also have found the immigrants better suited for breaking unions than the children of workers with roots in the communities.[62]

The Youth Labor Market, 1920–1941

In many respects the youth labor market during the pre-World War II years was remarkably similar to today's market. Youth who worked during this period did so largely in low-skilled and low-paying jobs, as is evident from the data on the industrial distribution of young workers presented in table 4.2.

Like today's young people, the youth in 1930 tended to find employment in the industries most likely to provide secondary jobs. Sixty-eight percent of

Table 4.2
Industrial Distribution of Nonagricultural 10-17 Year Olds, 1930 (in percentages)

Industry	Men 10-17	Men All	Women 10-17	Women All
Mining	3.1	4.0	0.2	0.06
Building industries	3.7	8.8	0.1	0.2
Manufacturing	39.0	33.1	41.5	24.1
Transportation, communication	8.6	14.0	4.1	4.3
Banking, insurance, real estate	2.2	3.5	2.2	4.0
Wholesale, retail	23.2	14.5	12.8	12.4
Public services	0.6	3.2	0.1	1.2
Professional services	1.3	4.7	2.3	16.5
Recreation, amusement	2.2	1.0	0.6	1.3
Hotels, domestic, laundry	6.6	5.7	31.6	32.0
Miscellaneous	7.9	6.1	3.4	3.2

Source: Alba Edwards, *A Social Economic Grouping of the Gainful Workers of the United States* (Washington, D.C.: U.S. Government Printing Office, 1938), pp. 142-181.
Note: I created these categories to conform as closely as possible to modern usage.

male youths were employed in manufacturing, wholesale and retail trade, hotels and laundries (compared with 53 percent of male adults), and 85 percent of young women found employment in these industries (compared with 68 percent of adult women).

These broad categories, though useful, can be misleading. A single category can include a wide range of skill levels, pay, and promotional opportunities. A better flavor of the nature of the jobs held by youths comes from the descriptions and judgments of observers of youth jobs. The consensus of these reports is that youth jobs, then as now, were secondary in nature.

A 1932 report by a Massachusetts commission on employment noted: "Many of the jobs commonly given to children provide irregular employment, almost if not completely casual in nature. . . . Young boys and girls are hired because they are cheap and because they can be laid off without qualms of conscience as to family obligations." A national survey concluded that "in urban areas, child labor under 16 persists mainly in the street trades and in miscellaneous small retail and service establishments," and the chief of the United States Children Bureau observed in 1937 that "the child labor picture today shows a shift to the employment of boys and girls under 16 from factories . . . to occupations in trade services."[63]

This phenomenon was not limited to very young workers. Youth just out of high school also worked in similar establishments. A 1938 survey of high school graduates and dropouts in New York State found that over 40 percent were employed in the first years after school in small stores, filling stations, garages, small businesses, and contractors with five or fewer employees and concluded that "if these boys and girls are to receive higher pay than they now earn, most must leave their present jobs." The transition was also observed in 1932 in Rochester, New York: "As boys and girls grow older and have longer work experience they tend to drift out of errand and messenger work and into factory work."[64]

As is true today, the confinement of young people to secondary jobs was partly due to the hiring practices of primary employers and partly to the preference of the youth themselves. The hiring practices of primary firms were characterized in 1942 as follows: "Except for juvenile occupations . . . it is not easy to find urban employers of standing who will hire young people under the age of 18. Many employers have been accustomed to hire young men of 20 or 21 only if they seemed above the average of maturity for their age."[65]

The other explanation of the casual nature of youth employment is the attitudes of the young themselves. There is scattered evidence that the attitudes of the young in this earlier period were similar to the attitudes of young people today. The author of the 1938 survey of high school graduates and dropouts in New York State remarked that the youth "were unmindful of their future," and went on to say: "The boys and girls who succeed in getting jobs are more concerned with the superficial conditions of their work, or the satisfaction of having any kind of job, than with the particular opportunities which their jobs offer."[66]

Another youth worker remarked, concerning efforts at job placement, "We are dealing, of course, with adolescent boys and girls, many of whom are naturally restless and prone to change jobs frequently for the most trivial reasons."[67]

A 1929 survey of employees at Macy's Department Store in New York City found, as did a separate survey at Aetna Insurance Company, that absences and lateness declined sharply with age.[68] The Rochester survey found that 65 percent of the youth stayed with their first employer after school for three months or less and that over 60 percent of the youth averaged between two and four employers per year.[69]

Unemployment reflects the interaction of supply and demand forces. Unemployment rates are very high for young teenagers and decline until the early twenties, when the rates approximate those of adults. This pattern reflects the behavior of youth and the hiring practices of firms. The pre-World War II labor market was structurally similar to today's, which is clear from the data in table 4.3

Schools and Schooling

Schools came to play a prominent role in the youth labor market. As a result young people have increasingly delayed their entrance into the full-time labor market and have stayed longer in school. Part-time and summer employment accounted for a growing fraction of youth jobs.[70] Schools increasingly intervened directly in the youth labor market, initially with employment certificates and later through vocational education and its curricular offspring. At a deeper level, the schools and the growth of credential-oriented employment practices became important in the allocation of jobs to youth.

The growth of schools and their increasing role in the lives of the young are documented in table 4.4.

Table 4.3
Unemployment Rates by Age (percents)

Age	1936, Maryland (Out-of-School)	1937, United States
15	—	41.4
16	56	50.0
17	49	46.5
18	39	41.6
19	29	34.7
20	29	—
21	25	—
22	22	—
23	20	—
24	20	—
15–19	—	41.2
20–24	—	24.3

Source: Column 1: Howard Bell, *Youth Tell Their Story* (Washington D.C.: American Council on Education, 1938), p. 55; column 2: American Youth Commission, *Youth and the Future* (Washington, D.C., 1942), p. 12.

Table 4.4
Trends in School Attendance

Year	High School Graduates as a Percentage of 17-Year-Olds	First-Time College Students as a Percentage of High School Graduates
1900	6.3	—
1910	8.6	—
1920	16.3	—
1930	28.8	39*
1940	49.0	35
1950	57.4	40
1960	63.4	52
1970	75.6	61

Source: *Historical Statistics of the United States*, Series H598-601, H587-597.
* This figure is actually for 1932.

The role of schooling—the impact of the overall system of education—is at the heart of much economic and sociological theory. There is considerable evidence that schools perform a sorting function for the economy, helping to determine the allocation of desirable and undesirable jobs. From a meritocratic or human capital viewpoint, this allocative function is both fair and necessary for economic efficiency. From other perspectives, ascriptive characteristics—race, sex, social class—are the organizing principles of the sorting scheme.

A correlary to this allocative role of schooling has been the escalation of educational requirements for jobs. As late as 1929 a leading personnel journal ran an article asking "Is there a place in industry for the college man?"[71] The absurdity of this question today is testimony to the escalation of educational requirements for jobs. Whether this escalation truly reflects growing skill requirements or whether some other explanation is more persuasive is a difficult question, but in either case the impact of the development on the youth labor market is obvious.

These issues concerning the role of schooling are extremely interesting in themselves and are also vehicles for a serious examination of the social system. They would, however, take us too far afield. Instead, I will take up the narrower question of the direct relationship between schools and the labor market. I will stray from this stricture in only one respect—in the next section the role of schooling as a custodial device will be discussed in the context of a more general discussion of the enclosure of youth.

Through the mid 1910s the high school, despite the pressure of increased enrollments, remained largely an academic institution, with a traditional classical curriculum, and many of its graduates went directly into teaching.[72] However, the impact of growing enrollments and the broadening social composition of the students proved too strong for traditionalists to resist. Much of the intellectual history of educational theory from the mid 1910s onwards can be read as an effort to define and come to terms with the work-related services that schools might provide. In the words of George Counts:

Our secondary school has already responded in many ways to these profound changes which have transformed the social order. . . . the extraordinary expansion of the curriculum, the almost feverish search for subjects, the readiness with which new devices are tried and abandoned . . . would all seem to be inspired by a more or less conscious recognition of the demolition of the social foundations upon which the older programs of secondary education rested.[73]

The implication of this remark is that schools were followers, not leaders, and this was true (although Counts argued, vainly, that schools should create and implant new social values). The school curriculum in many ways expanded to prepare youth for work. Successive national commissions of educators acknowledged this function for schools and sought to find ways to better integrate activities in the school and in the work place.[74]

One can imagine schools in local communities playing a lead role by designing courses to teach real skills and then placing youths in jobs. There are, of course, examples of such activism. Early in the period when the effectiveness of the compulsory education law was still in doubt, the most efficient enforcement device was employment certificates issued by schools, without which youth could not be legally employed. These devices permitted school officials to decide which youth could work, and there is evidence that issuance of the certificates varied with labor market conditions.[75] There were also examples of a more direct relationship. In Chicago the Swift Meat Company established on the company premises a continuation school for employees, a school accredited, staffed, and furnished by the local school board.[76] The Atlanta school system systematically rated students through high school and then sent these ratings to a community employment service organized by local businessmen.[77]

In fact, however, schools generally failed, then as now, to play an important direct role in the youth labor market. The best evidence of this failure can be found in the school programs expressly designed to have an impact: vocational education and placement counseling.

Vocational education had its origins in manual training, a curriculum reform designed to bridge the gap between work and schools.[78] With the passage of the Smith-Hughes Act in 1917, vocational education acquired federal support and the program grew. In 1920 enrollments in vocational education courses numbered under 100,000; by 1930 the figure was 300,000, and in 1940, 950,000.[79]

Vocational educators have proved themselves remarkably adept at bureaucratic battles for money and turf. In 1938 President Roosevelt complained: "Much of the apparent demand for the immediate extension of the vocational education program under the George-Dean Act appears to have been stimulated by an active lobby of vocational teachers, supervisors and administrative officers in the field of vocational education, who are interested in the enrollments paid in part in Federal funds."[80] In the 1960s the vocational education system succeeded in capturing, against the wishes of the Labor Department, an important fraction of employment and training programs.

Vocational education has been considerably less successful at preparing students for work. Most evidence today suggests a minimal effect even with respect to placement in jobs whose skills are related to those studied in school,[81] and the pre-World War II picture seems not to have been much different. A 1938 survey in New York State concluded that "in most instances the curriculum themselves do not produce different kinds or degrees of out-of-school competence."[82] In 1934 the U.S. Office of Education found that 150,000 students had received bookkeeping training, yet the maximum number of openings was 34,000.[83] A presidential commission lent weight to this in 1938, when it concluded that "vocational education in trades and industries has tended to produce a supply of labor without reference to the demands for it."[84]

The general ineffectiveness of vocational education was matched by the performance of guidance and placement functions in general. The New York survey found that the schools knew little about the background of their pupils, provided little information to the youth on curiculum choice, and had little active concern for vocational adjustment;[85] "the high school's opinion of its pupil's social competence bears little relation to the actual success of these boys and girls in getting jobs."[86]

A 1930 survey of 150 school systems found that 33 percent had a placement service and that the ratio of vocational counselors to youth varied between 1 to 1595 in small systems and 1 to 3340 in large systems.[87] A 1938 national review of secondary schools concluded that the "guidance service is probably less well organized and operating less effectively than any other phase of secondary school activity."[88]

Obviously schools failed during the pre-World War II period to intervene effectively in the labor market. Observers concerned with youth employment problems bemoaned these difficulties and suggested remedies ranging from local labor market surveys to cooperative education and work study arrangements.[89] Anyone familiar with current discussions will recognize similar criticisms and often identical policy suggestions.[90] That schools have for so long been relatively unimportant and ineffective in the youth labor market suggests that the cause is not lack of ideas or competency but the essential structure of the labor market itself, in particular the extended period between leaving school and settling down. The remarkable growth of school systems during this period affected the youth labor market not directly but through the schooling issues raised earlier and also because of the school's role in keeping youth out of the job market.

Enclosure

The most fundamental theme of the 1920–1940 period is the institutionalization of the exclusion of youth from the central sectors of the labor market. This exclusion was not, of course, purely involuntary. As personal incomes rose and the number of children per family fell, youth and their families tended to consume more education and more leisure, that is, to delay labor market entrance. The average age of entrance rose steadily during this period.[91]

Nonetheless, youth were systematically excluded from most sectors of the labor market and "enclosed" either in schools or in youth work programs, an institution that emerged during this period. One clear set of evidence documenting this exclusion is the refusal of primary employers to hire youth.

Apparently many urban employers give no consideration whatever to employment of young people under the age of 18, and in some occupations the attainment of age 21 has been made a significant factor by law or custom.[92]

Young persons are sometimes barred from consideration through standards of hiring that appeared designed mainly to simplify the problem of choosing.[93]

Almost every employer has in mind a range of ages within which he prefers to hire. . . . For many years the upper limits have been dropping and the lower age limits have been rising.[94]

There has been a steady trend since 1910 to exclude youth under 21 from employment.[95]

These developments are, of course, a continuation of the trend that started at the turn of the century. However, an important shift of emphasis emerged, especially during the Depression. In the earlier period those seeking to exclude youth from work were in some sense "friends" of the youth. That is, the central pressure groups were child and youth advocates. Later many of those in the forefront of the effort to limit youth employment were representatives of adult workers who saw youth workers as a threat to their constituencies' employment chances. These feelings are expressed in the statements of union leaders in support of the National Youth Act:

A large number of unemployed youth without any means of support and consequently ready to work for any wage, no matter how small, constitutes a serious danger to our union standards [ILGWU].[96]

[Youth are used] as a bludgeon to defeat those things which the trade union movement has fought for many years [Textile Workers].[97]

As far as we are concerned, it is our object to keep youth off the sea until they are old enough, and anything that will keep them in school . . . has our support [Maritime Union].[98]

With millions of unemployed youth available for industrial exploitation today they present a constant threat to the employed worker [Electrical Workers].[99]

This attitude has not changed substantially.

The exclusion or enclosure of youth was managed through the use of the schools to perform a custodial function, national legislation to make the employment of youth difficult and unprofitable, the emergence of federal youth employment programs that performed an important custodial function, and work-place rules that made the employment of youth difficult.

Educators, public officials, union leaders, and others came to see an important role for the schools in keeping youth out of the labor market. In 1931 and 1932 back-to-school drives occurred throughout the country, and the intent of these activities was made quite explicit.[100] For example, the Massachusetts Commission on the Stabilization of Employment, in its final report, recommended "a progressive increase in the age at which children are permitted to leave school for work. . . . this would remove from the labor market, already increasingly overcrowded, as a result of depression, perhaps 9000 children. In more normal times the number might be as high as 15,000."[101] Labor leader Sidney Hillman argued "the educators could do more to keep the youth from the competitive field, keep them employed in some way. . . . we must find a way not to have youth competing with adults."[102] These efforts, as well as the tendency of youth to stay in school when labor market opportunities are poor, had the intended effect: between 1930 and 1932 high school enrollment increased by 704,000, compared with an increase of 488,000 in the previous two-year period.[103]

Schools responded to this new influx by reorganizing curricula into more explicit tracks and by redefining subjects to make them more "useful" to students when they finally left school.[104] Throughout the period school officials showed an awareness of this custodial function, and although there were occasional complaints that "unprepared" students were being forced to remain in school, officials tended to welcome their new role.[105] The U.S. Commissioner of Education noted in 1941: "We still have a huge reservoir of unemployed workers. . . . withdrawal from school into the labor market would only result in continued unemployment of older workers."[106] In fact, educators sought to expand this function through political struggles against the expansion of federal youth programs such as the National Youth Administration on the grounds that these programs usurped the proper role of schools.[107] Throughout the period, in national conferences, in hearings on youth legislation, and in other forums, there was frequent discussion of raising the age of compulsory schooling in order to keep more youth out of the labor market. In fact, the pressure was so great that one observer complained in 1940: "Youth can no longer be shoved out-of-sight and thus out-of-mind by being sent back into the school system."[108]

Schools thus became an important holding ground for youth. In part this was the result rather than the cause of the exclusion of youth from the labor market. However, as the back-to-school drives and the operation of compulsory education laws illustrate, to a certain extent the schools were an active instrument of the exclusion. On balance, as in so many other aspects of school-economy linkages, the schools were probably followers, not leaders. They performed, albeit with increasing enthusiasm, a custodial function thrust upon them.

A consistent objective of child labor opponents since the turn of the century had been the enactment of federal legislation abolishing child labor. Several bills were ultimately passed by Congress but were ruled unconstitutional by the Supreme Court. As a result, reformers sought to pass a child labor amendment to the Constitution. The amendment was passed by Congress but failed to gain the necessary number of approvals by state legislatures. Although never passed, the dying amendment gained new life with the onset of the Depression. In 1933 fifteen new states approved the amendment (only five had previously approved it), often with the explicit goal of limiting youth competition to adult workers.[109]

Although the constitutional amendment strategy failed, the goal of federal restrictions was achieved, first through the codes enacted under the National Recovery Act (NRA) and later, when that legislation was declared unconstitutional, through the Fair Labor Standards Act. The NRA, operating through the industry codes, sought to limit youth labor through age limitations and through minimum wages. Of the first 455 codes, 420 set a minimum age of 16, and two-thirds of the codes excluded youth under 18 from hazardous work. Interestingly, 15 codes permitted youth under 16 to work, largely in secondary industries—theaters, retail, and newspaper distribution.[110] In addition, the early codes frequently included an apprentice or learner's rate set at 80 percent of the minimum. However, organized labor opposed this on the grounds of potential substitution of youth for adults, and the later codes generally included a provision limiting the wages paid to learners and apprentices to 5 percent of the total wage bill.[111]

The effectiveness of these provisions is difficult to determine. The consensus of estimates seems to be that between 35,000 and 50,000 youth between 14 and 16 lost work as a result. The head of the Children's Bureau reported that the year after the NRA was declared unconstitutional, the number of youth leaving school for work increased by 182 percent.[113]

With the end of the NRA codes, the major legislative efforts to exclude youth from work were the Fair Labor Standards Act and youth relief programs—the Civilian Conservation Corps (CCC), the National Youth Administration (NYA), and the proposed American Youth Act. The hearings on the Fair Labor Standards Act, as it related to child labor, contained repeated references to the NRA, and it seems clear that the intent was to duplicate the success of the NRA in preventing youth from competing with adults. Interestingly enough, in view of the modern debate about the effects of the minimum wage, the proponents of the bill clearly understood that it would reduce youth employment. This was an explicit purpose.

The youth relief programs also had the explicit goal of removing youth from the labor market. Early in the discussions concerning the possible programs of the National Youth Administration, there was considerable talk of attacking the structural features of the labor market that caused high youth unemployment. However, as the activities of the program developed, it became clear that the real effort was simply to provide money to youth and keep them off the job market.[114] For example, the minutes of a 1939 meeting of NYA, AFL, and National Education Association officials reported general agreement that "the probabilities are that the trend towards a later employment age for youth apparent even before the depression and greatly accentuated by it will continue in the face of a large measure of business improvement. . . . [Hence a] new type of program of work and education is urgently needed."[115] Union support for the CCC and the NYA was conditional upon careful efforts to keep the youth in the programs from competing with adult workers, and this concern led to considerable controversy about wage rates and the type of work performed. Union support for the proposed American Youth Act was explicitly motivated by the effort to keep youth out of the labor market.[116] This concern was shared by groups other than unions, as an official of the American Youth Commission made clear in a statement supporting financial aid for students on the grounds that it would "reduce adult unemployment by removing many youthful workers from an already glutted labor market."[117]

Developments at the work place also served to limit the economic opportunities of youth. One important union strategy was to limit the extent of apprenticeships. This was important because "in times of depression, employers in the absence of apprenticeship regulations, are likely to keep apprentices at work and lay off journeymen."[118] Hence prior to the Depression 11.5 percent of the union agreements covering apprenticeship specified a ratio of apprentices to journeymen of 1 to 10 or more; after 1929, 41 percent specified such a ratio.[119] There were also widespread efforts to raise the wages of apprentices relative to those of journeymen, thus making youth more expensive, and to limit the fraction of the total wage bill accounted for by apprentices.

The emergence of seniority rules also tended to exclude youth by vesting the adult work force with job rights and by placing a priority on recalling laid-off adult workers. Seniority agreements became a much sought after goal during the Depression, an effort that met with some success. In Slicter's sample of 388 agreements signed between 1923 and 1929, 145 contained layoff or recall restrictions, while 290 of 400 agreements signed between 1933 and 1939 contained such provisions.[120]

In summary, schools, national labor legislation, youth relief programs, and work-place activities all tended to restrict the economic opportunities of youth. Youth employment and unemployment became a structural problem, and by 1940 both the definition and discussion of the problem was essentially identical to that of today.[121] The Lynds, in their 1935 book *Middletown in Transition,* perceived and characterized the problem with great accuracy:

What we appear to be seeing here is the slow emergence of a social problem likely to be momentous in the future, namely the presence in Middletown even in the prosperous 1920's of a jobless and schooless population, an idle, in-between group commencing in the mid-teens and culminating in the after-school age of nineteen. . . . with the growing pressure on available jobs from steadier workers past their teens, Middletown's industries may be absorbing less and less of the population under twenty, leaving a helpless group too old for school and too young to get jobs. Under the circumstances, the prolonging of schooling through high school and into college may represent not only a desire for more education but a slowly growing necessity to choose between school and idleness.[122]

5 Unemployment and Labor Market Structure

Without doubt the major explanation for current interest in the youth labor market lies in high youth unemployment. With the unemployment rate for 16-19-year-olds near 20 percent, this interest is understandable. Even more pressing than youth unemployment's causes and consequences is the issue of racial differentials in unemployment rates. Regardless of one's attitude toward high youth unemployment in general, it is impossible to be sanguine about the fact that the unemployment rate of young blacks is double that of young whites. The next chapter will take up these racial differentials in detail.

Structural sources of high unemployment rates are the relationship of unemployment to schooling, the hiring and firing practices of different kinds of firms, and the behavior of youth in the labor market. Most unemployment among the young can be attributed to these three causes. The minimum wage is another structural characteristic of the youth labor market that has been given considerable attention. These topics are structural in the sense that they go to the question why youth unemployment rates consistently exceed the overall unemployment rate by a factor of more than two. In taking this approach I abstract from cyclical issues. It is not surprising that expansions or contractions in the economy affect youth unemployment, but more interesting is the gap between youth and adult rates. This chapter also abstracts from a supply and demand explanation of youth unemployment. Examining the determinants of supply and demand curves makes sense because unemployment, certainly in an arithmetical and perhaps in a substantive sense, is the difference between supply of and demand for youth labor at a given wage, but for now I focus on the institutional setting in which those curves operate.

One important justification for my focus on structural explanations is the stability of the relationship between youth and adult unemployment, at least for white youth. Table 5.1 contains regressions of the unemployment rate of 16-19-year-olds on the white adult male unemployment rate (a proxy for demand), a constant term, and a time trend. The time trend, for whites, men and women, although significant, is very small. Of course, this relatively stable relationship is somewhat deceptive since it obscures important shifts such as the growing school enrollment rate, an important development because the labor force participation and unemployment rates of students and nonstudents differ. This relationship, along with the explanation for the large time trend in the black equations, is considered in chapter 6. This chapter focuses on the structural characteristics of the economy that underlie both the large constant term and the large coefficient on adult unemployment in table 5.1

Unemployment and Schooling

One of the most important sources of high unemployment among young people is the relationship between schooling and work. This may seem paradoxical, since one motive for encouraging youth to remain in school has been a desire to remove them from the labor market. While this strategy can succeed in terms of reducing labor force participation and hence total numbers of youth at work and unemployed, it does not reduce the unemployment rate. Many youth in school continue to work, generally part-time, and these youth have high unemployment rates. Furthermore, during the transition from school to full-time labor force participation a youth is especially susceptible to unemployment.

The relative importance of school-related unemployment is apparent from some simple data. In October 1976, 54 percent of unemployed 16-21-year-olds were enrolled in school; an additional 8 percent reported themselves as unemployed because they had just left school and were looking for an entry job.[1] Thus 63 percent of all unemployed 16-21-year-olds were either in school or in their entry period. A comparable picture emerges from the National Longitudinal Survey. In 1969-1970, 51.1 percent of the total weeks of unemployment experienced by 17-19-year-olds were ac-

Table 5.1
Unemployment Regressions, 16-19-Year-Olds, 1954-1978

Group	Constant	U35WM	Time	R^2	Durbin-Watson Statistic
White men	.0584 (6.44)	2.3415 (11.00)	.0009 (2.27)	.904	1.77
Black men	.0751 (4.26)	3.2286 (6.76)	.0071 (9.49)	.927	2.04
White women	.0696 (5.16)	1.5720 (7.09)	.0016 (2.29)	.876	2.12
Black women	.1631 (6.81)	1.9900 (3.19)	.0071 (6.72)	.870	2.09

Source: U.S. Department of Labor, Employment and Training Report of the President, 1977, p. 170; Employment and Earnings, 1978, 1979
Note: The independent variables are the unemployment rates of 16-19 year olds of each race-sex group. The independent variable is the unemployment rate of 35-44 year old white men and a time trend. The equations were estimated with the Cochrane-Orcutt technique. t-statistics are given in parentheses.

counted for by youth either in school or in the entry stage.[2] The relationship between interfirm shifts and entry is also revealing. In the NLS data 58.8 percent of the 17-19-year-olds who worked in 1969 and in 1970 and who were in school both years had the same employer both years; 64.4 percent of the out-of-school group did, while only 25.1 percent of the entry group did. Entry is associated with job shifts, and job shifts are associated with unemployment.

The entry issue, however, must be treated with some care. The literature tends to point out that a large fraction of unemployed youth consists of new entrants and to conclude from this that unemployment among this group is to be expected, that their unemployment is due to entry and not to a prior quit or layoff. However, the surveys define a new entrant as a youth who has never previously worked two consecutive weeks in a full-time job. Many youths who have held part-time jobs and are hence experienced workers may be new entrants by this definition. The effect is thus to overstate the importance of inexperience and to understate the importance of quits and layoffs as causes of unemployment among youth.

An additional source of school-related unemployment is, of course, unemployment during the summer. Until very recently most federal youth employment programs were devoted to summer jobs. The magnitude of the seasonal movement of youth into the labor market is evident from the figures for April and July 1978. In April 8.7 million youth were in the labor force; in July the figure was 11.8 million. In April 1.3 million youth were unemployed; in July, 1.9 million.[3] Approximately 900,000 youth were enrolled in federal youth employment programs in July. These youth are counted in the labor force statistics as employed, but it is clear that a large fraction would have been unemployed without the program, raising the 1.9 million figure considerably.

Thus it is clear that the rhythm of the school year results in considerable unemployment. Apart from the federal programs, 600,000 additional youth were unemployed in July; without the employment programs the figure would rise to over 1 million (not all youth in these programs would otherwise be unemployed). However, these youth are not being deprived of career opportunities as a result of their unemployment. Summer labor markets are the clearest example of the marginal nature of youth employment and of how the treatment of youth—in this case the school calendar—imposes that marginality.

Another result of schooling is that an important fraction of the teenage work force is part-time. In 1976 34.9 percent of all teenage labor force participants were either working part-time (voluntarily) or looking for part-time work. Put another way, 33.4 percent of all unemployed 16-19-year-olds were looking for part-time work.[4]

Much of the widespread feeling that youth unemployment is a less important problem than it seems is due to the close relationship of unemployment and schooling. Because so many youth are looking for part-time jobs, it is argued, they work primarily for spending money and unemployment, while galling, is not serious. It is also argued that unemployment associated with the school-to-work transition (entry) should not be of great concern, because it tends to be of relatively short duration.[5] These arguments, while superficially persuasive, are based on the assumption that unemployment, even "casual" unemployment, takes no long-term toll. Very little work has been done to test this assumption and I will take this up later.

Young people who are still in school seek casual, generally part-time, work in sectors of the economy that are especially unemployment prone. For example, in October 1976, 47.1 percent of employed 18-19-year-olds who were enrolled in school were working in wholesale and retail trades.[6] The 1976 unemployment rate for all experienced workers in this industry was 8.6 percent compared with an average of 7.3 percent for all industries taken together.[7] This comparison suggests that a second "structural" source of youth unemployment is the industrial distribution of young workers as well as the nature of demand for youth labor.

The Demand for Youth Labor

High youth unemployment obviously implies inadequate demand. However, this is too pat an explanation. Certain features of the youth labor market assure that demand can never be "adequate." The huge influx of youth in the summer, for example, puts a considerable strain on the capacity of the labor market to absorb them. Unemployment associated with entry is unlikely to be eliminated by more extensive demand for young workers because finding a job takes time. Unemployment caused by the behavior of youth — quits for example — is unlikely to be eliminated easily. Thus demand-oriented explanations of youth unemployment are necessarily incomplete.

Nonetheless, the structure of the demand for youth labor clearly contributes to unemployment. Most firms that offer stable employment prefer not to hire young workers, at least at going wages. Young workers are at the bottom of the hiring queue and are, to use a hackneyed phrase, the last hired and the first fired. Firms that do exhibit some preference for young workers typically do not provide stable employment.

The distribution of young workers by industry does not, at least at the crude one-digit level, explain the age pattern of unemployment. Table 5.2 contains frequency distributions, calculated for the NLS, of workers aged 17–19 and 25–27 by 1969 industry. The sample is limited to youth with a high school degree or less, a necessary control when comparing across two age groups.[8] As is apparent from these figures, the industry distributions of the two age groups differ. For example, the younger workers are more heavily concentrated in retail trade and less heavily concentrated in durable manufacturing than are the older. However, contrary to what one might expect, the different industrial distributions do not explain very much of the gap in experienced unemployment. When the younger group is "given" the older group's industry distribution but keeps its own within-industry unemployment rates,[9] the predicted unemployment is 3.92 weeks, insignificantly different from the actual 3.99. The explanation, of course, is that within industries young workers find employment in the less desirable firms, and within firms young workers face greater risk than older workers.

The argument that within given industries younger workers tend to work in the least desirable firms is difficult to document using the NLS because of

Table 5.2
Industrial Distribution (in percentages) and Unemployment, 1969

Industry	17–19 Year Olds		25–27 Year Olds	
Agriculture	13.6	(2.77)	5.7	(0.41)
Mining	0.6	(1.50)	1.9	(0.0)
Construction	12.7	(3.86)	14.0	(2.15)
Durable manufacturing	20.1	(4.04)	30.0	(2.62)
Nondurable manufacturing	13.8	(3.45)	16.1	(0.34)
Transportation	5.4	(3.02)	9.3	(0.65)
Wholesale trade	4.4	(4.12)	5.5	(0.44)
Retail trade	9.7	(4.57)	2.7	(0.30)
Finance	1.4	(6.88)	1.7	(0.00)
Business services	4.1	(4.76)	4.2	(0.35)
Personal services	3.2	(5.75)	0.6	(7.00)
Entertainment	2.4	(5.60)	0.4	(0.00)
Professional services	6.2	(4.65)	2.3	(0.36)
Public administration	2.5	(5.75)	5.5	(0.05)

Note: The figures in parentheses are the average weeks of unemployment in 1969–1970 within each industry. The sample is limited to those with a high school degree of less.

the absence of good institutional detail on the characteristics of firms. One clue, however, is unionization, since this is more likely to be associated with primary than with secondary firms. In 1969, 55 percent of the employed 17-19-year-olds with a high school degree or less worked in firms where wages were set by collective bargaining, compared with 87 percent of the 25-27-year-old-group. This is not a spurious relationship caused by the difference in the industrial distribution of the two groups. The older group had a higher rate of unionization in 9 of the 11 one-digit industries.[10] This is evidence for the strong inference that younger workers find employment in less desirable firms.

Even within a given firm, young workers face a higher probability of being laid off, because of seniority systems, formal and informal, as well as the aversion of firms to hiring youth and their consequent desire to get rid of them as soon as possible. The annual layoff rate (NLS data) for out-of-school 17-year-olds in 1969-1970 was 0.29; for 21-year-olds it was 0.18, and for 27-year-olds, 0.13. (Why do not wages adjust to compensate firms for those characteristics of youth that lead firms to place them at the bottom of the hiring queue. If youth are to some degree substitutable for adults (and the evidence is that they are),[11] then at a low enough wage firms should be happy to hire them. Part of the answer is that firms are reluctant (except in the tightest of labor markets) to adjust wage structures as part of a hiring strategy.[12] However, another part of the answer is that the wages of youth have an institutionally established floor in the minimum wage.

The Minimum Wage

The minimum wage is frequently cited, in both the professional and the popular literature, as a major structural source of youth unemployment. The effects of the minimum wage have become an issue of great concern in recent years, because of rising unemployment rates among the young and recent increases in the minimum wage. Legislation passed in 1977 raised the hourly minimum wage in steps from $2.65 on January 1, 1978, to $3.10 on January 1, 1980. In addition, coverage in the federal law has been extended. The Fair Labor Standards Act of 1938 virtually exempted government, agriculture, and retail trade and had major exemptions for service industries and construction. The effect was to exclude many youths from coverage, since the excluded industries tended to be the ones in which youth were heavily represented. With the expanded coverage of the law in recent years, many youth-intensive industries have been under the scope of the act.

For example, the 1966 amendments added hospitals, schools, laundries, hotels, motels, and restaurants to the list of covered industries. In 1947 only 56 percent of employed persons were in firms covered by the minimum wage; by 1968 the figure had risen to 79 percent.[13]

The imposition of a minimum wage above the market-clearing wage (the wage that would prevail in the absence of a minimum) leads firms to move up their demand curves and thus reduce the amount of labor they employ. Employment therefore falls. The impact on unemployment is, however, ambiguous. If the minimum wage covers all sectors of the economy, then the only question is whether workers remain in the labor market awaiting a job. If some do, then unemployment rises. If there is an uncovered sector, then some workers from the covered sector may seek jobs in the exempt sector, and some workers in the exempt sector may find it worthwhile to look for jobs in the covered sectors. Other workers may simply become discouraged and leave the labor force. The net effect on unemployment rates is not clear.[14] However, the net effect on employment is unambiguous.

The greatest effects of the minimum wage fall on workers whose wage was previously below the minimum. This is clearly a low-wage group. Although some adults fall into this category, most in this group are likely to be youths. Workers whose wages normally lie just above the minimum may benefit, since employers have an incentive to search for workers whose productivity justifies paying the minimum.

As with much else in economics, an important question is not simply the predicted direction but also the magnitude of the effect. The effect of an increase in the minimum wage may be so small that it is of little practical importance. If, for example, the demand curve for youth labor is relatively inelastic with respect to wages, the net effect will be small. Alternatively, the imposition or increase in the minimum wage may lead employers to compensate, not by reducing labor demand, but by eliminating inefficiencies in their operations.[15]

The empirical work on the effect of minimum wages is far from inspiring.[16] The typical technique is to employ national time series data and to estimate a relationship for some combination of sex-age-race subgroups. Most studies have been flawed for one of two reasons. First, studies that use the unemployment rate as their dependent variable are misleading because the minimum wage reduces employment but can have either positive or negative effects on labor force participation. Thus in an unemployment regression interpreting the effect as the sign of the minimum wage variable is highly suspect. Second, most studies have failed to control for the extent of coverage, and thus the key variable of interest is misspecified.

Five recent studies have avoided these errors by estimating employment rather than unemployment relationships and by controlling for coverage. Kaitz, Mincer, and Regan use as their dependent variable employment-to-population ratios for teenage subgroups. Welch uses the ratio of total teenage to adult employment, and Gramlich uses total youth employment.[17] The first four studies include on the right-hand side the minimum wage variable and the adult unemployment rate, while Gramlich employs a minimum wage variable and total output. In addition, Welch and Regan include quarterly dummies, while Mincer and Kaitz do not. Regan and Welch include the proportion of youth in federal training programs, Kaitz uses yearly dummies to control for this, and Mincer does nothing. Mincer, Kaitz, and Welch control for the proportion of youth in the armed services, while Regan does not. Kaitz and Welch include the school enrollment rate while Mincer and Regan do not. Regan, Kaitz, and Gramlich include a control for the size of the youth pool, while Welch and Mincer do not. Mincer and Gramlich include a time trend, while the other studies do not.

All this variation, and the resulting confusion of interpretation, is disheartening and is the consequence of poorly specified models. For example, the use of relative population terms seems to confound demand relationships with supply variables, while the school enrollment rates are clearly endogenous. Nonetheless, it is worth examining the results of the models.

1. Kaitz estimates his model for whites and nonwhites stratified by sex and age (16-17, 18-19). For whites the minimum wage coefficient is negative and significant at the 5 percent level in three of the four equations, failing only for 18-19-year-old women (in which case it is positive and insignificant). For blacks the minimum wage coefficient is never significant at 5 percent and is positive in three of four equations. In one equation it is positive and significant at the 10 percent level.

2. Mincer estimates his model for all teenagers (16-19) stratified by race and for 20-24 year old males stratified by race. (He also estimates his model for adults, as does Gramlich.) The minimum wage coefficients are negative in all four cases and are significant at the 1 percent level in three, failing only for black teenagers.

3. Welch estimates his model for all teenagers using several specifications. In equations omitting the armed forces, enrollment, and manpower program variables, the minimum wage coefficient is negative and significant at

the 5 percent level; in equations including these variables, the minimum wage term is not significant, although it is negative.

4. Regan estimates equations stratified by age (16-17, 18-19), sex, race, and school enrollment status. For men the coefficient is negative all eight times and is significant five times. For women the coefficients are negative four times out of eight and are significant twice. The magnitudes are generally greater for blacks than whites.

5. Gramlich estimates his model for all teenagers (with no subgroups) and finds that the minimum wage has a very modest impact on aggregate teenage employment but that it tends to shift employment from firms offering full-time jobs to those with only part-time employment. Thus he concludes that the "quality" of youth employment is adversely affected.

These results are clearly open to question. In general, the effects are much stronger for men than for women, in terms of both the magnitude of the coefficient and the significance. No one offers an explanation of this result, although it may be possible to argue that the actual coverage varies by sex. Furthermore, the results for blacks are less reliable than those for whites, and more so for statistical significance than for magnitude. Welch suggests that differences in the sample sizes of the black and white Current Population Survey may account for this. On the basis of this work one could say that the minimum wage reduces employment and that the effect is more pronounced for blacks than for whites, but one could not draw this conclusion with much certainty.

The minimum wage does not account for the high unemployment levels of youth. It does have an effect, but the effect is not large enough that eliminating the minimum wage or imposing a dual minimum would reduce the unemployment of the young to acceptable levels. Regan, whose findings are consistent with the other studies, estimates that if the 1966 minimum wage amendment (which greatly expanded coverage and raised the minimum from $1.25 to $1.65) had not been enacted then in 1972, the teenage unemployment rate would have been 12.4 percent instead of 16.2 percent and 30.5 percent instead of 33.5 percent for nonwhites. These effects, although not trivial, are not as large as the attention given to the topic would lead one to expect. Nor are their welfare implications clear. Some of the jobs lost by teenagers undoubtedly went to adults, and some of the disemployed teenagers returned to school, a use of their time that may well have been more productive in the long run.

The conclusion that the minimum wage has an adverse effect on youth employment is anathema to major segments of the liberal political, and (to a lesser extent) economic, establishment. However, it should come as little surprise, for the minimum wage was one of the major legislative tools employed in the 1930s to reduce youth employment and limit their competition with adults. The minimum wage was intended to have these deleterious effects on the youth labor market. It was an important element in the restriction of the young to a marginal economic role. That this remains so is clear from the recent debate about the passage of a subminimum wage for the young. Secretary of Labor Ray Marshall, speaking in opposition to a lower minimum wage for youth, denied that the minimum wage has disemployment effects but admitted his fear that "any youth differential would encourage employers to lay off adults with families to support and replace them with young people at lower wages."[18] George Meany, the former president of the AFL-CIO, also denied a disemployment effect but went on to remark: "The concept of 'evening out unemployment rates' means that for teenage unemployment rates to be lowered, unemployment rates will have to be increased for older workers. Does Congress really want to say to a teenager: 'The only way to get you a job is to pay you less than the minimum wage and fire an older worker, who may have a family, so that you may be hired'?"[19]

This argument is remarkably reminiscent of the 1930s argument for the restriction of youth. Also as in the 1930s, advocates of restricting the scope of youth pointed to federal youth employment programs as the solution.

It is possible that the value judgment implied in these arguments is correct. If jobs must be rationed, adults probably have a better claim than youth. There is, however, another argument in favor of the subminimum wage for youth. Supporters of the dual minimum wage argue that besides the obvious effect of fewer employment opportunities, minimum wages also have serious long-term consequences because youth are denied training opportunities. In the words of Martin Feldstein: "Firms cannot afford to offer useful on-the-job training to a broad class of young employees. . . . it is here that the minimum wage has an unambiguously harmful effect on some young workers. Even if an individual were willing to 'buy' on-the-job training by taking a very low wage for 6 months or a year, the minimum wage would not permit him to do so."[20]

Whether this is so, however, is far from clear. The minimum wage has historically reached only 50 percent of the average manufacturing wage shortly after increases.[21] In periods between increases, inflation and wage increases erode even this low level. The firms whose wages are at this level are almost entirely secondary labor market firms who provide little in the way of training or career ladders. The youth whose employment is reduced by the minimum are teenagers in the moratorium stage who are unlikely in any case to find work outside this sector. That this is true can be seen by examining the firms who actually campaign for a lower youth minimum. In the 1977 hearings the firms were restaurants, retail stores, convenience stores, laundries, and parking lot operators.[22] In the words of Senator Williams: "You know what happens when we deliberate the minimum wage. Almost a million dollar campaign is launched against it by these fast food campaigns (*sic*) with Big Mac No. 1."[23] These firms are unlikely to provide much in the way of training or salable experience.

The minimum wage reduces youth employment and raises unemployment, although it is not the principal cause of youth unemployment. It is not surprising that the minimum wage has this effect, since its purpose was originally to shield adult workers from competition. The minimum wage contributes to the enforced marginality of young workers.

The Behavior of Youth

An important part of the explanation for youth unemployment is clearly the behavior patterns of the youth. These patterns have both a direct and an indirect effect. The direct effect is that youth who quit jobs frequently or who move in and out of the labor force are likely to experience high unemployment rates. The indirect effect is that this behavior influences the hiring and firing practices of firms. Many firms, especially firms with well-developed internal labor markets and hence the prospects of stable employment, are reluctant to hire youth, reducing the demand for youth labor and forcing youth into less stable sectors of the labor market. In describing how the behavioral patterns of youth contribute to their unemployment patterns, I use quits as the measure of unstable behavior.

Table 5.3 presents the average number of quits per youth during 1969-1970 broken down by age and school status. As one would expect, given the impact of aging on behavior, quit rates decline quite sharply with age, a decline of over 67 percent between ages 17 and 27. The quit rates of youth who are in school or in the entry period are higher than those for youth who are out of school This is not surprising, given the peripheral attachment of in-school youth to the labor market and the tendency of youth in the entry period to change jobs.

Table 5.3
Quits by Age, 1969-1970

Age	Entire Sample	In School	Entry	Not in School
17	0.85	0.80	0.83	0.98
18	.77	.91	.71	.65
19	.65	.73	.96	.57
20	.54	.71	.70	.43
21	.58	.74	.54	.53
22	.44			.39
23	.44			.43
24	.42			.42
25	.32			.30
26	.34			.34
27	.27			.29

Source: National Longitudinal Survey.
Note: Only cells with 30 or more cases are reported.

The Nature and Consequences of Youth Unemployment

There is considerable controversy about the proper interpretation of youth unemployment. Because such a large fraction of it is associated with school attendance and entry because most unemployed youth live with parents and relatives and hence are not primary earners, and because the problem seems to disappear with age, many observers discount its importance. Indeed in other countries, for example Britain, youth who are in school and unemployed are not counted in national unemployment statistics. The National Commission on Employment Statistics has recently debated such a scheme for this country.

Other observers argue that youth rejected by the job market will develop destructive attitudes, ranging from self-hate to social anger. In addition, regardless of the long-term effects, some young people suffer considerable short-term financial hardship from prolonged unemployment. For example, 51 percent of youth between 16 and 24 who were unemployed in 1976 came from families whose income was less than the Bureau of Labor Statistics lower living standard budget.[24]

The 77 youth in the East Boston sample experienced a total of 58 spells of unemployment or periods out of the labor force.[25] The youth were asked several questions designed to determine the degree of hardship involved in the spells of unemployment. They were asked whether it bothered them not to be working, and why or why not, whether they were in financial trouble during the spell, how much (if any) money they had coming in and from what source, and a series of questions about job search.

For 43 percent of the spells the youth reported that they were not upset or bothered by not working. The key variable predicting this attitude is age. The youth were not bothered in 60 percent of the spells that occurred when they were 20 years old or younger; this was true in only 17 percent of the spells that occurred when the youth was over 20. This finding is to be expected, given the nature of the moratorium stage. The pattern is closely associated with the living arrangements of the youth; in only 8 percent of the spells for those 20 or under was the youth not living with parents, while the comparable figure is 56 percent for the over-20 group. There is also a significant difference between the younger and the older groups in their reason for being upset by not working. The younger group cited boredom 64 percent of the time as the major source of discomfort, while this was cited by the older group only 30 percent of the time.[26] This finding reflects the differences in living arrangements and in the financial needs of the two groups and their attitudes toward work. (For some subgroups, for example inner-city blacks from poor families, financial hardship is a real problem. I do not wish to minimize this; rather I am describing what I regard as the modal situation.)

These results are suggestive and clearly supportive of the ideas developed about the relationship between youths' attitudes and labor market behavior. However, it is important to examine the issue more carefully with a larger and more representative sample. The NLS does not provide information on how the youth feel about unemployment, but it can be used to examine the long-term consequences of unemployment.

Very little is known about the long-term consequences of unemployment. Adult unemployment clearly brings financial hardship and psychological suffering as well as interrupted careers and potentially permanent setbacks.[27] However, because of the special nature of youth unemployment, it is difficult to be certain about its effects. Thernstrom presents some evidence that youth who entered the labor market during the Great Depression experienced a permanent setback to their careers, but it is obviously difficult to generalize from this period.[28]

One certainty is that both longitudinally and in the cross section youth unemployment diminishes rapidly with age. This is shown in table 5.4. Reading down the columns shows the experience of different age groups in a given year. Reading along the diagnals shows the experience of the same cohort as it ages. This pattern in the national data reflects the adjustment

Table 5.4
Unemployment Rates over Time by Age, Race, and Sex

	1970	1972	1976
White males			
16-17	.157	.164	.197
18-19	.120	.124	.155
20-24	.078	.085	.109
Black males			
16-17	.278	.351	.377
18-19	.231	.262	.340
20-24	.126	.147	.207
White females			
16-17	.153	.170	.182
18-19	.119	.123	.151
20-24	.069	.082	.104
Black females			
16-17	.369	.383	.460
18-19	.329	.387	.350
20-24	.150	.174	.217

Source: Employment and Training Report of the President, 1977, pp. 169-170.

processes described earlier, not simply the later entry of better educated and more qualified workers.[29] Unemployment at early ages may not have lasting consequences.

The question here is whether young workers who experience unemployment show its effects in later years. In particular, what impact does unemployment have on wage rates and on the extent of unemployment in subsequent years. If a youth experiences unemployment in year t, what is the effect on wages and unemployment in yeams $t + 1$, $t + 2$, ane so forth. In answering this question I distinguish between the effects of unemployment experienced at younger ages, say 17-19, and that at older ages, say 20-24. I also distinguish between the effects of unemployment experienced in and out of school. Finally, I shall try to discern any racial differences in the effects of unemployment. Because these questions involve effects on individuals over time, the National Longitudinal Survey is the natural source of data.

Table 5.5 displays the basic patterns in the data and illustrates the fundamental difficulty to be overcome. The data are organized into two groups: those who did and did not experience unemployment in

Table 5.5
Characteristics of Youth Who Did and Did Not Experience Unemployment, 1968–1969

Youth Characteristics	No Unemployment	Some Unemployment
1. Weeks of unemployment, 1970	1.20	4.96
2. Weeks of unemployment, 1971	1.91	5.37
3. Hourly wage, 1970	$3.55	$2.98
4. Hourly wage, 1971	$3.79	$3.28
5. Years of education completed, 1970	11.57	10.82
6. KWW test	34.11	31.76
7. Weeks of unemployment, 1967–1968	0.81	4.23
8. Hourly wage, 1968	$2.84	$2.46

Source: National Longitudinal Survey of Young Men.

1968–1969. The experience of these two groups in subsequent years is displayed in the first four rows of the table. As is apparent, the group with no unemployment does considerably better with respect to both later unemployment and later wages than does the group that experienced unemployment. In addition, the effect of the 1968–1969 experience seems to decay with time; the wage gap between the two groups is narrower in 1971 then in 1970, and the ratio of the weeks of unemployment experienced by the groups falls from 4.13 in 1970 to 2.81 in 1971.

These crude patterns thus seem to imply that unemployment has a telling effect in later years. The difficulty with this interpretation emerges very clearly in rows 5–8. Rows 5 and 6 show that the group that experienced no unemployment in 1968–1969 averages more education and scores better on a test of knowledge of the world of work than the group that experienced unemployment. More dramatically, rows 7 and 8 show that in the years prior to the 1968–1969 unemployment, the group without unemployment did better than the group with unemployment. This clearly implies that the differences observed in 1970 and in 1971 cannot be attributed simply to the experience of unemployment in 1968–1969. The following picture emerges:

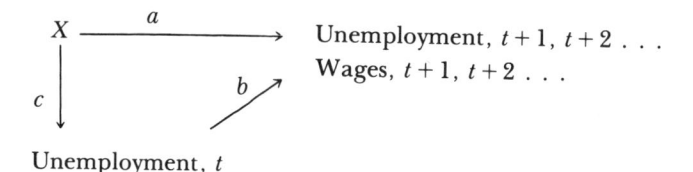

$$X \xrightarrow{a} \text{Unemployment}, t+1, t+2 \ldots$$
$$\text{Wages}, t+1, t+2 \ldots$$
$$c \downarrow \quad \nearrow b$$
$$\text{Unemployment}, t$$

where X represents the characteristics of the individual (both personal and situational) that "cause" unemployment in time t (path c) and the outcomes in $t+1$, $t+2$, and so forth. Since we are interested in focusing on path b, we need to control for paths a and c.

The central distinction is between the causal impact of early unemployment on later unemployment and the persistence of unemployment. By causality I mean the impact of the early experience on the later experience after statistically controlling for the characteristics of individuals that might explain both events. The analysis focuses on this question. However, unemployment can persist in the absence of causality, and the data in table 5.5 suggest that it does. Therefore even if early unemployment does not beget later unemployment in the strict causal sense, it does not follow that youth unemployment is of no concern. Its persistence suggests that some youth are in trouble, and unemployment is a symptom. That symptom should trigger intervention especially for older youth who experience persistent unemployment when they should be settling down.

The basic wage model is

$$W_{t+1} = \alpha + \beta_1 U_t + \beta_2 W_{t-1} + \beta_3 \text{Age}_{t+1} + \beta_4 \text{Age}^2 + e.$$

In this model the wage at time $t+i$ is a function of (1) the wage in the period prior to the unemployment, (2) the experience of unemployment, and (3) age.[30] By including the wage for the period prior to unemployment, we control for the personal characteristics of the individuals (the X variables in the diagram) and thus isolate the independent effect of unemployment. This formulation makes it possible to avoid the dilemma. It rests on the reasonable assumption that in the absence of unemployment the individual's wage in period $t+i$ is well predicted by previous wage and age. The coefficient on the unemployment term thus measures the effect of unemployment on later wages.[31]

The results of this analysis are presented in table 5.6 for men aged 16–26 in 1968 who were out-of-school between 1968 and 1971. Panel A presents results for the entire sample, while panels B and C subdivide the sample by age to reveal the differences, if any, in the effects of unemployment for older and for younger youths. The arguments developed throughout this book suggest that the effect is more important for the older group. To make the two age groups as comparable as possible, the subsamples are limited to youth with a high school degree or less.

I have measured the unemployment variable with a dummy that takes the value 1 if the youth experienced unemployment in 1968–1969 and 0

Table 5.6
Wage Equations Measuring the Consequences of Unemployment

Wage	Constant	Unemployment	Wage68	Age	Age²	$\bar{R}^2$	F
A. Entire sample, out-of-school, 1968–1971							
1970	−91.069	−16.951*	0.968	12.552	−0.218	.498	326.33
		(7.891)	(0.029)	(19.596)	(0.411)		(4,1303)
1971	180.135	−7.636	1.011	−10.301	0.272	.476	298.63
		(8.601)	(0.032)	(21.361)	(0.448)		(4,1303)
B. Ages 16–19 in 1968, high school degree or less, out-of-school 1968–1971							
1970	−2416.636	11.589	0.765	247.092	−6.026	.304	92.51
		(11.819)	(0.071)	(266.116)	(6.717)		(4,277)
1971	−5668.671	2.733	0.743	579.053	−14.402	.230	22.232
		(13.826)	(0.084)	(311.297)	(7.858)		(4,277)
C. Ages 20–24 in 1968, high school degree or less, out-of-school 1968–1971							
1970	−1491.987	−30.009*	0.994	126.147	−2.532	.440	100.18
		(14.022)	(0.051)	(145.399)	(3.020)		(4,500)
1971	−2591.287	−24.086	0.987	220.415	−4.515	.464	110.17
		(13.207)	(0.048)	(136.950)	(2.844)		(4,500)

Note: Standard errors are given in parentheses. The dependent variable is the 1970 hourly wage in cents.
* Significant at the 5 percent level.

otherwise. An alternative formulation is the weeks of unemployment experienced in 1968–1969, a variable that can range from 0 to 52. The results of this formulation do not differ from the dummy variable and are reported in footnotes. The dependent variables are wages in 1970 (one year after the 1968–1969 experience) and wages in 1971, two years later.

Looking first at panel A, the significant coefficient on unemployment for the 1970 wage equation implies that those who experienced unemployment in 1968–1969 had a 1970 wage $0.16 per hour lower than those who did not (after controlling for their earlier wage and age). This effect implies that their annual income is $372 lower, on the assumption of 2080 hours worked per year. It is also apparent in panel A that the effect is cut in half and loses statistical significance by 1971.

Panels B and C show, however, that this pattern varies with age. Panel B shows that for the younger group the effect of unemployment is never large or significant, as the discussion of the moratorium stage implies. On the other hand, for the older group the effect is large and significant for 1970 and nearly as large and approaching conventional (5 percent) significance in 1971. Evidently unemployment does have a deleterious effect when experienced by the older group.[32]

It is also of some interest to examine the impact on later wages of unemployment experienced in school. Table 5.7 shows the results of the equations estimated for the group that was in school during the 1968-1969 period and out of school subsequently. These results show quite clearly that unemployment experienced in school has essentially no effect on later wages, again much as one would expect given the earlier analysis.

To summarize thus far, these results show that for out-of-school 16-26-year-olds and for out-of-school 20-24-year-olds there is a significant loss of subsequent earnings due to unemployment, particularly in the year immediately following the experience. However, for the younger group and youth in school there is not discernible effect.

The analysis for determining the effect of unemployment in one period on unemployment in subsequent periods is slightly more difficult than that for examining the effect of unemployment on wages. The same procedure would yield an equation of the form

$$U_{70} = \alpha + \beta_1 U_{69} + \beta_2 U_{68} + \beta_3 \text{Age} + e.$$

This is obviously unacceptable, since it fails to avoid the dilemma posed at the beginning of this section. That is, simply correlating current with previous unemployment fails to isolate the effects of unemployment per se, since some people may be unemployment prone. To avoid this problem I work with an equation of the form

$$Z = U_{70} - \hat{U}_{70} = \alpha + \beta_1 U_{69} + \beta_2 \text{Age}_{70} + e.$$

Table 5.7
Wage Equations for Those in School in 1968 and Out of School in 1969-1971

Wage	Constant	Unemployment	Wage68	Age	Age²	$\bar{R}^2$	F
A. Entire sample, in-school 1968, out-of-school later years
1970	8.570	−7.339	.498	4.125	0.251	.439	44.44
		(15.569)	(.078)	(41.352)	(0.936)		(4,218)
B. Ages 16-19 in 1968, in-school in 1968, out-of-school later years, high school degree or less
1970	−419.284	2.081	.539	63.589	−1.729	.104	4.80
		(15.319)	(.124)	(329.504)	(8.565)		(4,127)

Note: Standard errors are given in parentheses.

Here the dependent variable is the difference between actual weeks of unemployment in 1970 and the weeks predicted by an auxiliary equation regressing 1970 or 1971 unemployment on a set of independent variables.[33] This model implies that deviations from expected current unemployment can be attributed to the effect of past unemployment. This formulation is acceptable provided that the auxiliary equation includes all relevant independent variables. The omission of an important (perhaps unobserved) variable will bias the coefficient on weeks of 1969 unemployment, since such a variable would lead to a positive correlation between the deviation of actual and expected unemployment (Z) and 1969 unemployment. To determine the importance of this I also estimate the equation for a subset of youth who experienced no unemployment in 1967–1968 (the previous year, $t-2$). This group should be more homogeneous with respect to any omitted variable.

Table 5.8 contains the results of the equations for the entire sample and

Table 5.8
Effects of 1968–1969 Unemployment on Later Unemployment

Z	Constant	Unemployment	Age	$\bar{R}^2$	F
A. Entire sample, out of school					
1970	1.258	2.763* (0.406)	−0.063 (0.052)	.037	26.29 (2,1293)
1971	3.879	2.756* (0.566)	−0.176 (0.073)	.025	17.56 (2,1255)
B. 1968 age 16–19, out of school, high school degree or less					
1970	28.699	2.406* (0.991)	−1.474 (0.497)	.043	7.48 (2,283)
1971	15.543	0.969 (1.276)	−0.823 (0.660)	0007	1.09 (2,265)
C. 1968 age 20–24, out of school, high school degree or less					
1970	−1.240	03.000* (0.513)	0.029 (0.126)	.060	17.16 (2,501)
1971	5.885	3.469* (0.873)	−0.247 (0.213)	.030	8.93 (2,495)

Note: The sample excludes youth unemployed at the time of the 1969 interview because, unless they found a job the next day, their inclusion would bias the results toward finding an effect of 1969 unemployment on the 1970 experience. Standard errors are given in parentheses.
* Significant at the 5 percent level.

the two subgroups.[34] These results show a clear effect of 1968-1969 unemployment on 1969-1970 and 1970-1971 unemployment for the entire sample and for the older group. For the older group, for example, the experience of unemployment in 1968-1969 implies that the 1969-1970 experience will be three weeks more unemployment than that predicted by the auxiliary regression. The young group, unlike the case of wages, also shows a significant effect for 1970 although it sharply diminishes and becomes insignificant by 1971.[35]

These results lose some of their strength, however, when the sample is limited to those who experienced no unemployment in 1967-1968. The results for this group are presented in table 5.9. As is apparent, the results are robust for the entire sample. However, for the younger group the coefficients become insignificant for both years, while for the older group the coefficients remain significant for 1970 but not for 1971. These results weaken somewhat the implications of table 5.8, but since it is doubtless too stringent a test to eliminate all those with previous unemployment, it seems fair to conclude on balance that unemployment has an effect on later unemployment for the sample taken as a whole and for the older subgroup.

Finally, the effect of unemployment experienced in school on later unemployment is also of interest. Table 5.10 contains the results of equations estimated for youth in school 1968-1969 and out in subsequent years; it shows, as was true in the case of wages, that there is no significant effect.

To consider whether the effect of unemployment varies by race, I ran equations of the same form as reported in tables 5.6 and 5.8 with the addition of two variables. The first was a race dummy variable, which was 1 if the youth was black and 0 otherwise. The purpose of this variable was to control for racial differences in the level of wages or unemployment. The second variable was an interaction term constructed by multiplying the race dummy by the unemployment dummy. This variable, the one of interest, tells us whether the effect of unemployment varies by race.

The results of this analysis are presented in table 5.11. The letters A, B, and C refer to the subgroups. The analysis for wages reveals no significant coefficient on the interaction term; in fact, four of the six coefficients are of the "wrong" sign. This does not mean that blacks experience no adverse effect from unemployment; rather it means that the effect does not vary by race. The results for unemployment are somewhat different. There five of the six coefficients are positive and three are significant. Evidently unemployment has a racially differential (and adverse) effect on the chances of later unemployment for blacks. Furthermore, these results in-

Table 5.9
Effects of 1968–1969 Unemployment on Later Unemployment, No Unemployment in 1967–1968

Z	Constant	Unemployment	Age	$\bar{R}^2$	F
A. Entire sample, out of school					
1970	−0.131	2.274*	−0.007	.017	9.93
		(0.517)	(0.057)		(2,993)
1971	3.440	1.905*	−0.160	.012	7.12
		(0.674)	(0.076)		(2,985)
B. 1968 age 16–19, out of school, high school degree or less					
1970	28.940	1.595	−1.496	.031	4.01
		(1.364)	(0.608)		(2,185)
1971	16.225	0.757	−0.861	−.002	0.766
		(1.67)	(0.776)		(2,177)
C. 1968 age 20–24, out of school, high school degree or less					
1970	−6.325	1.636*	0.239	.019	4.66
		(0.638)	(0.134)		(2,375)
1971	3.434	1.203	−0.151	−.0001	0.969
		(1.036)	(0.217)		(2,379)

Note: Standard errors are given in parentheses.
* Significant at the 5 percent level.

Table 5.10
Effects of Unemployment in School on Out of School Unemployment

Z	Constant	Unemployment	Age	$\bar{R}^2$	F
1970	A. Entire sample, in-school 1968, out of school later years				
	2.767	1.848	−0.145	.054	4.15
		(0.994)	(0.148)		(4,216)
	B. 1968 age 16–19, in-school 1968, out of school later years, high school degree or less				
	16.949	2.322	−0.944	.018	2.22
		(1.407)	(0.688)		(2,131)

Note: Standard errors are given in parentheses.

Table 5.11
Race Coefficients

	Race 1970	Race 1971	Race × Unemployment 1970	Race × Unemployment 1971
Wages				
A.	−40.258*	−42.731*	26.121	6.547
	(7.885)	(8.588)	(16.213)	(17.657)
B.	−34.187	−57.337*	−15.155	−2.745
	(14.421)	(16.678)	(24.091)	(27.861)
C.	−24.871	−20.611	27.863	7.889
	(12.815)	(12.079)	(28.394)	(26.763)
Unemployment				
A.	−0.596	0.531	1.889*	0.125
	(0.377)	(0.525)	(.837)	(1.168)
B.	−2.009	0.167	3.576	−0.783
	(1.136)	(1.500)	(2.018)	(2.264)
C.	−0.636	0.332	2.754*	5.076*
	(0.440)	(0.740)	(1.061)	(1.800)

Note: Standard errors are given in parentheses.
* Significant at 5 percent level.

dicate that that effect is strongest for older blacks (20–24) and seems to intensify (the coefficient for 1971 is larger than that of 1970).

Summary

Youth unemployment is a structural problem arising from the marginality of youth labor. Even under the best possible macro regime youth unemployment would remain quite high. Furthermore, at least for whites, there has been little appreciable long-term trend.

Structural sources of the high youth unemployment are the relationship of work patterns and schooling, the hiring pattern of firms, and the behavior of youth. Together these characteristics of the youth labor market guarantee high unemployment rates, implying that any policy intended to effect a significant reduction in youth unemployment (beyond that possible from macro policy) will come up against some very difficult barriers.

One of the mysteries concerning youth unemployment is whether it has any long-term consequences. In the East Boston interviews the attitudes of youth toward unemployment vary quite sharply with age. The younger group tended either to be unconcerned about unemployment or to cite boredom as the chief difficulty, while the older group expressed more standard economic and psychological concerns. Analysis of the NLS data showed that unemployment experienced at 17-19 seems to have few deleterious effects on subsequent wages or unemployment, while unemployment experienced at later ages does portend difficulties. The pattern does not differ by race with respect to wages, but there is at least a hint in the data that the consequences of prior unemployment on later unemployment are more severe for blacks.

6 Racial Differentials in Youth Unemployment

Regardless of the importance attached to youth unemployment in general, it is impossible to minimize the importance of the unemployment of black youth. Their unemployment rates are astronomical. While youth unemployment as a general phenomena is a consequence of the marginal nature of the youth labor force, something else is at work in the case of blacks.

The Facts and the Paradox

From the mid 1960s onward, the labor market situation of young blacks—as measured by income, wages, educational attainment, and occupational status—improved considerably. For example, in 1959 the income of 18-24-year-old nonwhite males was 70 percent of the national average for that group; for females it was 55 percent. Yet by 1969 the ratio had risen to 85 percent for men and 92 percent for women.[1] As another example, an index of the penetration of blacks into professional jobs was 0.39 for men in 1950 and 0.47 for women (1 signifies equality); by 1975 the index stood at 0.65 and 0.83.[2]

These figures do not imply, even by the measures used here, that the situation of black and white youths have been equalized. Important gaps remain, but there is an improving trend. However, some analysts take the argument further. There is still a racial gap in earnings between young blacks and whites. In 1970 in the NLS data out-of-school black men between the ages of 18 and 28 averaged $2.73 an hour while whites averaged $3.79, 38 percent more per hour. Many economists find it useful to decompose this gap into the fraction caused by differences in the personal characteristics that the youth brings to the labor market and the portion attributable to differences in the value that the labor market attaches to those characteristics. This is a useful distinction because it helps to pinpoint the source of the wage differential. To make this distinction concrete, one can imagine two polar situations. Before the mid 1960s blacks with a college education earned less than whites with only a grade-school background. The source of the racial gap in earnings was overwhelmingly due to differences in the labor market's treatment of blacks and whites. Today some economists argue that the situation is the opposite—holding endowment constant blacks do as well as whites. If this is true, then the existing racial gap in earnings is due to differences in the average characteristics (endowments) that the two groups bring to the labor market (which, of course, in turn may reflect previous discrimination).

A useful way to test the relative importance of these two sources of the racial differential is to estimate an earnings regression and then to decompose the racial gap in the dependent variable into differences attributable to the coefficients and differences attributable to the mean values of the variables. The coefficients represent labor market treatment and the mean values represent endowments. Imagine that the following (overly simple) regression is estimated separately for blacks and for whites.

$$W = B_0 + B_1 \text{ED} + B_2 \text{TRN} + B_3 \text{TENURE} + e$$

where W is hourly wages, TRN is months of vocational training, TENURE is years on the job, ED is years of schooling, and e is an error term. Then the racial differential in earnings ($W_W - W_B$) can be decomposed as follows:

$$(W_W - W_B) = (B_0^W - B_0^B) + \sum_j \overline{X}_j^B (\beta_j^W - \beta_j^B) + \sum_j \beta_j^W (\overline{X}_j^W - \overline{X}_j^B)$$

The first term on the right side is the portion of the racial gap attributable to differences in the constant terms. This represents differences in treatment that are unexplained by the variables used in the regression. The second term also represents differences in treatment; in this case it tells us how much of the gap is due to the differences in the black and white coefficients. The third term tells how much of the gap is due to differences in the racial means of the variables (differences in endowments).

Table 6.1 contains estimates of earnings equations for blacks and whites and table 6.2 presents the results of the decomposition. From the coefficients and mean values for the education variable, the distinction between endowments and treatment is clear. On the one hand, blacks receive a lower return to schooling than do whites (0.03 as opposed to 0.05). On the other hand, blacks also have on average fewer years of schooling (10.5 as opposed to 12.3). The decomposition helps in the sorting of these effects.

It is clear from the decomposition (table 6.2) that the three most important sources of the overall gap are KWW, ED, and TENURE. In all three cases blacks suffer both because of lower endowments and because of lower rates of return. Overall, the results show that more of the racial gap is due to differences in endowment than in treatment. If blacks kept the same equation structure (treatment) but their endowments were made equal to whites, their earnings would be 23 percent higher ($e^{0.207}$). If they kept the same endowments but faced the white equation structure, their earnings would be 14 percent higher ($e^{0.128}$). If both treatment and endowment changed to that of whites, the racial gap would be wiped out.[3]

There are two important lessons. The first is that the new labor market argument is probably overstated. The decomposition reveals that earnings

Table 6.1
Wage Equations

Variable	Blacks	Means	Whites	Means
KWW	.008 (.002)	27.26	.010 (.001)	36.40
ED	.039 (.010)	10.59	.051 (.006)	12.31
UNION	.329 (.040)	0.34	.216 (.024)	0.308
TRAIN	.0008 (.0007)	8.25	−.0006 (.0003)	14.46
TENURE	.021 (.021)	2.03	.073 (.017)	2.52
TENURE^2	−.001 (.002)	7.41	−.005 (.001)	10.85
EXPER	−.0006 (.011)	4.08	.018 (.006)	2.65
EXPER^2	.0004 (.0009)	32.18	−.0007 (.0006)	19.52
HEALTH	−.098 (.090)	0.044	−.093 (0.42)	0.076
MAR	.075 (.038)	0.625	.120 (.026)	0.728
CONSTANT	4.678		4.530	
$\bar{R}^2$	.373		.286	

Note: The dependent variable is the log of 1970 hourly earnings in cents. The sample is limited to youth out of school between 1969 and 1970. The independent variables are defined as follows: KWW, score on the test of knowledge of the world of work; ED, years of school completed; UNION, 1 if a union member, 0 otherwise; TRAIN, months of training completed elsewhere than a regular school; TENURE, years on the current job; EXPER, years since left school minus TENURE; HEALTH, 1 if health limits work, 0 otherwise; MAR, 1 if married with a spouse present, 0 otherwise. A Chow test rejects the hypotheses that the two equations are equal with $F = 4.96\ (10,1208)$.

Table 6.2
Decomposition of Racial Earnings Differentials

Variable	Total	Attributable to Treatment $\overline{X}^b (B_W - B_B)$	Attributable to Endowments $B^w(\overline{X}^w - \overline{X}^b)$
KWW	.172	.054	.118
ED	.214	.127	.087
UNION	−.004	−.038	−.006
TRAIN	−.014	−.011	−.003
TENURE	.140	.105	.035
TENURE^2	−.046	−.029	−.017
EXPER	.050	.075	−.025
EXPER^2	−.027	−.035	.008
HEALTH	−.0018	.0002	−.002
MAR	.040	.028	.012
		.276	.207
$B_W^o - B_B^o$		−.148	
		.128	

Note: A negative sign is favorable to blacks.

for young black men would be 14 percent higher if they were treated like whites. An open question is whether the endowments are a legitimate basis for differentials. However, this exercise shows considerable progress for blacks. When a similar analysis was performed on data from before the mid 1960s, the fraction of the differential due to treatment swamped that due to endowments.[4]

At the minimum, both the narrowing of the wage differential and the improvement in the coefficients for young blacks represents progress. Some observers go a step further and argue that discrimination is no longer a labor market problem on the grounds that the near equality of the β's shows that blacks receive a return equal to whites for productive characteristics. This argument implies that the explanation for the differential now lies largely in the institutions that lead young blacks to enter the labor market with poorer endowments than young whites. Schools and the structure of black families are the most often cited culprits.[5]

Whether one accepts this view depends in important part on what one believes are legitimate sources of earnings differentials. For example, in the earnings equations an important fraction of the wage gap was due to differences in the mean educational attainment of blacks and whites. One interpretation is that education is directly related to either productivity or lower training costs and that employers are therefore justified in paying a premium for better educated workers. Another interpretation is that for many jobs there is little difference in the productivity of workers with different amounts of schooling and that employers, knowing that blacks have on average less schooling, use educational attainment as a device for screening them out. This debate would take us far afield, but it is important to keep this caveat on the new-labor-market view in mind.[6]

Whether one accepts the strong or weak version of the new-labor-market argument it is clear that on a number of dimensions there has been considerable progress in recent years for young blacks. The paradox is that with respect to unemployment and labor force participation (and hence employment-to-population ratios), the position of young blacks has deteriorated seriously.

Table 6.3 presents, for both men and women, racial ratios of employment-to-population rates. As is quite apparent, the situation of young blacks is not only poor but has worsened. Nor is this situation limited to the more poorly educated group in the cohort. For example, in October 1976 the unemployment rate of 20-24-year-old blacks enrolled in college was 17.2 percent compared with 7.4 percent for whites.[7]

Several facts stand out:

1. White men have been able to maintain their position. Their employment-to-population ratio has not declined since the late 1960s; if anything it shows a slight secular improvement.
2. Black men have not been so fortunate. Their employment-to-population ratio, which was roughly equal to that of white men until the early 1960s, has shown a steady decline since then. Hence their situation has worsened, both absolutely and relative to white men.
3. White women have experienced a sharp increase in their employment-to-population ratio since the mid 1960s. The ratio hovered around 0.35; now it is near 0.45. This sharp increase is due to a rising labor force participation rate in this group. In 1965 the rate was 0.39; in 1975, 0.52.
4. The situation of black women has not deteriorated appreciably in absolute terms but is well below that of white women (and both groups of men) and has worsened relative to white women as the latter group's rate has risen.

Two issues require explanation. First, why does the absolute difference exist between the experience of blacks and whites? For example, why was

Table 6.3
Ratios of Employment to Population, 16-19-Year-Olds

	Men			Women		
Year	White	Black	Black/White	White	Black	Black/White
1954	.50	.52	1.05	.36	.25	.68
1955	.52	.52	1.00	.37	.26	.71
1956	.54	.52	.97	.39	.28	.72
1957	.52	.48	.92	.38	.27	.70
1958	.47	.42	.88	.35	.23	.65
1959	.48	.42	.86	.35	.20	.58
1960	.48	.44	.91	.35	.25	.70
1961	.46	.42	.91	.35	.23	.67
1962	.47	.42	.90	.35	.23	.67
1963	.45	.37	.84	.33	.21	.64
1964	.45	.38	.84	.32	.22	.67
1965	.47	.40	.84	.34	.20	.60
1966	.50	.40	.80	.38	.23	.61
1967	.50	.39	.78	.38	.25	.66
1968	.50	.39	.78	.38	.25	.65
1969	.51	.39	.76	.40	.25	.63
1970	.50	.31	.72	.40	.23	.57
1971	.49	.32	.64	.39	.20	.52
1972	.52	.32	.63	.41	.20	.48
1973	.54	.34	.63	.44	.23	.52
1974	.54	.32	.59	.44	.22	.51
1975	.51	.28	.54	.43	.22	.51
1976	.52	.27	.53	.44	.20	.46
1977	.55	.27	.50	.46	.20	.44
1978	.56	.30	.52	.49	.23	.48

Source: U.S. Department of Labor, *Employment and Training Report to The President*, (Washington D.C.: Government Printing Office), 1979.

the employment-to-population ratio in 1978 0.56 for white men while it was 0.30 for black men. Second, why has the situation deteriorated over time? Although related, these are two distinct issues. For example, there is some evidence that blacks have poorer access than whites to job-contact networks. This can help explain the level difference, but it cannot explain the trend. There is no reason to believe that the contact networks of blacks have worsened or that those of whites have improved over time nor is there any evidence that the importance of these networks has increased in recent years.

Although there are no even widely accepted explanations for the poor employment situation of young blacks, there are a variety of hypotheses, many of them plausible but unproven and in some cases contradictory.

One common explanation is the growth in cohort sizes—the baby boom. In 1955, 16-19-year-olds accounted for 9.0 percent of the population, while in 1975 they accounted for 12.7 percent. This implied a growth in absolute numbers from 8.8 million to 16.6 million.[8] Such an enormous growth might well be expected to create severe labor market problems, and popular writing has made a good deal of this. In fact, at least for whites, the baby boom has had a relatively minor effect; that this is so is illustrated by the small time trend in time series unemployment regressions for whites in table 5.1 and the fact that the employment-to-population ratios for whites have not worsened. There are two reasons for the small effect. First, until recently, the extension of schooling kept many of these youth out of the labor market. The percentage of youth between 18 and 24 who were enrolled in school grew from 14.2 percent in 1950 to 31.1 percent in 1970.[9] Because students have lower participation rates than nonstudents, this dampened and delayed the impact of the baby boom and shifted its effect away from the noncollege youth labor market.[10] Thus while the 18-24-year-old cohort grew in absolute numbers by 52 percent, their share of the total labor force rose more moderately, from 15.9 percent to 17.8 percent. The second point is that the economy responded reasonably well to the influx of youth. The teenage share of total employment roughly kept pace with the growth in their share of the labor force, growing from 5.8 percent in 1954 to 8.3 percent in 1975.[11]

All this implies that the baby boom is not quite the villain it is made out to be for whites. The story may be different for blacks, since the baby boom was larger for them. Between 1960 and 1970 the white 15-19-year-old population grew by 41.0 percent; the growth for blacks was 67.5 percent.[12] The difficulty with this explanation, however, is that in the absence of other aggravating factors, a rapid increase in black relative to white teenage population should not affect black relative to white unemployment. To draw an analogy: suppose that the number of redheads in the labor market suddenly increased. If redheads were just like blonds and brunettes in other respects, then the effects would be to raise the unemployment rate of all groups, not simply that of redheads. If, however, there were some other characteristic of the labor market that made redheads less likely than others to find work, then the population boom could help account for the worsening position. This is not to say that the baby boom played no role. The growing number of white youth may have crowded black youth out of jobs. However, we need to discover what characteristic led to this outcome or what other aspects of labor markets have retarded the growth of black relative to white youth employment.

In searching for such a characteristic, it is useful to think of the potential sources of the problem in four categories: secular shifts in the enrollment patterns and regional distribution of black youth, structural characteristics of local labor markets, the characteristics or behavior of the youth, and employer behavior.

Enrollment and Regional Shifts

Two secular changes in the status of black youth — their growing enrollment rates and the movement of blacks from the South — might be expected to play some role in the decline of the black youth employment-to-population ratio. In the instance of school enrollments the case is quite clear. In-school youth have lower labor force participation rates than their out-of-school brethren, and as a consequence their employment-to-population ratios are lower. Therefore, as a growing fraction of black youth remain in school — a development most observers would applaud — one consequence will be a decline in the overall employment-to-population ratio of the cohort. This decline is probably not a source of concern, and it is important to get a sense of its magnitude. The impact of the movement from the South is less clear. In part this movement represents a decline in the importance of farm employment to blacks, and since farm youth seem likely to have higher reported employment-to-population ratios, the situation is similar to that of enrollment rates. On the other hand, a movement out of the region where racial discrimination is sometimes thought to be the most virulent might be expected to raise the black employment-to-population ratio.

Turning first to school enrollments, the basic trends are reported in table

6.4. Two facts are apparent: the enrollment rates of young blacks have been rising, and the enrollment rates of whites have been declining. Together, these trends imply that black employment-to-population ratios should decline, both absolutely and relative to those of whites. (The 1975 figures probably understate enrollment rates relative to 1960 and 1970. The 1960 and 1970 data are taken from the census, which records actual school enrollment, while the 1975 figures are taken from the Current Population Survey, which asks for the major activity in the past week. Thus part-time enrollments are likely to be missed in 1975. However, the trends are unmistakable.)

A useful technique for determining the importance of these developments is to ask what black and white employment-to-population ratios would have been at time t if they faced the labor market at that time but had the enrollment patterns that existed at time t-1. In other words, at time t (say 1970 or 1975) assign the then existing employment-to-population ratio *within* each enrollment class but distribute the youth across the classes according to their t-1 (say 1960) distribution. Thus if the hypothetical 1975 employment-to-population ratio is higher than the actual ratio, then the difference represents the extent to which the black ratio declined due to shifts in enrollment patterns as opposed to shifts in the treatment of blacks in the labor market.

Tables 6.5 and 6.6 show the results of these calculations for the period 1960-1975 and 1970-1975. The findings confirm the expectations, and the effects are strong. The greatest movement, not surprisingly, is for the entire 1960-1975 period. Here, for example, the employment-to-population ratio

Table 6.4
Enrollment Rates, 1960-1975

	1960	1970	1975
16–19-year-olds			
White male	.71	.79	.63
Black male	.61	.67	.70
White female	.61	.70	.60
Black female	.56	.64	.61
20–24-year-olds			
White male	.22	.31	.17
Black male	.13	.16	.18
White female	.10	.17	.11
Black female	.09	.11	.11

Source: 1960, U.S. Census Summary, vol. 1, table 253; 1970, U.S. Census Summary, vol. 1, table 289; 1975, May 1975 Current Population Survey Tape.

Table 6.5
Impact of Enrollment Rate Changes, 1960–1975

	Actual Employment-to-Population Ratio, 1975	Hypothetical Employment-to-Population Ratio, 1975
16–19-year-olds		
White male	.50	.48
Black male	.25	.29
Black/white males	.50	.60
White female	.41	.41
Black female	.20	.23
Black/white females	.49	.56
20–24-year-olds		
White male	.74	.71
Black male	.59	.62
Black/white males	.80	.87
White female	.57	.58
Black female	.44	.46
Black/white females	.77	.79

Source: 1960, U.S. Census Summary, vol. 1, table 253; 1970, U.S. Census Summary, vol. 1, table 289; 1975, May 1975 Current Population Survey Tape.

for 16–19-year-old black men would have been 0.29 had the enrollment shifts not occurred, but because of these shifts the ratio was 0.25. This in itself may not seem like a large difference, and 0.29 is still an unacceptably low rate. But taken with the effect working in the opposite direction for whites (their enrollment rates declined over the period), the racial ratio rises from 0.50 to 0.60. Again, a ratio of 0.60 is not within an acceptable range but it is nontrivially higher than 0.50. Similar effects are apparent for all subgroups. The effects in the 1970–1975 period are considerably smaller for blacks but larger for whites. This reflects the sharp decline in school enrollment reported in the Current Population Survey, and this effect may be exaggerated.

These findings cast no doubt on the level of treatment of black youth; even after corrections, their employment-to-population ratios are well below those of whites. But these findings do raise the question whether the deterioration in the labor market prospects of black youths relative to those of whites is an artifact of the change in enrollment patterns. A useful way to get at this issue and control for enrollment rates is to examine the relative

Table 6.6
Impact of Enrollment Rate Changes, 1970–1975

	Actual Employment-to-Population Ratio, 1975	Hypothetical Employment-to-Population Ratio, 1975
16–19-year-olds		
White male	.50	.45
Black male	.25	.26
Black/white males	.50	.57
White female	.41	.39
Black female	.20	.20
Black/white females	.49	.51
20–24-year-olds		
White male	.74	.63
Black male	.59	.63
Black/white males	.80	1.00
White female	.57	.56
Black female	.44	.45
Black/white females	.77	.80

Source: 1960, U.S. Census Summary, vol. 1, table 253; 1970, U.S. Census Summary, vol. 1, table 289; 1975, May 1975 Current Population Survey Tape.

treatment of out-of-school youth. Table 6.7 reports the ratio of the black to white employment-to-population ratio for nonenrolled youths over the period 1964–1977. In each subgroup, the situation of blacks relative to whites has worsened in recent years. It seems clear, then, that the earlier perception concerning trends over time remains correct, although a certain amount of the trend even in the out-of-school group may be due to the shifting enrollment patterns. As black enrollment rates rise, the "quality" of the remaining out-of-school pool worsens, while as white enrollment rates decline, the "quality" of their out-of-school pool improves. Available data do not permit adequate controls for this, but it is difficult to believe that the effect is strong enough to account for a shift, say for 16–19-year-old men, from a ratio of 0.86 in the mid 1960s to 0.60 in the mid 1970s.

The impact of regional shifts is quite weak compared with the role of enrollment trends. Table 6.8 shows the ratio of black to white employment-to-population ratios broken down by region. The movement from the South would be an important factor only if, in 1970 (the latest year for which adequate data are available), the pattern in the South differed in important

Table 6.7
Ratio of Black to White Employment-to-Population Ratios for Nonenrolled Youth, 1964–1977

Year	Males 16–19	Females 16–19	Males 20–24	Females 20–24
1964	.85	.90	.96	1.06
1965	.89	.68	.98	1.13
1966	.88	.70	.95	0.96
1967	.89	.67	.91	1.00
1968	.79	.70	.93	1.01
1969	.88	.63	.96	1.03
1970	.73	.60	.88	0.93
1971	.81	.67	.88	0.88
1972	.78	.58	.92	0.86
1973	.84	.55	.87	0.86
1974	.76	.58	.88	0.85
1975	.60	.56	.83	0.75
1976	.58	.55	.77	0.78
1977	.61	.53	.79	0.74

Source: Special Labor Force Reports, *The Employment of School Age Youth*, various years.

Table 6.8
Ratios of the Black to White Employment-to-Population Ratio by Region, 1970

	16–19 Enrolled		16–19 Not Enrolled		20–24 Enrolled		20–24 Not Enrolled	
Region	Male	Female	Male	Female	Male	Female	Male	Female
North East	.56	.63	.61	.63	.98	1.04	.80	.88
North Central	.55	.60	.61	.62	.96	1.02	.79	.91
South	.56	.58	.78	.71	.79	.85	.86	.98
West	.55	.63	.61	.71	.98	1.04	.76	.98

Source: 1970 Census Summary, vol. 1, table 289.

respects from elsewhere. On balance the South appears little different from other regions. Its treatment of enrolled black youth is slightly worse than average, and its treatment of youth not in school is somewhat better. Since most 16–19-year-olds are enrolled, this implies that the movement out of the South helped them, and thus the overall decline in the employment-to-population ratio is understated, an offset to the enrollment effect discussed before. For most 20–24-year-olds out of school, however, the movement from the South hurt.

In short, the changing pattern of enrollment rates has played an important role in the decline of black employment-to-population ratios, both absolutely and relative to whites. Even so, the situation of blacks is poor and is worsening.

Structural Change in Local Economies

One source of the difficulties faced by young blacks may be shifts in the structure of local labor markets. Three possibilities seem plausible: (1) a decline in the availability of youth jobs; (2) increased availability of competing groups; and (3) the suburbanization of jobs.

There has been considerable concern in the popular literature that youth face a reduction in entry-level jobs. For example, Charles Silberman has written:

Technical change is said to be destroying unskilled jobs, most especially the traditional "entry jobs" through which teenagers used to make their way into the labor force—i.e. jobs that could be filled by youngsters with little education and no particular skill or training, but that might lead to more skilled and better paying jobs later on.[13]

In response to this argument Kalachek notes that "a summary of the technical literature provides not one iota of support for this contention."[14] Kalachek is right in the definitional sense that every job ladder must have an entry job. In a more substantive sense both the success of the economy in matching growth in the youth labor force with growth in jobs and the absence of an important time trend in unemployment equations for whites suggest that the entry-job argument needs to be viewed with some skepticism. However, it is possible to argue that changes in the job structure have had an adverse effect on young blacks.

Early in their careers youth tend to work in the secondary sector of the economy. Blacks may be disproportionately located in SMSAs in which youth-intensive activities have experienced either a secular decline or stagnant growth. In the country as a whole between 1960 and 1970 the share of all jobs accounted for by construction and nondurable manufacturing declined while the share of retail jobs remained unchanged.[15] If blacks live in SMAs which experience a contraction this might have two effects that would hurt them relative to whites. First, if the employers in the secondary labor market hire via a labor queue—ranking potential employees in terms of desirability—then the shrinking of the youth job pool could leave the position of whites unchanged but leave blacks without jobs if blacks are ranked below whites.[16] In other words, whites would capture a larger share of a shrinking pool of jobs. Second, whites may be better able than blacks to move outside the range of traditional youth jobs and find employment in other sectors. Employers may be more willing to substitute white than black youth for other labor. Either scenario would explain why a shrinking (absolute or relative to the labor force) of youth jobs would hurt blacks relative to whites.

A second structural change that might have similar implications is the increase in the availability of competing labor force groups, particularly women, white youth, and illegal aliens. These groups, for reasons of preference and discrimination, are likely to work in the secondary sector populated by black youth. Between 1960 and 1976 the labor force participation rate of married women with children between the ages of 6 and 17 rose from 39.0 percent to 53.7 percent.[17] Although good data are not available, most observers believe that in many urban labor markets there has been an influx of illegal aliens in recent years. And, of course, the numbers of white youth increased with the baby boom. Again, to the extent that these groups are preferred by employers to young blacks, then the employment impact will be adverse.

A final possible shift in local economies frequently cited as a major problem is the suburbanization of jobs. The perception that jobs have moved to the suburbs while black youth have been trapped in the inner city is correct. Between 1970 and 1974 central-city employment in the United States increased by 2.7 percent while employment outside central cities grew by 18.1 percent. In 1976, 75 percent of black 16-19-year-olds lived in central cities while the figure for whites was 34 percent.[18] As a result of these trends a large literature has emerged concerning the impact of these developments on black employment. John Kain initiated the debate and argued that black employment was reduced because of difficult physical access to jobs, lack of information, and the reluctance of employers to "import" blacks into white communities.[19]

Whatever the merits of the argument for adults, it seems plausible for youth. Their geographical scope of job search is likely to be more limited, both because of limited access to automobiles and because many work part-time after school and hence are unlikely to take jobs that require considerable travel. There is also some casual evidence to support this argument: the unemployment rate of center-city nonwhite youth in 1976 was 40.8 percent while for those residing in the suburban ring it was 33.0 percent.[20]

However, white residential dispersion has accompanied the job shift, so the popular view that suburbanization of jobs hurts the employment chances of black youth is no longer clear. As white youth move to the suburbs, black youth may have a better chance at downtown jobs even if the number of these jobs has decreased. On balance their possibility of being employed may rise. Furthermore, large concentrations of blacks living and shopping downtown may lead firms sensitive to consumer preferences to hire more blacks. Evidence supporting this point, and hence contrary to Kain, was recently presented by Offner and Saks.[21]

There are thus three possible explanations of the worsening position of young blacks that rely on structual changes in the local economies. Shifts in local industrial structure, increased availability of competing groups, and the suburbanization of jobs may help account for the plight of black youth. A second class of explanations rests on changes in the behavior of the youth themselves.

The Behavior and Characteristics of the Youth

Changes in the characteristics of black youth would appear to point to lower, not higher, relative unemployment rates. By all measures black youths who enter the labor market today are better prepared than comparable cohorts a decade ago. This is best seen in terms of educational attainment. The median years of school completed by blacks in 1959 was 8.7, while for whites it was 12.1. By 1976 the gap had essentially disappeared, with the figure for blacks being 12.3 and for whites 12.6.[22] Furthermore, there is evidence that the quality of predominantly black schools has improved over the decade.[23] However, several lines of argument imply that the behavior of black youths has changed in a manner that leads to higher unemployment rates. The first two arguments paradoxically rest on hypothetical responses of black youth to the improvements in the general economic conditions of blacks and to the political events that lie behind these changes.

Robert Flanagan has argued that black unemployment rates have worsened because more black youth have been drawn into the labor force in response to the improvements in their treatment.[24] Because the process of entry brings with it higher probabilities of unemployment, this response raises black unemployment rates. It does so presumably because black teenage participants as a group will contain a higher proportion of new entrants than will whites. In support of this argument Flanagan presents data showing that for *experienced* workers (nonentrants) over 25 years old the racial unemployment ratios have improved over time. The difficulty with Flanagan's position is that it seems inconsistent with the secular decline in the labor force participation rates of young blacks. To reconcile Flanagan's assertion that the pool of teenage blacks is becoming more heavily weighted with new entrants with the secular decline or stagnation in participation rates (for those in school and those out of school), one would have to assume a large withdrawal of experienced workers from the labor market. In a sense this is simply a redefinition of the problem, not an explanation of it.

A second supply-side explanation has been presented by Piore.[25] He suggests that the impact of the Civil Rights movement in the 1960s led young blacks to refuse the menial, low-paying jobs that had been acceptable to their parents. The parents, many of whose frame of reference was the rural South, had accepted these jobs and the discriminatory treatment they entailed because the jobs seemed an improvement over prior conditions and because of the implied promise that the conditions of their children would improve. The next generation whose frame of reference was the North and whose consciousness had been raised by the Civil Rights movement insisted on better treatment.

There are several ways in which this development might lead to more unemployment. The changing behavior of black youth might be interpreted as an inward shift of young black supply curves to certain jobs. This would have the effect of raising their wages and reducing their employment. In an earnings function, which is really a reduced form of a supply and demand system, one would observe an improvement in black wages, but the cause would be a supply shift and the consequence would be more unemployment due to the reduction in employment and the extended search of blacks for jobs that treated them better. Alternatively, if the new attitudes of young blacks led them to become a less tractable work force, less willing to submit to arbitrary and discriminatory treatment, employers would perceive this as a rise in the cost of black labor and would move up their demand curves, reducing their demand for black labor. Under either interpretation unemployment would rise as a result of these new attitudes.

A final supply-side hypothesis is that the work orientation of young blacks is poor relative to that of white youths. Perhaps because of inadequate preparation in homes or school or perhaps because of the ready availability of income in the illegal economy, relatively more young blacks than young whites do not want to work.

Market Failure

There are two important market-failure hypotheses. The first is that for some reason, perhaps affirmative action pressure, the wages of young blacks have not adjusted to excess supply to the same extent as the wages of young whites. Because their wages are "too high," the employment of young blacks has lagged behind that of whites. The second market-failure hypothesis is that racial discrimination continues to be an important factor in the labor market. Although this discrimination has eased somewhat with respect to wages, it has not done so in terms of employment. The arena of discrimination has shifted from inside the firm to the hiring gate.

Empirical Analysis

The different explanations can be classified into two categories: (1) explanations that rely on racial differences in the behavior of individuals; (2) explanations that emphasize the nature of the economic structure confronting individuals. In the former category are the supply-side explanations. Arguments about differences in the aspirations and behavior of black and white youth can best be tested by data on individuals; the National Longitudinal Survey is an obvious choice. Through an analysis of racial differences in quit rates, layoff rates, reservation wages, and aspirations I hope to identify the role, if any, of racial differences in behavior in explaining unemployment differentials.

These data are not well suited for examining the structural hypotheses described earlier. Arguments concerning local industrial structure, the role of competing groups, and suburbanization of jobs require considerably more detail on specific labor markets than is available in the NLS. Furthermore, data on individuals cannot be employed to estimate demand curves or shifts in racial demand curves over time. Thus examining the role of labor market structure and aggregate demand and supply curves requires another source of data. For these purposes cross-sectional census data on

Standard Metropolitan Statistical Area (SMSA) labor markets is a good choice. These data are rich with respect to the variables of interest.

At this point the reader who is not comfortable with modestly complex regression analysis should be warned that the next several sections will be heavy going. The chapter summary provides a fairly detailed review of the important findings.

The Research Strategy

In this section I attempt to understand youth employment levels and the worsening racial unemployment differential by estimating a model of the youth labor market employing aggregate SMSA census data. I estimate and discuss an employment model using first the 1970 census and then the 1960 data. The strategy is to use the 1970 model to explain youth unemployment levels and the racial differential and then to compare the 1970 and 1960 models to understand changes over time. The procedure will then be repeated for labor force participation and school enrollment.

Although these data permit study of local labor market structure, they also have important limitations. The most general is the difficulty of inferring time series changes from cross-sectional data. This problem arises because proxies for cyclical effects, such as the local unemployment rate, may actually reflect differences in local labor market equilibrium. Another problem is that census SMSA data are poorly suited for fully capturing and controlling for differences in individual or group skills, training, or ability. Thus any comparison between, say, the demand curves for two groups will be marred by the omission of adequate controls. Finally, the 1960 census was taken during a slack economy, while the economy was tight at the time of the 1970 census. Thus comparisons between the two years should be interpreted cautiously.

Previous econometric efforts directed toward the youth labor market have focused on labor force participation, school enrollment, labor demand, including attention to industrial structure, and the minimum wage.[26] However, in much of this literature, with the exception of the work of Katz,[27] the modeling is limited either to single-equation efforts or to multiple-equation models of particular facets such as labor force participation. Here I attempt to account for the interrelationships of demand, school enrollment, labor force participation, and wage levels.

The observations are SMSAs with a population in 1970 of 500,000 or more which reported data separately for blacks. Fifty-four SMSAs met this criterion.[28] The equations are estimated separately for 16–19-year-old black and white men and women. (Data on Spanish-speaking people have been excluded from all appropriate variables.) The 1960 equations were estimated with data from the same SMSAs with a few variables omitted.[29]

The Employment Model

The structure and estimation techniques of the employment models are as follows:

Model I

$$\text{EMP} = \beta_0 + \beta_1 \text{ own wage} + \beta_2 \text{ wage of competing youth group} + \beta_3 \text{ adult women's wage} + \beta_4 \text{YOUFRAC} + \beta_5 \text{SUB} + \beta_6 \text{Q} + e$$

Model II

$$\text{EMP} = \beta_0 + \beta_1 \text{ own wage} + \beta_2 \text{FRACLF, competing youth group} + \beta_3 \text{FRACLF, adult women} + \beta_4 \text{YOUFRAC} + \beta_5 \text{SUB} + \beta_6 \text{Q} + e$$

All variables are measured in natural logs. The estimating procedure is three-stage least squares applied to each sex equation pair for each model. The youth wage variables are endogenous, and the additional instruments were MIN, UADULT, and MANWAGE. All variables are weighted by the square root of the SMSA population.

The variables in the model are defined as follows. (Additional details are provided in the appendix to this chapter.)

Variables defined for 16–19-year-olds of each race and sex group:

WAGE
Hourly wage (measured for 1969 and adjusted for seasonal differences in hours worked)

EMP
Number employed during the census week

ED1619
Median years of school completed

ER
Enrollment rate during the census week

LFPER
Labor force participation rate of enrolled youth

LFPNER
Labor force participation rate of nonenrolled youth

MARFRAC
Fraction of the cohort married (for women)

Variables defined separately for all blacks and whites in the SMSA:

ED25
Median educational attainment of adult men 25 years old and older

RESDISP
Ratio of the population living in the central city to population living outside the central city

SUB
The ratio of all the SMSA's jobs located in the central city to jobs located outside the central city divided by RESDISP

FAMIC
Median family income

Variables defined for the entire SMSA:

Q
Total personal income in the SMSA

YOUFRAC
For men, the fraction of the SMSA's jobs accounted for by construction, manufacturing, and trade; for women, the fraction of the SMSA's jobs accounted for by trade

SOUTH
A dummy taking on the value 1 if the SMSA is located in the South

MIN
A dummy taking on the value 1 if the SMSA was predominantly located in a state which in 1969 had a minimum wage exceeding the federal minimum wage

EDDOL
Per capita expenditure on education in the SMSA's major city

UADULT

The SMSA unemployment rate of adult men during the census week

URBAN

The fraction of the SMSA's population living in urban areas

WOMENWG

Hourly wage of adult women

FRACLF, competing with youth group

The labor force of the competing youth group (same sex, other race) divided by the SMSA's total employment

FRACLF, adult women

The labor force of adult women divided by the SMSA's total employment

The equations are intended to answer several questions. First, differences in the structure of the equations by race suggest separate demand curves, which in turn implies discrimination (subject to the caveat concerning the absence of personal characteristic controls). For example, a common finding is that the wage elasticity of employment is larger for blacks than for whites, and this can be taken as evidence of discrimination.[30] The comparison of the 1960 and 1970 equations makes it possible to detect shifts in the demand equations.

The equations also make it possible to determine the importance of several aspects of local labor market structure. The first of these is competition from other groups. The equations focus on two such groups: adult women and the other racial youth group of the same sex. Thus, for example, the question is whether the employment of black teenage males is influenced by the availability of adult women and of white teenage males. This issue is examined in two ways. In Model I, a traditional demand equation, the impact of the potentially competing groups is measured by the wage cross-elasticities. The notion behind Model II is that of a labor queue, rather than wage competition, and the impact of competing groups is captured by variables measuring their availability. If the competing groups play an important role, then in Model I the sign on the cross elasticity terms should be positive (indicating, for example, that in SMSAs in which the wages of adult women are high the employment of youth increases); in the queue models the sign should be negative (indicating that in SMSAs in which adult women are more available the employment of youth declines).

The impact of the suburbanization of jobs is examined via the SUB variable. This variable, which measures the ratio of central-city jobs to race-specific central-city population, should have a positive sign if a favorable spatial distribution of jobs increases youth employment. Finally, the measures of industrial structure, which are sex specific, should make it possible to determine whether the presence of youth jobs is important and whether the importance varies by race.

The results for both models for 1970 are reported in table 6.9. In general the equations perform well, and several important findings emerge:

1. The own-wage elasticity of employment is considerably higher for blacks than for whites. This is true for both men and women in Model I though only for men in Model II. This finding is consistent with several hypotheses other than discrimination. It may be, for example, that a given black youth is a less qualified worker and that wage levels do not fully compensate. However, the differences in the elasticities are so large that it is difficult to believe that discrimination does not play some role.

2. Black youths and whites youths, of both sexes, compete with each other for jobs, but evidently the competition centers not around wages, but rather around the availability of the two groups. However, the competition is symmetrical. Whites are sensitive to the availability of blacks as well as the reverse. It is not the case that whites are in effect guaranteed the number of jobs they require while blacks get the remainder. Furthermore, the discrepancies in the elasticities are in part only indicative of the different sizes of the two groups, not of asymmetrical treatment. To understand this imagine that the size of each group increases by 1 percent and that the additional workers are allocated to "white jobs" and "black jobs" in proportion to the existing distribution of those jobs. Thus, for men, the 1 percent increase in the white youth labor force would produce an additional 227 white workers of whom 11 percent would take black jobs (black male employment is 11 percent of all male teen employment) and thus reduce black employment by 25 jobs, a reduction of 1 percent, implying an elasticity of 1. A similar 1 percent increase in the black youth labor force would imply an increase of 32, of whom 89 percent would take white jobs, reducing white employment by 0.1 percent, implying an elasticity of 0.1. Thus the expected ratio of the elasticities is 10. The expectations are essentially the same for women. Thus in the case of men the racial competition is somewhat adverse to blacks (the ratio of elasticities is worse than expected), while in the case of women the competition is favorable. White men are taking more jobs away from black men than would be expected if the two groups were treated equally, while black women do not face this problem.

Table 6.9
Employment Equations, 1970

Variable	White Men	Black Men	White Women	Black Women
Model I				
Own wage	−1.3328	−7.0562	−0.781	−6.3574
	(1.52)	(2.58)	(0.64)	(1.87)
Competing youth wage	1.4622	1.1958	1.4717	−1.5076
	(1.41)	(0.55)	(1.18)	(0.41)
Adult women wage	0.8915	−1.9121	0.3298	0.0515
	(1.36)	(1.18)	(0.47)	(0.02)
YOUFRAC	0.3237	2.0136	0.3483	−4.0181
	(0.88)	(1.98)	(0.46)	(1.97)
SUB	−0.0587	−0.1721	0.0031	−0.1229
	(0.78)	(1.49)	(1.35)	(1.04)
Q	0.9160	0.9768	0.9566	1.0405
	(10.97)	(4.27)	(10.04)	(3.65)
Constant	1.9669	4.9617	1.6614	−3.8697
	(2.55)	(2.64)	(1.43)	(1.19)
Model II				
Own wage	−1.2062	−8.2791	−0.6943	−0.5337
	(3.72)	(3.63)	(0.69)	(0.35)
FRACLF, competing youth group	−0.1928	−2.4669	−0.3390	−1.6440
	(4.11)	(3.09)	(5.63)	(4.08)
FRACLF, adult women	−1.1270	−5.5348	0.6646	1.2510
	(2.03)	(1.72)	(0.93)	(1.00)
YOUFRAC	0.5702	2.5674	−0.7292	−1.4148
	(2.59)	(2.42)	(1.30)	(1.27)
SUB	−0.0735	−0.1306	0.0035	−0.0502
	(1.48)	(0.88)	(1.84)	(0.63)
Q	0.9743	0.9366	0.9614	0.8971
	(16.21)	(3.78)	(11.94)	(6.61)
Constant	0.8169	−8.1265	−0.3663	−6.7012
	(1.05)	(1.73)	(0.40)	(2.90)

Note: t-statistics are given in parentheses.

3. Competition from adult women is somewhat different. Again there appears to be no wage competition. However, in Model II adult women appear to compete with both white and black men but not with teenage women. This is an unexpected finding since, given the occupational segregation that characterizes labor markets, one would expect the competition to be more intense among the female groups. This result casts doubt on the reliability of the findings concerning competition from women, but if those doubts are held in abeyance it is clear that women pose a greater threat to black than to white teenage males. (The logic of the discussion in the second finding does not hold here because the base of a 1 percent increase in the number of adult women is the same for both groups. That is, if there was an increase of, say, 1000 adult women and they were allocated to black and white jobs in proportion to the relative numbers of those jobs, then the elasticities would be equal.) If it is true that women pose a greater threat to black men, then the rapid growth in their labor force participation clearly plays a role in the problems encountered by black teenage men.

4. A major interest is the impact of the suburbanization variable. The data show a vast racial difference in the suburbanization of population. The mean value of RESDISP (the ratio of central-city to non-central-city population) is 10.5 for blacks and 0.84 for whites. Although I argued before that the effect of job dispersion and residential dispersion of whites could either benefit or hurt blacks, these results suggest that there is no effect one way or the other. Hence even if the Kain argument is plausible for youth, as it seems to be, it is offset either by the reduction in competition that black youth face for the remaining central-city jobs or by the pressures that a numerically more dominant black population places on firms to hire black youth.

5. The industrial structure variable is positive and significant in all four male equations but significant only once in the female equations.[31] In the male equations the size of the coefficient is substantially larger for blacks than for whites. This result suggests that while both groups are dependent on the availability of youth-intensive industries, in cities with an adverse industrial distribution whites can either capture a larger share of available youth jobs or penetrate other sectors. Furthermore, this finding suggests that secular shifts in industrial structure have been adverse to blacks. In 1960 the mean value of the male YOUFRAC variable was 0.659; by 1970 it had declined to 0.525. These results suggest that this shift in the industrial

composition in these SMSAs had an adverse impact on black men. At the same time the weak results for women suggest that a similar effect is not in operation for them.

1960 Results

The employment equations were reestimated for 1960 (with the suburbanization variable omitted); the results are presented in table 6.10. In general, the structure of the equations is strikingly similar across the decade; however, a few important shifts emerge:

1. The own-wage elasticities for blacks tend to worsen (take on larger absolute values) between 1960 and 1970. This is consistent with the hypothesis that the arena of discrimination shifted from treatment on the job to the hiring gate. The competition faced by black men from both competing groups also intensified between 1960 and 1970.

2. The industrial structure variable was insignificant in 1960 for black men, yet by 1970 the variable became significant and important. Thus black men have become increasingly dependent on a particular industrial configuration.

3. The results from Model II suggest that the own-wage elasticities for whites of both sexes improved between 1960 and 1970. However, this finding should be treated cautiously because the pattern is not present in Model I.

Labor Supply

The ratio of black to white labor force participation has worsened secularly. In these data the lower black participation rates are reflected by mean values of 0.370 for men and 0.291 for women, compared with comparable white values of 0.491 and 0.385. Although contributing by definition to lower unemployment, these relatively low black participation rates are a further sign of pathology in the labor market. The racial differential cannot be attributed to compositional effects arising from schooling, enrollment rates are lower on average for blacks (0.695 for men and 0.644 for women, compared with 0.799 and 0.708 respectively for whites), and the participation rate of out-of-school youth is higher than the rate of those in school.

The comparison between the 1970 and the 1960 labor supply equations sheds light on the decline of black relative to white participation. However, these results should be treated with some skepticism. Labor force participa-

Table 6.10
Employment Equations, 1960

Variable	White Men	Black Men	White Women	Black Women
Model I				
Own wage	1.1569	−4.3402	−1.0609	−2.0438
	(0.84)	(2.74)	(0.93)	(1.06)
Wage, competing youth group	0.1107	−5.7863	0.2676	0.2669
	(0.18)	(1.60)	(0.39)	(0.08)
Wage, adult women	−0.7456	1.1636	0.6054	−3.1549
	(0.98)	(0.58)	(1.07)	(1.97)
YOUFRAC	0.0553	0.1118	0.0626	0.1696
	(0.73)	(0.56)	(0.76)	(0.73)
Q	0.9521	0.9082	0.9925	1.1273
	(12.52)	(4.51)	(14.49)	(5.81)
Constant	1.9621	0.8366	1.2849	−0.3609
	(4.44)	(0.71)	(2.96)	(0.29)
Model II				
Own wage	−3.3369	−5.4662	−1.7942	−3.3283
	(3.92)	(4.67)	(4.21)	(3.41)
FRACLF, competing youth group	−0.3436	−0.5913	−0.3362	−1.6480
	(4.53)	(1.29)	(6.15)	(4.61)
FRACLF, adult women	0.3170	1.0913	0.3931	1.4989
	(0.66)	(0.71)	(1.12)	(1.33)
YOUFRAC	0.4334	0.6141	0.4357	1.0355
	(3.52)	(1.34)	(4.43)	(6.82)
Q	1.0186	0.7803	1.0694	1.6696
	(16.86)	(4.60)	(21.13)	(5.33)
Constant	0.6321	0.7230	0.0920	−2.9881
	(1.03)	(0.29)	(0.19)	(1.26)

Note: t-statistics are given in parentheses.

tion is an ambiguous concept in the youth labor market. The labor market is volatile, with youth moving in and out of the labor force. Attachment to the labor force is not as secure as it is for adults. Many youth who are reported out of the labor force are in fact available for work and may even be looking in a casual way. At the same time, youth who are currently looking or working have a weak attachment and may soon be out of the labor force. There is also considerable disparity in reported participation between census estimates, in which a parent generally reports the status of a youth living at home, and surveys that ask the youth directly.[32] Thus the following discussion should be taken cautiously.

The model contains three supply equations: an enrollment and two labor force participation equations, one for those in school and one for those out of school. The equations themselves are conventional in structure. Participation is a function of wages, family income, adult unemployment, the fraction of the cohort that is married (in the female equations), and one unusual variable—the residential dispersion of the racial group. This variable is intended to test the hypothesis that inner-city youth, particularly black youth, are especially discouraged.

The enrollment equation is also conventional, though again there are several measures of the impact of spatial dispersion of population. The conventional wisdom concerning this equation is that high unemployment rates encourage youth to remain in school, adult education levels are a proxy for taste and hence the effect should be positive, family income incorporates several effects but is most likely to be positive,[33] and urbanization is associated with higher enrollment rates. Per capita expenditure on education should have an ambiguous effect since it may reflect either higher-quality schools or more serious problems, though on balance its effect should be positive.

The estimation procedure is the same as for the demand equations with the third stage applied to the participation and enrollment equations of each sex-race group. The equations are estimated using a logit specification.

It is apparent in table 6.11 that there are some important racial differences in the structure of the 1970 labor force participation equations, and, with one significant exception, they argue for lower black participation rates. In the in-school equation, both black men and women show significant negative wage effects but whites do not.[34] In the out-of-school equation black women show a significant negative wage effect while the effect for white women is positive. On the other hand, the coefficient is

Table 6.11
1970 Labor Supply Equations

Variable	White men	Black men	White women	Black women
Enrollment				
FAMIC	0.00001	−0.00005	−0.00003	−0.00005
	(1.26)	(1.77)	(0.34)	(1.73)
RESDISP	−0.0389	−0.0025	−0.0283	−0.0007
	(1.46)	(1.68)	(1.57)	(0.52)
EDDOL	−0.0001	−0.0009	0.0003	−0.0009
	(0.31)	(1.54)	(0.92)	(1.67)
UADULT	2.3614	7.1914	2.1721	4.3172
	(1.17)	(2.59)	(1.50)	(1.71)
ED25	0.2027	0.1097	0.1405	0.0650
	(3.65)	(3.10)	(3.60)	(1.54)
URBAN	−0.0337	−0.8671	−0.4401	−1.4919
	(0.11)	(2.33)	(2.29)	(4.46)
Constant	−0.8544	1.0013	−0.5140	1.7677
	(1.46)	(2.35)	(1.16)	(3.98)
Labor Force Participation, Enrolled				
UADULT	−1.4139	3.4422	−3.8892	−3.0517
	(0.53)	(0.92)	(1.26)	(0.82)
WAGE	0.0891	−0.7485	0.3146	−0.9237
	(0.92)	(1.80)	(0.73)	(1.67)
FAMIC	0.00006	0.0001	0.00008	0.0003
	(3.81)	(2.16)	(3.90)	(5.14)
RESDISP	−0.0034	−0.0007	0.0181	−0.0042
	(0.10)	(0.41)	(0.44)	(1.83)
MARFRAC	—	—	−2.4268	3.9534
			(1.89)	(1.83)
Constant	−0.6975	−0.7278	−1.8326	−2.6333
	(2.64)	(1.90)	(2.18)	(3.46)
Labor Force Participation, Not Enrolled				
UADULT	−7.5635	−15.9161	−8.1433	−8.8451
	(2.85)	(3.98)	(4.68)	(2.98)
WAGE	−0.1703	1.2084	0.9262	−0.8270
	(1.71)	(2.69)	(3.67)	(1.83)
FAMIC	0.00005	−0.00008	0.00002	0.0002
	(3.34)	(1.59)	(2.25)	(4.21)
RESDISP	0.0075	−0.0021	0.0828	−0.0021
	(0.23)	(1.16)	(3.62)	(1.15)
MARFRAC	—	—	−4.5322	2.4740
			(6.29)	(1.40)
Constant	1.4325	−0.3584	−0.6822	−0.4670
	(5.33)	(0.87)	(1.40)	(0.75)

Note: t-statistics are given in parentheses. The dependent variables are in logit form.

positive for black men. Thus there is some, although not overwhelming, evidence of a stronger income effect for black than for white youth.

The equations demonstrate that the conventional wisdom concerning the relationship between unemployment and enrollment is correct; the coefficient is large and positive in all four equations and significant in two. The coefficients on the education level of adults also perform as expected. The only surprising result is the consistently negative sign on the urbanization term, a finding contrary to expectation. This cannot be attributed to the quality of central-city schools, since the urbanization index counts most suburbs as urbanized.

The shifts between 1960 and 1970 in the labor force participation equations do not present as clearcut a picture as the employment equations do. For whites the shifts between 1960 and 1970 are not consistent across the sexes. However, for blacks the shifts are consistent and help explain secular trends in participation rates.

In table 6.12 the discouraged worker effect for white men is considerably stronger in the 1960 compared with the 1970 equations, for both those in and those out of school. On the other hand, while the 1960 equations share the classic pattern of a positive wage term and negative family income term by 1970 the wage term is insignificant and the family income coefficient is positive. Thus the structure of these equations changes, but the changes are offset and there is very little overall movement in observed participation rates. For women there is little change in the discouraged worker effect and an inconsistent wage effect pattern. The term in the out-of-school equation becomes positive and significant in 1970, while the coefficient for the in-school term loses significance. The somewhat inconsistent picture — for example, the move away from the "classic" patterns in the 1960 white male equations, is comparable with Field's work on adult women which shows a similar disintegration in expected participation patterns over time.[35]

The shifts in the black equations tell a more consistent story. For both black women and men the 1970 equations show a considerably more powerful discouraged worker effect than do the 1960 equations, and this doubtlessly explains the adverse participation trends over the decade.

Individual Behavior

An important limitation of the analysis thus far has been its focus on aggregates — SMSA employment, labor force participation rates, and so forth. While this approach has its advantages, it is incomplete in important respects. In particular, it obscures the behavior of individuals and makes it impossible to control adequately for differences in the background

Table 6.12
1960 Labor Supply Equations

Variable	White men	Black men	White women	Black women
Enrollment Equation				
UADULT	2.0853	9.4278	0.9660	0.9643
	(1.21)	(2.21)	(.43)	(0.27)
ED25	0.1107	0.3180	0.0394	0.0826
	(4.72)	(4.96)	(1.23)	(1.48)
FAMIC	0.00001	−0.0002	0.0001	−0.00006
	(0.47)	(3.02)	(3.24)	(0.78)
Constant	−0.4614	−1.5622	−0.7625	−0.3897
	(1.60)	(3.4933)	(2.02)	(1.00)
Labor Force Participation, Enrolled				
UADULT	−0.70845	−8.22227	−5.6091	−2.3099
	(1.78)	(1.48)	(1.54)	(0.50)
WAGE	5.13645	0.8836	0.9807	0.1561
	(4.41)	(1.03)	(1.79)	(0.29)
FAMIC	−0.0003	−0.0000002	0.00004	0.0001
	(2.90)	(0.002)	(0.58)	(2.24)
Constant	−4.2026	−1.8545	−2.0640	−2.2820
	(5.63)	(3.60)	(3.76)	(4.15)
MARFRAC	—	—	−1.6895	−2.0634
			(1.98)	(1.75)
Labor Force Participation, Not Enrolled				
UADULT	−11.1303	6.7276	−8.2155	−5.9216
	(2.65)	(1.11)	(2.62)	(1.59)
WAGE	3.7160	−1.3197	10.3118	−1.0836
	(2.87)	(1.44)	(0.64)	(2.48)
FAMIC	−0.0001	−0.00007	0.00002	0.0001
	(1.17)	(0.55)	(0.39)	(2.45)
Constant	−1.5705	2.0974	1.7427	0.2019
	(1.91)	(3.78)	(3.65)	(0.44)
MARFRAC	—	—	−6.0109	0.8754
			(8.044)	(0.90)

Note: t-statistics are given in parentheses. The dependent variables are in logit form.

characteristics of people. For these reasons the aggregate SMSA analysis must be supplemented by studying individual micro data.

A useful way to examine the hypotheses concerning the impact of individual behavior on the racial differences in unemployment rates is to decompose the unemployment experience of individuals into a portion attributable to frequency of spells of unemployment and a portion attributable to the length of each spell. In particular, the annual weeks of unemployment experienced by a person is a product of the probability that the person will experience a spell and the expected duration of a spell when it is experienced. This distinction between spells and duration is important. For example, a group may suffer high unemployment rates either because of a disproportionate number of spells, though each spell may end quickly, or because unemployment lasts a very long time when it does occur. Issues of behavioral differences versus opportunity arise in both cases. For example, a group may experience frequent spells because they tend to quit jobs frequently. (This would normally be taken as a behavioral difference, although people may also be forced to quit by bad treatment on the job.) Alternatively, a group may have frequent spells because they are more likely to be laid off. Similarly in the case of duration a group may experience long durations becaue their reservation wages are too high or because firms refuse to hire them.

Duration of Unemployment

The model employed here is drawn from the implications of various search theories.[36] An individual's duration of unemployment is determined by a two-equation system, one equation determining the reservation or acceptance wage, the other determining the duration of a spell. This system can be summarized as

$R = R(K,D,C)$ \hfill (1)

$D = D(U,R,K)$ \hfill (2)

with

$$\frac{\partial R}{\partial K} > 0, \frac{\partial R}{\partial D} < 0,$$

$$\frac{\partial R}{\partial C} < 0, \frac{\partial D}{\partial U} > 0,$$

$$\frac{\partial D}{\partial R} > 0, \frac{\partial D}{\partial K} < 0,$$

where

D = Duration of spell
K = Skill level
R = Reservation wage
C = Cost of search and time spent unemployed
U = Distribution of job vacancies

A straightforward approach to searching for racial differentials in duration is to estimate this system for blacks and whites and test for the differences across the equations. In particular, it would be interesting to know whether there are differences in the rate at which the reservation wage falls in response to duration, differences in the extent to which skill levels reduce duration, and differences in the impact of cost-reducing factors, such as unemployment insurance, in increasing the reservation wage.

Estimates of this system are provided here, but there is a serious difficulty. Although this system provides an estimate of the determinants of reservation wage, the measure of duration is biased. Rather than measuring completed spells, which is what we want to measure with respect to the complete system of unemployment, the simultaneous system provides a measure of spells in progress. The use of duration in progress provides a biased estimate of the length of completed spells largely because long spells have a higher probability than short spells of being sampled at a point in time.[37]

Because of this problem, the emphasis here is on a reduced form of (1) and (2), namely

$$D = D(U, K, C), \qquad (3)$$

where D is now length of completed spells. Unfortunately, this introduces some ambiguity into the expected signs of the variables and the interpretation of the coefficients. For example, a high skill level would reduce duration by making more vacancies accessible but might also increase duration by raising the reservation wage. Furthermore, a negative coefficient on marriage, for example, may result either because married workers are more eager to find work (and thus reduced their asking wage) or because they are more attractive to employers and hence receive more or better offers.

Information from two survey periods of the National Longitudinal Survey is employed, 1969-1970 (collected in 1970) and 1970-1971 (collected in 1971).[38] These periods were chosen because they are the first for which complete information is available on every job held and on each spell of unemployment. The sample was limited to whites and blacks (other non-whites were excluded). The analysis is limited to out-of-school youth.[39]

In the analysis of the reduced-form equation (3), the unit of observation is each completed spell of unemployment that occurred between 1969-1971. This procedure insures that the theoretically proper dependent variable is being measured.[40] In addition, only spells associated with job change, entrance, or return to the labor market are included. Thus spells associated with temporary recalls are excluded. Whatever the importance of this class of spells for adults, they are not important for youth[41] and are excluded because of expected differences in the pattern of job search. The dependent variables are:[42]

Skills and Personal Characteristics

AGE
Age in years, measured at the beginning of the year.

KWW
This is the score on a test of knowledge of the world of work, administered by the interviewers. In addition to the possible direct importance of such a measure in explaining ability to find a job, it is also a good proxy measure of intelligence.

EDUCATION
Years of education, measured at the beginning of the year.

DEPEN
Number of dependents, excluding the wife, measured at the beginning of the year.

DRAFT
1 if eligible for the draft, 0 if not, measured at the beginning of the year.

MAR
1 if married at the beginning of the year, 0 if not.

Search Cost Variables

UI
The fraction of wages replaced by unemployment insurance. The variable is (total UI dollars received) ÷ (hourly wage of most recent job × 35 × weeks unemployed that year).[43] It is measured with error since data on the amount received are available for the entire year but not for each spell.

NONWG
This is nonlabor income (excluding transfer payments) received during the year. The availability of such income should permit, and perhaps encourage, more extended search.

Demand Variables

U
The local unemployment rate, measured in tenths of a point.

DU
The local unemployment rate at the end of the year minus the rate at the beginning of the year.

Other Variables

LINE
1 if the spell began when the respondent left a previous job and had the next job lined up in advance, 0 otherwise.

LAYOFF
1 if the spell began with a layoff from a previous job, 0 otherwise.

OLF
1 if time during the spell of unemployment was spent out of the labor force, in addition to time unemployed, 0 if not. Time out of the labor force spent in school or in the armed forces is not included in this measure.

The results of the duration equation are presented in table 6.13.[44] The two racial equations were tested for equality by means of the Chow test, and the hypothesis of equality was rejected at the 0.05 level ($F = 2.3$). In addition, race was fully interacted with the variables in a pooled equation to test for significant differences among specific coefficients. The coefficients of DRAFT, U, and LINE are significantly different at the 0.05 level and the coefficients of AGE differ at the 0.10 level.

The interpretation of these coefficients must be tempered by the realization that the equation is a reduced form. Still there are several interesting results. Time spent out of the labor force, neither working nor looking, reduces the duration of unemployment. This is plausible since many jobs are found through word of mouth, and the word can easily be passed to someone not actively looking. Thus, for youth the distinction between time unemployed and time out of the labor force can be tenuous. The impact of

Table 6.13
Duration Equations

Variable	Black	White
AGE	0.511	0.006
	(0.206)	(0.174)
KWW	−0.024	−0.013
	(0.079)	(0.059)
DRAFT	5.141	0.055
	(1.474)	(0.029)
DEPEN	0.402	−0.092
	(0.449)	(0.601)
EDUCATION	0.535	0.223
	(0.255)	(0.210)
MAR	−3.246	−1.577
	(1.393)	(1.049)
LAYOFF	3.243	0.643
	(1.106)	(0.841)
LINE	2.314	−2.598
	(1.893)	(1.353)
U	−0.003	0.073
	(0.028)	(0.022)
DU	0.055	0.055
	(0.031)	(0.029)
UI	−0.271	0.268
	(0.466)	(0.585)
NONWG	0.001	0.003
	(0.007)	(0.001)
OLF	−3.303	−2.385
	(1.589)	(1.059)
CONSTANT	−10.140	1.600
N	247	412
F	3.421 (13,233)	2.44 (13,398)
SE	8.395	7.952
$\bar{R}^2$	0.113	0.043

Note: Standard errors are given in parentheses.

unemployment insurance seems marginal, and coefficients in both equations are insignificant and of opposite sign. However, this variable is measured with potentially serious error, and there are additional possible biases in its use.[45] A change in the unemployment rate (DU) has an identical impact on black and white duration, although the level of unemployment has opposite racial effects.[46] Finally, nonlabor income increases the duration of spells for both races, although the effect is statistically significant only for whites.

A useful technique for summarizing the results of these equations is to decompose the differential into portions due to differences in the values of the variables of the two groups and differences due to the structure of the equations. This decomposition is reported in table 6.14.[47] In this decomposition negative items are favorable to whites. The results indicate that the difference in the structure of the equations implies that blacks have durations 1.200 weeks longer than they would be if they were treated or behaved like whites. Given that their actual duration is 7.915 weeks, they suffer durations 17 percent "too long." On the other hand, black characteristics are slightly "favorable." In particular, they have less education and nonwage income than whites, both of which increases white duration. The sum of these favorable characteristics reduces their durations relative to whites by 0.403 weeks and this, when subtracted from the differential due to equation differences, leads to an actual differential of 0.797 weeks.

Spells of Unemployment

Racial differences in frequencies of spells of unemployment may be due to differences in endowments or to differences in treatment and behavior. The most important conclusion that emerges from my attempt to disentangle these effects is that, unlike the case of duration, the racial differences in spells of unemployment are due largely to differences in either background characteristics or behavior, but apparently not to differences in treatment.

In this section I estimate separate racial equations for the probability of a spell of unemployment and compare the equations. However, it is important to distinguish between quits and layoffs. The same variable, for example the unemployment rate, has an opposite expected impact on quits and layoffs and, therefore, I have estimated a separate model for each.

Not all quits and layoffs lead to unemployment. In both instances, though presumably more so for quits, a separation can be followed by immediate acquisition of another job. Furthermore, the separation can also

Table 6.14
Decomposition of Unemployment Duration

Variable	Difference Due to Characteristics	Difference Due to Equation Structure
AGE	−.003	−10.988
KWW	−.086	0.297
U	.018	3.559
DU	.116	0
DEPEN	.057	−0.513
EDUCATION	.258	−3.294
UI	.014	0.079
DRAFT	−.002	−1.087
LAYOFF	.048	−1.152
NONWG	.124	0.021
LINE	−.015	−0.455
MAR	−.012	0.581
OLF	−.114	0.012
Total	.403	−12.940
Constant		11.740
Total		−1.200

be followed by movement out of the labor force. The distribution of quits and layoffs into these categories is shown in table 6.15. The figures in the table are the average of the 1969–1970 and 1970–1971 quit and layoff rates for young people out of school in those periods, and the data reflect all job changes that occurred in those periods.

Both the overall layoff rate and the overall quit rate are higher for blacks than for whites, the quit rate being 7 percent higher and layoff rate 20 percent higher. These results are not surprising; one expects to find blacks laid off more frequently than whites because of discrimination and lower endowments. Furthermore, the poorer jobs held by blacks would lead them to quit more frequently. What is surprising is that for layoffs and quits resulting in unemployment, the differential remains roughly the same for layoffs (23 percent) but widens considerably for quits, to 62 percent higher than the white rate. Evidently while blacks do not in general quit much more frequently than whites, they are considerably more likely to be unemployed after quitting and less likely to find another job immediately. It remains, of course, to see whether this pattern persists after controlling for differences in personal characteristics.

Table 6.15
Annual Quit and Layoff Rates

Separations	Whites Rate	Whites Percentage	Blacks Rate	Blacks Percentage
Layoffs				
Resulting in unemployment	.073	46.2	.096	50.5
Resulting in withdrawal from labor force	.011	6.9	.010	5.2
Followed by another job	.074	46.8	.084	44.2
Total	.158	100	.190	100
Quits				
Resulting in unemployment	.072	22.1	.117	34.0
Resulting in withdrawal from labor force	.035	10.7	.033	9.5
Followed by another job	.218	67.0	.194	56.3
Total	.325	100	.344	100

Note: The rates are averaged for two periods, 1969-1970 and 1970-1971. Only out-of-school youth are included. Percentages may not add up to 100 due to rounding.

This table also supports the common view that most voluntary job changing does not result in unemployment. However, it is surprising to learn that a considerable fraction of layoffs (46.8 percent for whites and 44.2 percent for blacks) are also immediately followed by another job.

The next step is to estimate quit and layoff models. Attention will be limited to quits and layoffs followed by spells of unemployment. The quit equations can be motivated by search theory, human capital theory, or some amalgam of the two. Accumulation of specific human capital and high wages should, if the other variables are held constant, reduce the probability of quitting. Other opportunities, indexed in this model by the unemployment rate, should increase the probability of quitting. Personal characteristics, such as marital status, dependents, and age, have an ambiguous effect depending on their impact on the individuals' needs and taste for risk.

The new variables in the quit equation are TENURE, which measures years on the job, UNION, a dummy variable that takes the value of 1 if wages are set by collective bargaining and 0 otherwise, and WAGE, the hourly wage measured in cents. In addition, a variable is introduced to test the hypothesis that one source of black quitting is discrimination on the job. The variable WTDIF is constructed by fitting a wage equation for whites, estimating what each individual (white or black) would receive, and taking the difference between that value and the actual hourly wage.[48] A positive value for blacks indicates a wage below that predicted by the white equation and may be correlated with quitting.

In the layoff model specific human capital and a high skill level are expected to reduce the probability of a layoff, while increases in the unemployment rate should increase the probability. Temporary layoffs are again excluded from the analysis.

In all the equations the dependent variable is dichotomous and takes the value 1 if a quit or layoff followed by unemployment occurred during the year and 0 otherwise.[49] As was the case in the duration analysis, the sample is pooled for two years, 1969–1970 and 1970–1971, and only youth out of school at the beginning and end of the period are included.

The equation was estimated to fit the logit functional form[50]

$$P = 1/(1+e^{-BX})$$

where P is the dichotomous dependent variable, X is the vector of explanatory variables, and the B's are the estimated parameters. A maximum likelihood estimation procedure was employed. The results of the logit quit and the layoff equations are presented in table 6.16. Predicted probabilities for blacks using the mean values of the variables are provided in table 6.17. The implications of this equation are somewhat surprising.[51] The uncontrolled gap for layoffs (table 6.15) narrows, but the gap remains. Thus even when personal characteristics, demand, experience, and job skills are controlled, young black men still face a higher probability of layoff, but the gap is not strikingly large. With respect to quits the result is surprising: the gap widens. Blacks seem considerably more likely to quit into unemployment.

In terms of the mechanics of the equations the key variables are AGE, EDUCATION, TENURE, and WAGE. Increases in the values of the first two variables decrease the probability of white quits but increase the probability of black quits. TENURE decreases the probability for both groups but much more so for whites. The only offset is WAGE, in which a high wage decreases the probability of quitting more for blacks than for whites.

The variable employed to test for quitting due to differential treatment, WTDIF, performs as expected in both sign and significance, lending support to the notion of shifts in supply as well as demand curves; however, the magnitude of the effect is small.

The explanation for the quit differential is elusive. The differential in overall quits, as opposed to quits into unemployment, is considerably smaller; hence the structure of a general quit equation may be more similar

Table 6.16
Quit and Layoff Equations

	Quit		Layoff	
Variable	Black	White	Black	White
CONSTANT	−2.178	0.208	−1.740	−0.461
	(2.074)	(0.185)	(1.918)	(0.584)
AGE	0.055	−0.082	−0.026	−0.003
	(1.033)	(1.499)	(0.679)	(0.089)
EDUCATION	0.153	−0.148	−0.033	−0.198
	(1.735)	(1.741)	(0.579)	(4.418)
TENURE	−0.037	−0.619	−0.243	−0.514
	(0.584)	(4.736)	(2.881)	(6.491)
DRAFT	0.556	−0.338	0.255	0.087
	(1.854)	(1.108)	(0.839)	(0.323)
DEPENDENTS	0.025	−0.157	—	—
	(0.265)	(1.262)		
MAR	0.368	−0.324	−0.428	−0.449
	(1.044)	(0.923)	(1.818)	(2.252)
UNION	0.293	0.045	−0.714	0.428
	(0.527)	(0.091)	(2.483)	(2.215)
WAGE	−0.016	−0.001	0.002	0.0001
	(2.365)	(0.248)	(2.504)	(0.135)
KWW	0.034	0.040	0.0006	−0.003
	(1.494)	(1.937)	(0.036)	(0.297)
U	−0.001	0.010	0.002	0.022
	(0.248)	(1.943)	(0.325)	(4.986)
DU	0.015	0.010	0.038	0.012
	(1.787)	(1.811)	(4.061)	(2.548)
WTDIF	0.014	0.0006	—	—
	(2.143)	(0.100)		
−2*log likelihood	554.318	807.896	550.046	989.624

Note: Absolute values of t-statistics are given in parentheses.

Table 6.17
Predicted Probabilities of Quits and Layoffs for Blacks

	White Equation	Black Equation
Quits	.034	.120
Layoffs	.078	.089

across the races than the unemployment quit equation. Thus blacks may quit no more frequently than whites, but they have difficulty lining up their next job.

Table 6.18 summarizes the results of the several duration and spell equations and indicates how much additional unemployment can be attributed to each of the divergences between the actual black values and the value predicted by each of the white equations. As is apparent in each instance — quits, layoffs, and duration — blacks experience more unemployment than they would had they been treated (or behaved) like whites. The difference in quit behavior accounts for nearly half of the additional unemployment, followed in importance by layoffs and duration. In the period 1969-1971 the average annual weeks of unemployment for out-of-school youths was 4.145 for blacks and 2.252 for whites; thus the differential was 1.893 weeks. The fourth column of table 6.18 shows the fraction of the total differential accounted for by the difference between actual values and those predicted by the white equations. This calculation implies that 55 percent of the total differential is due to differences in behavior or treatment while the remaining 45 percent can be explained by differences in personal characteristics.

Behavioral Differences

The analysis thus far suggests that 55 percent of the disparity between blacks and whites in annual weeks of unemployment is unexplained by differences in background characteristics. As with the analysis of wage differentials, questions about the legitimacy of the background characteristics in "justifying" the differential should be kept in mind. In the case of unemployment the percentage differential is larger than was true of wages, and the fraction unexplained by background characteristics is large. Is the

Table 6.18
Summary of Racial Differentials for the Full System

Outcomes	(1)	(2)	(3)	(4)
Quits	0.096	0.034	0.490	25.8%
Layoffs	0.117	0.078	0.308	16.2
Duration	7.915	6.715	0.255	13.4
			55.4%	

Note: (1) Actual values for blacks. (2) Predicted values using white equations and black characteristics. (3) Extra annual weeks of unemployment due to divergence of (1) and (2), holding remaining outcomes constant. (4) Fraction of annual differential in annual weeks of unemployment accounted for by (3).

unexplained differential due to differences in treatment or to differences in behavior?

It is, of course, very difficult to resolve this directly because the behavior of youths in the labor market or their treatment by firms is not observed directly. In investigations of housing discrimination it is common to have blacks and whites try to rent or buy the same housing unit and to compare their treatment, but such investigations are rare in the case of employment. The success of many Title VII race discrimination lawsuits is suggestive. In a direct experiment Phyllis Wallace had young black women apply for jobs and record their experience.[52] Evidence of discrimination emerged from this experiment, but the sample size was very small. In the absence of direct investigation, only indirect and inferential tests are available.

The differential in the duration of completed spells of unemployment may be due to difficulties that blacks face in finding jobs or to racial differences in the reservation wages. Differences in reservation wages would proxy behavioral differences and would cause longer durations. If young blacks have an "unreasonably" high reservation wage or if their reservation wage declines less rapidly than it does for whites in the face of unemployment, then the consequence would be longer duration.[53]

Table 6.19 presents a two-stage least-squares estimate of the reservation wage equation for youth unemployed at the time of the 1970 or 1971 surveys. All the variables have been defined previously, with the exception of EXXP, which is (AGE−EDUCATION−5). This is the standard experience variable employed in many earnings functions. The sample is limited to youth who were out of school at the time of the unemployment and were unemployed for reasons other than a temporary layoff, a labor dispute, or that they were waiting for a new job to begin.

The results in table 6.19 imply that little of the observed difference in duration can be attributed to differences in reservation wage formation. The coefficient on duration is only $0.05 per week apart for the two races.[54] When black mean values are substituted into the white equation, the predicted reservation wage is $2.41 an hour, slightly higher than the actual value of $2.38. Thus the white and black reservation wage structures are essentially the same, and there is no evidence that black youth unemployment is due to unrealistically high reservation wages. These results are supported by a study conducted by Stephenson which, employing a different data-set and a different specification, found that the reservation wage of black youth declined more rapidly than that of white youth as the duration of unemployment increased.[55]

Table 6.19
Two-Stage Least-Squares Reservation Wage Equations

Variable	Whites	Blacks
DURATION	2.471	7.025
	(6.411)	(4.384)
MAR	69.296	−26.195
	(28.99)	(36.011)
LINE	−100.162	3.994
	(154.009)	(82.679)
DRAFT	41.385	−29.418
	(24.989)	(27.549)
OLF	−37.601	55.067
	(21.958)	(27.565)
EXXP	22.149	6.451
	(16.245)	(10.750)
EXXP2	−0.890	−0.163
	(1.495)	(0.805)
UI	−9.601	32.963
	(8.735)	(21.073)
KWW	0.215	3.538
	(1.576)	(2.228)
DEPEN	33.625	10.155
	(20.259)	(13.984)
EDUCATION	21.507	−2.626
	(5.121)	(7.845)
CONSTANT	−95.572	64.831
	(70.105)	(105.36)
R^2	0.511	0.316
F	5.71 (11,60)	1.88 (11,45)
SE	74.7739	73.846
N	72	57

Note: The dependent variable is the hourly reservation wage in cents. Standard errors are given in parentheses.

A second important source of behavioral differences lies in the quit rates. The greater tendency of young blacks to quit into unemployment accounts for an important fraction of the unemployment differential. Although this result may seem clear evidence of behavioral differences, young blacks do not quit jobs more frequently than whites. I have estimated by means of ordinary least squares a linear probability model for all quits (employing the same variables found in table 6.16). When black mean values are substituted into the white equation, the predicted probability of a quit is 0.280, just slightly higher than the actual black mean of 0.264.[56] This stands in contrast with both the logit and the ordinary least-squares results for quitting into unemployment.

Thus young black men are not especially likely to quit. Rather their quits are more likely to lead to unemployment than those of whites. One possible explanation might be found in the motives for quitting, but table 6.20 seems to dispel this possibility. There is a clear difference in the reasons for quitting when quits are and are not followed by unemployment. For exam-

Table 6.20
Reasons for Quitting (in percentages)

Reason	Blacks	Whites
Followed by Unemployment		
Nature of job		
Hours, kind of work, conditions, interpersonal, location	36.8	44.6
Wages	15.1	6.1
Found better job	10.4	9.1
Health	8.5	14.4
Other*	29.2	25.7
Not Followed by Unemployment		
Nature of job		
Hours, kind of work, conditions, interpersonal, location	22.3	20.5
Wages	17.6	11.6
Found better job	26.8	24.0
Health	6.0	4.4
Other*	26.7	38.9

Source: National Longitudinal Survey of Young Men.
* Other includes return to school, military, prison, family and personal, and other.

ple, the category "found a better job" is more important (for both races) for quits not followed by unemployment. However, there do not seem to be major racial differences. For example, the nature of the job was cited by 51.9 percent of the blacks and 50.7 percent of the whites who quit into unemployment. Blacks cite wages more often while whites cite working conditions, but the importance of this difference is unclear (recall that the WTDIF variable was significant but unimportant in the quit equations).

A third test for behavioral differences concerns aspirations. Young blacks may have unrealistically high aspirations, perhaps because of an "oversensitive" antipathy to menial work caused by historical experience or by a misreading of the impact of racial progress on the continued importance of a training or skills. Neither hypothesis seems very convincing, but the idea is worth exploring because overly high aspirations could lead to inefficient job search and higher than necessary unemployment.

The NLS asked youth in the sample what jobs they would like to have at age 30; the responses were assigned Duncan scores.[57] This provides a metric for aspirations and aspirations can be regressed on background characteristics and the equations compared across races. If the black structure differs from the white in a direction of higher aspirations after background has been controlled, then this may be an indication of a behavioral difference.

Table 6.21 contains the regressions. The dependent variable is the Duncan score of the occupation desired at age 30; all the independent variables have been previously defined. These equations, although they differ in detail, provide no evidence of a racial difference. A Chow test ($F = 0.46$) rejects the hypothesis that the equations differ, and when the means of the variables for blacks are inserted into the white equation, the predicted value is 37.7, trivially different from the actual value of 38.5. Thus this test provides no support for the notion that young blacks have unrealistically high aspirations. A recent review of the sociological and psychological literature on work orientation also failed to find evidence of significant racial differences among youth.[58]

Finally, perhaps the strongest evidence that low motivation, unrealistic aspirations, and availability of alternative income sources do not play an important role is the sharp rise in labor force participation and employment that occurs when labor markets are tight. This is demonstrated both in the time series unemployment equations and the labor force participation equations presented earlier in the chapter. It is apparent that black youth respond to job opportunities, strongly suggesting that the problem is the availability of jobs rather than unwillingness to take those jobs.

Table 6.21
Occupation Desired at Age 30

Variable	Blacks	Whites
AGE	−0.508	−0.408
	(0.427)	(0.233)
KWW	0.385	0.251
	(0.183)	(0.106)
ED	3.962	4.273
	(0.576)	(0.314)
TRAIN	0.070	0.017
	(0.048)	(0.019)
HEALTH	0.179	−4.799
	(5.936)	(2.423)
Constant	−2.558	−4.187
$\bar{R}^2$	0.270	0.250
$\bar{X}$	38.52	47.61

Note: The dependent variable is the Duncan score of the occupation desired at age 30 (as specified in 1970). The sample is limited to youth out of school between 1969 and 1970. The Chow test is $F = 0.46$. Standard errors are given in parentheses.

The Role of Contacts

One possible explanation of the finding that young blacks are more likely to have a quit result in unemployment may be found in differential access to job contacts. Having decided to leave a job, whites may simply be more able than blacks to find the next job without experiencing unemployment. This may also be an explanation of the difference in durations. Most jobs are found through personal contacts,[59] so if blacks have fewer personal contacts than whites, they may experience difficulty locating jobs. Statistical controls for personal characteristics may fail to capture this important "unobservable," and since personal contact networks help people of every education and skill level land jobs, it is unlikely that the effect of this variable would be fully captured by other measured variables. The consequence may be that blacks, even after controlling for personal characteristics, may still have a harder time than whites in finding a job.

My interviews in East Boston and Roxbury lend some support to this hypothesis. The pattern of job-finding methods differs by race. Whites and blacks make essentially equal use of friends, but whites use parents and relatives twice as frequently as blacks. As a result, whites find 57 percent of their jobs through personal contacts, but blacks find only 33 percent in this manner. Furthermore, primary jobs are more frequently found through parents and relatives while secondary jobs are best found through friends. The relative inability of blacks to use parents and relatives thus seems to handicap them in their search for primary employment. Presumably blacks are less able than whites to use parents and relatives to help find jobs because past (and current) discrimination has prevented the parents from being in a position to help.

As a result, blacks are forced into greater reliance on formal institutions such as schools, employment agencies, and manpower programs. The proportion of blacks using these institutions is over twice that of whites. None of these institutions is notable for its success in placing clients in good jobs. Indeed, the originators of dual labor market theory developed their ideas by observing that the employment service and manpower programs seemed to recycle people through low-wage, unstable jobs.

The finding that blacks are unable to make effective use of personal contacts is not new. Lurie and Rayack reached the same conclusion in their study of a labor market in Connecticut.[60] However, there is also evidence to the contrary. In the NLS blacks and whites report essentially the same pattern of job finding. For youth out of school in 1969, 51.3 percent of the blacks and 44.2 percent of the whites found their jobs through personal contacts.[61] It still may be that personal contact referrals are more efficacious for whites, that they operate more quickly because white adults have better access to job contacts. Although plausible, this explanation is still speculative, and the issue of job contacts cannot be regarded as settled.

Another possible explanation of the quit patterns may lie in differential access to illegal activities. If the ghetto economy contains more illegal "jobs" than the white economy, then blacks who quit and show up in official statistics as unemployed may in fact be "working." Thus the differential in quits into unemployment may be misleading.

In the East Boston and Roxbury interviews there was evidence of illegal activities (unexplained periods of time, unaccounted income) but no evidence that such activities were more frequent in Roxbury than in East Boston. Other observers, however, have reached the opposite conclusion. For example, on the basis of extensive interviews in Watts and East Los Angeles, Paul Bullock concluded: "The subeconomy is probably the greatest single source of market income for youth in the center city."[62] To the extent that this is true these activities can explain the quit patterns, and they reduce normal employment because of the greater income possibilities and excitement of illegal activity. However, the existence of this sector cannot explain longer-term economic pathologies in inner-city labor markets. Illegal activities can best be conceptualized as the activities of youth in moratorium, as a form of secondary employment. Crime rates drop sharply with age, and youth who are ready to settle down do so in normal primary jobs if they are available. It is the unavailability of these jobs, not the existence of an alternative sector, that explains the difficulties of black youth.

A final market failure explanation is that black youth employment is high and rising because the wages that employers must pay young blacks are "too" high. The evidence underlying this argument is presented in table 6.22. In recent years the relative wages of white youths have fallen while those of blacks have not. The fall in the white wages was largely the result of the excess supply of white youths and the contraction of jobs available to them. These forces also affected blacks, but their wages did not fall, it is argued, because of affirmative action pressure and other barriers such as the minimum wage. The consequence is that black youths have become too expensive and their employment has fallen.

In a tautological sense this argument is correct. If black wages fell to zero, many more would be hired. However, this cannot be what advocates of this position mean; there must be some substantive content to the phrase "too high." The standard for the "correct" wage must be that the wage ratio should be equal to the ratio of productivity. In these terms the argument collapses. First, wages of blacks relative to white youths should have risen in recent years because their relative education and other endowments have risen. Second, when human capital earnings equations are estimated, the results show that young blacks in recent years have been approaching the fair, nondiscriminatory wage. They are beginning to receive an equal

Table 6.22
Ratio of Weekly Earnings of Full-Time Young Men to Weekly Earnings of White Men 25 and Over

Age	Whites 1969	Whites 1977	Blacks 1969	Blacks 1977
18	.54	.49	.44	.44
20	.66	.58	.63	.52
22	.79	.63	.59	.54
24	.87	.75	.60	.63

Source: May Current Population Survey Tapes; taken from Richard B. Freeman, "Why Is There a Youth Labor Market Problem?" paper prepared for the National Commission on Employment Policy, May 1979, p. 4.

return to what are presumably productivity-linked characteristics. In these terms it is "proper" for their wages relative to whites to have risen, and in the nontautological sense the relative wage explanation lacks validity.

Summary

The labor market situation of young blacks has improved in recent decades in a number of respects, but their relative unemployment and labor force participation rates have deteriorated. Several explanations for this deterioration have been proposed.

The secular decline in black relative to white employment-to-population ratios is in part due to the rising school enrollment rates of blacks and the declining rates of whites. Because in-school youth have low employment-to-population ratios, these developments depress the black relative to white ratio but do not signal a serious labor market problem. The magnitude of this effect is substantial, but the ratio of black relative to white employment-to-population ratios is poor even after controlling for the enrollment effect. Racial ratios for out-of-school youth also show a secular deterioration. Thus this explanation, while important, is incomplete.

Several explanations center around the supply characteristics of youth. First, it is sometimes argued that reservation wages for young blacks are too high, that aspirations or work orientation is poor, or that alternative income sources reduce the desire to work. These explanations do not stand careful scrutiny. Reservation wage equations do not reveal a significant racial differential, nor do equations for (an admittedly crude) measure of aspirations. Most important, the flow of black youth into employment when labor market conditions are favorable suggests that disinterest in work is not a major explanation.

A second supply-side explanation is that the qualifications of black youths are lower than those of whites, thus leading to a lower position in the hiring queue and to employment in less stable settings. There is some truth to this argument, as the analysis of the individual-level NLS data demonstrated. However, two important caveats are in order. First, whether educational credentials are a legitimate basis for differential outcomes is an open question, especially in the noncollege labor market. Second, differences in background characteristics cannot explain the worsening trend between black and white youth because at the same time that the trend has deteriorated, the educational and other qualifications of young blacks have improved.

Secular changes in local economies consist of the suburbanization of jobs, changes in local industrial structure, and increased competition from other demographic groups. The argument that suburbanization has reduced jobs for blacks is ambiguous in principle because both people and jobs have left the central city and thus the competitive position of black youths may not have worsened. In fact, evidence shows that suburbanization does not seem to have played an important role. Changes in the industrial structure, on the other hand, do seem important. The results show that employment among young black males is more sensitive than that of whites to the presence of youth-intensive sectors in the local economy. These sectors have exhibited a modest secular decline, and it appears that black youths have been less successful than whites in penetrating into other sectors.

The final category of structural changes is increased competition from other groups who are likely to be substitutes for black youth labor. The results for adult women at least suggested that their growing number in the labor force has reduced black youth employment. Another source of competition is white youth. Their employment-to-population ratios have not exhibited a secular decline, and this in conjunction with the baby boom implies that their absolute employment has increased sharply. White youths have been able to maintain their position in the labor market, to some extent at the expense of black youth. The evidence on both points is stronger for men than for women. Anecdotal evidence suggests that in some labor markets illegal aliens have also been competing with black youths for jobs.

Discrimination in employment is difficult to measure directly, but it must be accorded a central explanatory role. The analysis of the individual data suggests that residual factors account for roughly 50 percent of the unemployment differential, and it is conventional to interpret this residual as discrimination. The competition that blacks face from other groups in the job market is suggestive of discrimination. Absent an experiment, discrimination is difficult to prove but it is also difficult not to believe that much of the problem rests there.

More generally, the problem of high black youth unemployment rates is not simply a characteristic of the youth labor market. As black youths age, their unemployment rates decline and begin to reach the levels of black adults, but these levels are still much higher than those of white adults. This situation persists even for adults who entered the labor market during the late 1960s, the heyday of the "new labor market." For example, in 1976 the unemployment rate of 25–34-year-old white males was 5.6 percent, for white females, 7.6 percent. The rates for blacks of the same age were 11.0

percent and 13.0 percent. The situation of black youth thus cannot be understood without examining the persistence of discrimination throughout the labor market.

Appendix: Sources of Census Data

All labor force data refer to the civilian labor force. In the race-specific variables Spanish-speaking persons have been excluded. The census data (cited by table number) are taken from U.S. Census of Population, vol. 1, numbers 2-52 (Washington D.C.: G.P.O.), 1973.

EMP, ER, LFPER, LFPNER, table 166

ED16, table 147. The medians for each age group, 16-19-years-old, are treated as means, and the mean for the 16-19 year old range is calculated.

ED25, table 148

POP70, table 13

MARFRAC, table 165

WAGE, Hours are from table 166, weeks worked in 1969 from table 167, and income in 1969 (for 14-19-year-olds) from table 193. The hours worked are adjusted for seasonal differences through annual monthly hours reported in *Employment and Earnings*, table A-7.

RESDISP, SUB, table 190

YOUFRAC, table 187

WOMENWG, table 195 (full-year workers)

UADULT, table 165

FAMIC, table 205

EDDOL, Census of Governments, table 12

URBAN, City and County Data Book, table 3

TOTAL, Per capita income from table 89, population from table 13

FRACLFW, table 164

MIN, U.S. Department of Labor, *Youth Employment and Minimum Wages*, Bulletin No. 1657, (Washington, D.C.: U.S. Government Printing Office, 1970).

The 1960 data are defined analogously to the 1970 data and their source is described in Arnold Katz, "State Minimum Wages and Labor Markets for Youth," mimeographed (University of Pittsburgh, 1971). I have added the following additional variables from the 1960 Census of Population, vol. 1, numbers 2-52, (Washington, D.C.: G.P.O.), 1963.

FAMIC, table 139

YOUFRAC, table 75

ED16, tables 103 and 102

7 Conclusion

The structural characteristics of the youth labor market create many of the problems that modern youth face. The central characteristic of youth labor is its marginality, its exclusion from the stable portion of the economy. This marginality, in turn, results from the hiring practices of firms, the behavioral characteristics of youth, and the laws and institutions—such as schools—that place impediments in the way of youth employment.[1]

This institutional structure was put into place at the turn of the century, when the changing characteristics of technology and labor supply led to limitations in the economic activities of young workers and hence to the decline in youth labor force participation and the extension of schooling. With the Depression, the benign activities of the reformers gave way to a more deliberate effort to exclude youth in order to protect adult jobs. Youth were encouraged to remain in school, both legislation and union activity discouraged employers from hiring them, and federal employment programs were created to deal with surplus youth labor. The modern institutional structure was clearly in place by the end of the New Deal, and the discussion concerning public policy for unemployed youth had a remarkably modern ring.

The characteristics of this new institutional structure included extended periods in school, work activities limited to casual jobs, and the reluctance of primary firms to hire youth. The hiring practices of firms and the affluence of society are clearly important contributing factors to the behavior characterized as moratorium. In a different social setting youth would probably behave differently. At the same time, the stages have some deeper foundation. Probably the best way to conceptualize the relationship is to argue that the modern economic structure permits the expression of characteristic adolescent patterns.

Erik Erikson has argued that adolescence is a period of search and delay, a period of "psychosocial moratorium." The key task during this stage is identity formation, which in turn requires recasting childhood experiences into a form meaningful for future growth, establishing a consciously formed personality, and developing new ways of relating to family, friends, and potential sexual partners. It is a period of "free role experimentation."[2] Work is not always unimportant to youth, but it must compete with other concerns, particularly peer group and sexual relationships. Thus young people are in no hurry to establish occupational identities, to settle down. Not all young people can afford to wait, but the inclination is strong and is reflected in observed behavior.

The job patterns of young people can be understood in the context of a broader theory of labor market patterns. They start in secondary labor market jobs and over time move out of this sector. While in these secondary jobs, youth compete with other groups who are confined to that sector. In fact, an important finding is that the problems of black youth are exacerbated by competition from other secondary labor market groups. Most youth eventually move out into better jobs; for them the secondary jobs have the advantage of providing both the spending money and the freedom that they want in this stage. For groups trapped in this secondary market, the situation is much less auspicious. *Fortune* magazine recently published an article, "Who Will Do the Dirty Work of the Future?"[3] The problem has been partially solved by allocating the jobs to youth who pass through—an informal "national service"—but the tragedy is that some of this work is left over for groups without an escape.

The structure has proved quite stable. Popular writers who like to speak of a modern crisis in youth behavior, the erosion of work ethic, or the disappearance of youth jobs are generally wide of the mark. White youths show no important trend in unemployment rates. Nor is there any evidence of a secular tendency for youth to quit jobs more often than in the past or to experience greater turnover.[4]

At the same time the structure is not rigid. Within limits employers adjust their hiring patterns over the business cycle, and the economy has responded to pressures generated by the baby boom. The major development was an extension of schooling, both with respect to college and graduate school, a familiar response to excess supply. At the same time the economy grew rapidly enough to create new jobs for the enlarged supply of young entrants.

That the situation of youth in the labor market is fundamentally structural can be seen by examining the situation of youth in other industrialized countries. In most countries unemployment rates for young people are considerably lower than in the United States,[5] and this has elicited envious glances across the Atlantic. The explanations of the lower rates are complex and include differences in definition (Great Britain, for example, does not include in-school youth in the statistics), differences in demography (the growth rate of teenagers in the 1960s was much higher in the United States than elsewhere), and the generally lower unemployment levels in other societies.

A closer analysis, however, reveals that the situation of youth in most of the developed countries is more similar than implied by the level of unemployment rates. The key characteristic of the U.S. labor market is the differential, in treatment and behavior, between youth and adults. This structural characteristic is better examined through ratios than through levels, and when ratios are used the disparity between the United States and other countries diminishes. The ratio of teenage to adult unemployment in 1970 in other industrialized countries was very similar to that of the United States.[6]

A cursory examination of the literature on Great Britain suggests that the characteristics of their youth labor market are similar to those of the United States. For example, although their youth employment service is more organized than ours, surveys indicate that considerably less than half of those who leave school make use of it; even among these who do, there is considerable turnover in the first years on the labor market.[7] Other studies suggest that school leavers are more likely than adults to work in small firms, a finding that is at least suggestive of the labor market structure of the United States.[8] There is also some evidence that the behavior of youth is similar in other countries. Paul Willis described the job attitudes of youth in a factory town.

The pressure to go out at night . . . to buy modern clothes, smoke, take girls out — all of these things which are felt to constitute 'what life is really about' — put enormous financial pressure on 'the lads.' Shortage of cash is the single biggest pressure, perhaps at any rate after school, in their life. . . . all possible contacts in the family and amongst friends and casual acquaintances are exploited and the neighborhood scoured for jobs in small businesses, shops, on milk rounds, as cleaners, key cutters, ice cream salesmen, and as stackers in supermarkets.[9]

This is a clear description of youth in a moratorium stage who work in neighborhood secondary labor market firms for spending money.

Equally suggestive is Ronald Dore's description of the hiring practices of British firms for lower white-collar and blue-collar jobs.

Most of those recruited are men and women with experience. Neither factory, in fact, either seeks or admits school leavers for [semi-skilled operatives and laborers] since they take no one (except a few girls) below the age of 18 and nearly all workers in these categories leave school at 15.[10]

This description is similar to the American pattern. The hiring preferences of primary firms arise from their reluctance to risk hiring unstable youth. In Japan a new entrant into a large firm is expected to remain with that firm for life, implying that the firms would be willing to hire younger workers. Dore's evidence suggests that this is true. The average age of entry into the firms studied was over ten years lower in Japan than in Britain.[11] Furthermore, Japanese firms recruit workers directly from high school, and the schools play an important role in the hiring procedures.[12] The Japanese case suggests that where societal expectations and economic structure are sufficiently different the behavior of youth can adjust. At the same time, less than half the Japanese labor force is covered under the life-time employment system and very little is known about the uncovered sector. Thus there may be more similarities to the American case than is immediately apparent.

High youth unemployment follows logically from the structure of the youth labor market; it is not a transitory pathology. That this is so is illustrated by much of the discussion during the New Deal concerning youth unemployment. Paul David wrote in 1942 of the need to reduce the minimum wage for youth, encourage employers to end their antipathy to hiring youth, and expand federal training programs for the young. Howard Bell in 1940 called for improving the school-to-work transition by conducting better local labor market surveys and using the results to guide vocational education programs.[13]

The remarkable similarity between these ideas and current approaches, as well as the evidence that the current situation results from long-standing structural characteristics, has several implications for modern policy. It seems clear that to reduce youth unemployment substantially beyond that achieved by countercyclical policy will require serious intervention in the labor market structure. The hiring practices of firms will have to be altered. But the barriers to youth employment have not come about accidently; rather they have been created to protect the jobs of adults. Thus it would be technically difficult and politically impossible to intervene structurally in the youth labor market. Moreover it would be difficult to make a substantive case for doing so (with the exception of young blacks). Unemployment for teenagers does not generally portend later difficulty, though it can involve some financial hardships. Current federal youth programs, in particular the summer jobs program but also many others, are essentially income transfer programs designed to deal with the hardship and, as such, seem to be all that is required.

The goal of substantive policy should be to identify the youths who are having difficulty making the transition from moratorium to settling down behavior. These are the youth for whom the natural process is not working and who need help. The implication is that youth employment policy should focus, not on 16-19-year-olds, but rather on those in their early twenties. As a substantive matter, only at this age can those who require intervention be identified; as a practical matter, the younger group is very difficult to work with.

A second implication of this argument is that much of the policy focus on improving the "school to work transition" is misguided. Many analysts feel that the schools are failing to assist youth and that policy should be directed toward improving their capacity to do so. The ineffectiveness of schools is not a recent phenomenon, as we have seen, and the essential characteristics of the youth labor market make this inevitable. Because youth coming out of school are not ready to settle down and because primary firms are not prepared to hire them, there is a gap of several years between leaving school and settling down. Because there is little relationship between the first job after school and later jobs, it is not likely that the schools will be able to intervene effectively in the labor market. Educational policy is best directed toward improvements in basic skills (reading, writing, and arithmetic) while employment policy is better directed to helping the older group.

We should be more circumspect about what we expect from youth employment programs except in the case of black youth, whose serious employment problems deserve further consideration.

Designing policies to help young, unemployed blacks is not easy. If employers have been substituting adult women for black youth, for example, the immediate implication is that policy should discourage adult women from participating in the labor force, but such a policy is obviously neither feasible nor desirable. Similarly, the finding that black youth employment is sensitive to the industrial structure does not lead to any reasonable policy implications.

It seems useful to organize thinking concerning policy into two broad categories: policies designed to expand the pool of available youth jobs, and policies designed to alter the black share of a fixed job pool. Of course, in reality, there is some interaction between these two categories: it is easier to alter the black share of a labor pool that is expanding rather than stationary or declining. Nonetheless, as a first approximation, these distinctions are helpful.

Expanding aggregate demand and tight labor markets will do more for black youth employment than any conceivable alternative policy. Unemployment regressions showed that the employment situation of black youth is sensitive to the state of aggregate demand. When labor markets tighten, the situation of young blacks sharply improves, both in absolute terms and relative to whites. This central fact contradicts the arguments that black youth are uninterested and unqualified to work. Rather, black

Conclusion 155

youth find themselves at the end of the hiring queue. Tight labor markets break down discriminatory barriers and force employers to reach down in the queue. No other conceivable policy can do as much for black youth as a macroeconomic policy directed at full employment, although a considerable racial gap will remain and structural policies will still be necessary.

A second approach to evaluating policy is to take the pool of available youth jobs as fixed and to attempt to allocate those jobs equitably. A working definition of equitable in this case would be that a person's chance of being employed is independent of race. The job queue would be reshuffled to make the labor market race blind.

If this is the goal, then why does the queue not meet this criterion? Unemployed black youth fall into two categories. The first group consists of those who experience frequent spells or long durations of unemployment because of personal difficulty. The second group consists of those who are essentially ready for a job, but are unemployed because discriminatory practices have relegated them to a low place in the queue.

Those whose personal circumstances lie at the heart of the problem form a diverse group. Some may be single parents who need access to day care. Other have low reading and writing levels, some have lost confidence in their abilities and life chances, some are involved in criminal activities, while others have psychological problems. For this group supply-side human capital and social work-oriented programs make sense. Those who are equipped to function well in entry-level jobs but are unable to locate them need policies designed to alter hiring patterns and practices in the economy.

The distinction between young people who are in serious personal difficulty and those who need a job parallels the distinction between hard-core unemployed and those who are unemployed because of inadequate demand. The distinction seems useful, and the policy implications for the two groups are quite different. I have asserted that most black youths do not fall into the hard-core category, but it would be helpful to have some evidence on this point. Such evidence is, of course, difficult to obtain, but an inference can be drawn by examining the distribution of weeks of unemployment and spells of unemployment. Youths who experience many weeks or spells of unemployment over a period of several years are at least candidates for the hard-core designation. Tables 7.1 and 7.2 show for the NLS males who experienced some unemployment the fraction who experienced different amounts of unemployment and different numbers of spells. Table

Conclusion

Table 7.1
Distribution of Weeks of Unemployment among Out-of-School Male Youth Who Experienced Some Unemployment, 1969-1971 (in percentages)

| | 16-19-Year-Olds | | 20-24-Year-Olds | |
Weeks of Unemployment	White	Black	White	Black
1-4	32.8	42.6	45.3	28.8
5-8	19.5	15.0	18.6	14.0
9-12	11.8	13.6	13.2	17.8
13-16	8.8	4.8	4.8	6.6
17-20	3.4	0.9	4.8	8.9
20+	23.7	23.1	13.3	23.9
Total	100	100	100	100

Source: National Longitudinal Survey of Young Men.

Table 7.2
Distribution of Spells of Unemployment among Out-of-School Male Youth Who Experienced Some Unemployment, 1969-1971 (in percentages)

| | 16-19-Year-Olds | | 20-24-Year-Olds | |
Spells	White	Black	White	Black
1	28.6	20.5	47.4	21.4
2	28.6	16.6	26.1	37.2
3	19.4	37.4	13.8	18.2
4	9.9	17.2	9.5	12.1
5+	13.6	8.4	2.1	11.1
Total	100	100	100	100

Source: National Longitudinal Survey of Young Men.

7.3 presents similar data for both sexes using a different data source.

The implications of these tables are mixed. On the one hand, it is clear that a substantial fraction, probably a majority, of black youth who experience unemployment cannot be termed hard-core. Among the NLS 16-19-year-olds only 24 percent averaged more than eight weeks per year. The work experience survey can be expected to show more unemployment because it includes in-school youth and because census surveys consistently show more unemployment than the NLS. The results of this survey are more heavily weighted toward the hard-core interpretation, but even here it appears that more than half of the 16-19-year-old black women and over a third of the men who experienced some unemployment did so for eight weeks or less.

Table 7.3
Distribution of Weeks of Unemployment among Those Who Experienced Some Unemployment, 1977

Weeks	White Males	Black Males	White Females	Black Females
Ages 16–19				
1–4	34.0	26.0	41.8	45.5
5–14	33.7	29.9	34.6	27.2
15+	32.1	44.0	23.4	22.2
Total	100	100	100	100
Ages 20–24				
1–4	24.2	19.3	38.4	25.2
5–14	38.0	30.4	32.5	25.2
15+	37.7	50.1	28.9	49.6
Total	100	100	100	100

Source: March 1978 Work Experience Survey. Calculated from Robert Lerman, "The Nature of the Youth Employment Problems: A Review Paper," prepared for the Vice-President's Task Force on Youth Employment, November 1979, tables 11 and 12.

Still, a substantial number of youth qualify for the hard-core designation. The eight-week criterion is arbitrary, but surely those who are unemployed for three months or more should be classified as hard-core, and both data sets make it clear that a substantial fraction of the unemployed fall into this category. Perhaps more disturbing is the age pattern of the results. In both data sets the fraction of unemployed blacks who should be classified as hard-core is considerably larger in the older group. Thus with age the pool of unemployed becomes more heavily weighted toward those in some sort of personal difficulty.

These figures give only a rough approximation of the actual distribution of those who need services and those whose problems rest in the operation of the labor market. In particular, many of those termed hard-core by the analysis may well be ready for a job but may be the repeated victims of discrimination or inadequate job contacts. Thus the estimates of the numbers of youth who are hard-core should probably be treated as an upper bound. At the same time the analysis makes clear that programs of both types are necessary.

Two sets of policies are needed: policies aimed at remedying the personal problems of some youth, and policies aimed at altering the pattern of labor market hiring. Two important questions are what the characteristics of such policies should be and the extent to which current programs share these characteristics.

Conclusion

Programs seeking to deal with youth in personal difficulty should follow several operational principles. First, programs should be staffed by professionals trained to deal with the problem or problems involved. Counselors, reading specialists, health professionals, and others should be on the program staff or readily available to youth. Second, the program should be of sufficient duration to have a reasonable expectation of dealing with the problems involved. For youth who are in serious difficulty, short-term programs are not adequate.

Taken together, these two principles—a professional staff and a long-duration program—imply a seriousness of purpose. The simple notion is that people in difficulty need serious and sustained efforts to deal with their troubles. These principles are hardly startling; but they are not followed in most programs.[14] Most programs dealing with out-of-school youth are staffed largely by people who lack extensive training in relevant fields. The programs are designed to last one year, and youth who continue in the CETA system are rarely in an articulated treatment program. The programs are generally designed to keep the young participants busy with some task (housing rehabilitation, care for the elderly, filmmaking); services are a casual appendage. In short, the programs are not serious.

Two explanations for this situation stand out. First, most politicians and program operators do not think in terms of designing serious treatment programs. Rather, they are oriented toward short-term efforts intended to keep youth off the street. Second, the programs I have advocated are expensive, yet the bulk of monies go to in-school work experience (after-school employment) programs. Those programs perform a useful income maintenance function, but they claim too large a share of resources. The program operators have had long experience with these programs; they are essentially War on Poverty Neighborhood Youth Corp programs. Hence the programs run smoothly and with minimum difficulty. In addition, they serve large numbers of youth, a politically popular cause, and the agencies have become adept at capturing resources.

Many black youths, however, are in difficulty not because they lack skills but because they lack jobs. For them the central purpose of policy should be placement. What I have in mind are programs that provide a minimal amount of job readiness training (how to act in interviews, how to dress), place youth in jobs, and then stay with the youth for the first year or so, to assist the youth and to reassure and monitor the employer.

The central issue in this model, of course, is how the placement is to be achieved. Such placement is easier in expanding than in contracting economies, but the central problem of moving youth up the job queue remains. If, as I have argued, discrimination is the central reason that black youths are not hired, then placement programs must find ways to combat that discrimination. The difficulty with this suggestion (other than generating political support, a nontrivial problem) lies in designing such policies. Programs of this sort can be classified into three categories, each with its own difficulties.

1. *Hortatory Programs.* Policymakers periodically seek to persuade private firms to hire minorities by appealing to the firm's public spirit. Thus in the late 1960s the Johnson administration organized the National Alliance of Businessmen's JOBS program; now the Carter administration is emphasizing the Private Sector Initiative Program. Evaluations of the JOBS program indicate that little new net hiring occurred,[15] and there is little reason to believe that the new program will be more successful. If the problem is structural and rooted in economic self-interest or deeply embedded attitudes, it is hard to believe that "jawboning" will succeed.

2. *Financial Incentives.* Programs such as subsidized on-the-job training or the targeted income tax credit seek to lower the cost of hiring targeted groups and thus expand their employment. In formal terms the issue rests on the wage elasticity of demand for youth labor. Although the evidence is not strong enough to reject this strategy outright, the weak employer response to existing efforts to lower the cost of youth labor—for example, the on-the-job-training program and exemptions to the minimum wage— are not encouraging.

3. *Direct Intervention.* The third strategy is to employ a regulatory approach to force firms to hire more minority youth. For example, the Equal Employment Opportunity Commission (EEOC) or the Office of Federal Contract Compliance (OFCCP), the two agencies most directly concerned with the fair hiring of minorities, might focus on the problems of black youth. They could do so in cooperation with CETA by encouraging firms to employ CETA-sponsored workers. The chief difficulty is that the authorizing legislation and executive orders focus not on youth but on the employment of all minorities, and it would probably be age discrimination to direct a firm to hire a minority youth instead of an adult. Were this trade-off considered desirable—a highly debatable point—EEOC and OFCCP might seek to accomplish their goal indirectly by focusing enforcement efforts on firms that naturally hired large numbers of young people. The difficulty here is that these firms are likely to be low-wage, secondary employers that do not provide stable career jobs.

This survey of approaches seems quite pessimistic. The reason, I believe, is not that structural interventions are impossible but rather that so little creative effort has been spent along these lines. Manpower policy has been dominated either by income maintenance or personal characteristic approaches. Not until we recognize the need, and generate the political consensus for structural intervention, will sufficient energy be devoted to the design of workable strategies.

Appendix: The Interviews

The interviews were conducted in East Boston and Roxbury. East Boston was defined as Boston Ward 1, precincts 1-14; Roxbury as Ward 12, precincts 1-9. The source of the sample was the state census conducted in January 1977. The sample consisted of one in ten males born between 1951 and 1961. The interviewers went door to door, eliminating youth who were in school or who had attended college. Youth who had moved within East Boston and Roxbury were followed up, those who had moved out of the areas were dropped. The interviewers conducted three call-backs, and people who were not reached at the third visit were dropped from the sample. The questionnaire is reproduced here.

Part A

Interviewer: Ask questions A-1 to A-36 of all respondents.

A. 1 Age: _____

A. 2 City and State where born: _____

A. 3 Marital Status: _____ Married _____ Divorced or Widowed _____ Single

A. 4 Date Married: _____ Month _____ Year
_____ Not applicable

A. 5 Number of Children: _____
(Zero if none)

A. 6 Highest grade of regular school completed: _____
(for example, a high school degree is 12; a B.A. is 16.)

A. 7 When did you leave regular school: _____ month _____ year _____

A. 8 Why did you leave school then?

A. 9 Have you had any formal training (technical school, army specialty training, etc.) since leaving regular school?

If so, please give dates completed, area of training, and where you had the training for the two most recent such episodes.

Place	Kind of training	Dates

A.10 Highest grade of school completed by father: _____

A.11 Father's occupation most of his life: _____

A.12 Name and address of place father worked for most of his life:
_____

A.13 Highest grade of school completed by mother: _____

Appendix

A.14 Mother's occupation for most of her life: _____

A.15 Name and address of place mother worked for most of her life:
      _____

A.16 How long have you lived in (East Boston) (Roxbury)? _____ year(s)

A.17 Does your wife work? _____ No _____ Yes _____ Does not apply
      If yes, what is her occupation: _____
      Name and address of firm: _____

A.18 Do you live with parents or relatives now? _____ Yes _____ No
      If no, when did you leave? _____ month _____ year

A.19 For your three best friends:
      Age   Job title; name and address of place of work   Highest grade completed
      _____
      _____
      _____

A.20 For your brothers:
      Age   Job title; name and address of place of work   Highest grade completed
      _____
      _____
      _____

A.21 For your sisters:
      Age   Job title; name and address of place of work   Highest grade completed
      _____
      _____
      _____

A.22 For uncles and cousins (males):
                        Job title; name and address   Highest Grade
      Age Relationship of place of work   Completed
      _____
      _____
      _____
      _____

Appendix

Interviewer: If working, ask questions A.23–30; if not skip to A.31.

A.23 Do you think you could find another job fairly easily now if you had to?
_____ yes _____ no
why or why not:

A.24 How would you go about looking. Where and how would you look?

A.25 What kind of job would you most likely be able to get?

A.26 What kinds, if any, of jobs would you refuse to take? Why?

A.27 How much money would a job have to offer before you would take it?
_____ per _____

A.28 How would you feel if you lost your job now?

A.29 What would you do with yourself if you lost your job?

A.30 Would you be in a hurry to find another job? Why or why not?

A.31 When you got out of high school, what kinds of jobs did you want to get? For example, what were you looking for in terms of pay, how long you wanted to stay on the job, your future with that company, etc.

A.32 How about now? What kinds of jobs are you interested in?

A.33 If there has been a change, why?

A.34 How did you end up working as a _____ (current or most recent job)? Did you decide that's what you wanted to do or did you just luck into it, or what? How did it happen?

A.35 What would you like to see yourself doing five years from now?

A.36 Are you likely to be doing it? Why or why not?

Appendix

Part B

Interviewer: Collect the following data on all periods of working or not working since the respondent completed or dropped out of 11th grade. Use separate sheets if necessary.

Period No.	Date Began	Date Ended	Activity	School Status
	____month ____year	____month ____year		____no ____yes Describe:
	____month ____year	____month ____year		____no ____yes Describe:
	____month ____year	____month ____year		____no ____yes Describe:
	____month ____year	____month ____year		____no ____yes Describe:
	____month ____year	____month ____year		____no ____yes Describe:

Part C

Interviewer: For each period of working since leaving school identified in Part B, ask questions C.7 to C.38. Use separate packets for each period.

Period No. _____

C. 1 Where was this job? (Name and Address of company)

_____

C. 2 What was your job title? _____

C. 3 Briefly describe your duties.

C. 4 When did you start this job? _____ month _____ year

C. 5 Are you still there? _____ Yes

_____ No When left: _____month _____year

Why did you leave?

_____ Laid off

Appendix

_____ Quit (describe why)
_____ Other (describe)

C. 6 What were you doing just before this job?

   _____ Working someplace else

   _____ Looking for work

   _____ In school

   _____ Other (Describe) _____

C. 7 About how many people work at this place?

   _____ 1-5   _____ 101-500

   _____ 6-20   _____ 500 and up

   _____ 21-50   _____ Don't know

   _____ 51-100

C. 8 What does this company (or agency, etc.) do?

C. 9 Describe how you found this job.

C.10 Did anyone at the job you held before help you find this job? Describe.

C.11 Did any neighbors help you find the job? Describe.

C.12 Did any relatives or parents help you find the job? Describe.

C.13 Did any friends help you find the job? Describe.

C.14 When you were looking for this job, did you also look at other jobs?
      If yes, for each job indicate (a) the kind of job; (b) the location; (c) were you offered a job?; (d) if offered a job, why wasn't it taken?; (e) if not offered a job, why not?

Kind of job	Location (street, city)	Offered a job?	Why not Offered?	Why didn't take it?

Appendix

C.15 All together, how much do you earn before deductions (not counting overtime) at this job?

Starting: _____ per _____

Leaving or now: _____ per _____

C.16 At this job how many

_____ hours per day do you usually work? (Without overtime)

_____ days per week do you usually work? (without overtime)

C.17 How many parents or relatives worked there? _____
what positions do (did) they have

C.18 How many friends (who you knew before you had the job) worked there _____
what positions do (did) they have:

C.19 Is this job in the neighborhood? _____ yes _____ no

C.20 What do you mean by neighborhood?

C.21 About how many miles from where you live (lived) is this job _____

C.22 Now, the next questions are about how you learned to do the job.

a. Did you already know generally how to do the work?

_____Yes ___ ___No

If yes, how and where did you learn?

b. When you started the job, did you pick up any new skills on the job?

_____Yes _____No

If yes, describe the skills.

c. How did you learn these new skills?

d. Who was the person most responsible for teaching you?

e. Do you continue to learn new skills on the job?

_____Yes _____No

If yes, describe what new things and how you learn them.

f. About how long did it take you to learn how to do the job about as well as the other workers?

_____ Still haven't

_____ Months

C.23 How do you travel to the job? _____

Appendix

How long does it take? _____

C.24 Who was your <u>direct</u> boss?
Job Title: _____
Duties: _____

C.25 How did he supervise you?

C.26 How did you get along with him?

_____ Badly. Describe.

_____ OK. Describe.

_____ Were close. Describe.

C.27 Did (do) you think that there was/is any future for you on the job? Why or why not?

C.28 If you stay (had stayed) on this job, what do you think you would most likely be doing?

(a) After one year: _____ Same as now

_____ Different

Title and New Duties:

(b) After two years: _____ Same as after 1 year

_____ Different

Title and New Duties:

(c) After five years: _____ Same as after 2 years

_____ Different

Title and new duties:

C.29 Were your wages set by collective bargaining? _____ yes _____ no

C.30 Were you a member of a union? _____ yes _____ no
name of union _____

C.31 Did you regularly attend union meetings? _____ yes _____ no

C.32 Did you know who your officers were? _____ yes _____ no

C.33 Please list promotions you had at this firm: (starting with first job)
From:
_____ mo _____ yr
To:
From:
_____ mo _____ yr
To:
From:
_____ mo _____ yr
To:

Appendix 168

C.34 How did your boss go about keeping track of your work?

C.35 How often did you miss work (for reasons other than sickness?)
What happened to you?

C.36 How often were you late?
What happened to you?

C.37 Do you like the job? Why or why not?

C.38 Do you plan to stay on the job for the next year at least? Why or why not?

Part D

Interviewer: For each period of not working since leaving school identified in section B, ask question D-7 to D-17. Use separate packets.

Time Not Working No. _____

D. 1 What were the dates of this period of not working?

When started _____month _____year

When ended _____Still going on

_____month _____year

D. 2 What were you doing prior to this period?

_____ Working only

_____ In school only

_____ In school and working

D. 3 How did this period begin?

_____ Left school and did not have a job lined up.

_____ Quit a job: Why?

_____ Lost a job: Why?

D. 4 What did you mostly do with yourself during the time you weren't working?

D. 5 During a typical week, how much time, if any, did you spend looking for a job?
_____Hours per week.
What did you do the rest of the time?

D. 6 Did you leave town at all during this period?

Appendix   169

_____Yes _____No

If yes, how long, where, and why?

D. 7   Did you have any money coming in during this period?

_____Yes _____No

If yes, how much (_____per_____) and from where

D. 8   Were you married? _____yes _____no

Wife working: _____

_____

Number of children: _____ at the time.

D. 9   What was your living situation?

_____Living alone

_____Living with parents or relatives

_____Living with friends

_____Living with wife

D.10   What kind of jobs were you looking for?

D.11   How did you look for them?

D.12   In looking, did you get any help from:

relatives/parents (describe)

neighbors (describe)

friends (describe)

D.13   Were there any jobs which you were offered or think you could have gotten but which you didn't want? Describe the jobs and why you didn't want them.

Kind of job	Name and Address	Why didn't want

D.14   Were there any jobs which you applied for and didn't get?

_____yes _____no

Describe the jobs. Why do you think you didn't get them? (Be specific for each job)

Appendix

Kind of job	Name and Address	Why didn't get

D.15 Was the job you finally got (if working now or if spell ended) the first one you were offered? _____Yes _____No

D.16 Did it bother you very much not to be working? Why or why not?

D.17 Were you in money trouble during the period? Why or why not?

Notes

Chapter 1

1. *New York Times,* June 25, 1978.
2. *New York Times,* June 1, 1978.
3. U.S. Department of Labor, *Employment and Earnings* (Washington, D.C.: U.S. Government Printing Office, July 1978).
4. Organization for Economic Cooperation and Development, *Entry of Young People into Working Life* (Paris, 1977), p. 7.
5. For example, William Sewell and Robert Hauser, *Education, Occupation, and Earnings* (New York: Academic Press, 1975).
6. James Coleman et al., *Youth: Transition to Adulthood* (Chicago: University of Chicago Press, 1974).
7. In October 1976 the labor force participation rate of enrolled 16-19 year olds was 41 percent. A much larger percentage hold jobs sometime during the year. U.S. Department of Labor, *Students, Graduates, and Dropouts in the Labor Force,* Special Labor Force Report No. 200, October 1976, p. 41.
8. These figures are for 1976. See Special Labor Force Report No. 200, pp. 7-13.

Chapter 2

1. The National Longitudinal Survey was conducted by Herbert Parnes and his associates at Ohio State University. A complete description of the survey and sampling methods can be found in Herbert Parnes et al., *Career Thresholds,* Manpower Monograph No. 16 (Washington D.C.: Government Printing Office), 1970. The survey oversampled blacks. All the data in this chapter are reported separately by race, and the data have been weighted to maintain the oversampling of blacks but to weight for other characteristics. Thus within racial groups the data are nationally representative. Races other than whites and blacks have been excluded.
2. Edward Laezer, "Age, Experience, and Wage Growth," *American Economic Review* 66 (September 1976): 548-558.
3. The job here is the one held at the time of the survey in each year. Three-digit industries are much more detailed than the industry titles used in the tables. For example, "Wholesale and Retail Trade; Food and Related Products" is a three-digit industry title. An individual who is unemployed or out of the labor force either year is assigned a value of 0. As before, the data refer to those who are out of school in the years to which the entry refers.
4. Throughout this book the first job is defined as the first full-time or part-time civilian job held after leaving school for the last time. For a thoughtful discussion of the problems of defining the first job see Michael D. Ornstein, *Entry into the Labor Force* (New York: Academic Press, 1976), pp. 8-10. Ornstein limits most of his analysis to youth in the entry period and defines entry as 16 consecutive months of participation in the labor force, either in a full-time job or in searching for a full-time job (p. 24). Although this definition may be reasonable for his purposes, it is very restrictive for mine. Many youth move in and out of the labor force, thus violating his definition, and frequently hold part-time jobs. Many features of the youth labor market cannot be understood without considering these patterns.

Chapter 3

1. The industries included in the sample were printing, abrasives, machine tool, construction, refrigeration, gas stations, textile machinery, insurance, rolling mill manufacturing, banking, electrical machinery, telephone, hospital, retail stores, candy manufacturing, and utilities.
2. Percy Davidson and H. Dewey Anderson, *Occupational Mobility in an American Community* (Stanford, Calif.: Stanford University Press, 1937).

3. A. B. Hollingshead, *Elmtown's Youth and Elmtown Revisited* (New York: John Wiley and Sons, 1975), p. 277.

4. A national longitudinal panel survey on youth attitudes found some evidence that the prevalence of viewpoints that might seem associated with moratorium (for example, the desire for an easy job or a job without responsibility) decline with age. See Jerald G. Bachman, Patrick M. O'Malley, and Jerome Johnson, *Adolescence to Adulthood: Change and Stability in the Lives of Young Men* (Ann Arbor, Mich.: University of Michigan, 1978), pp. 158-159.

5. This is obviously not true for all youth, and I do not mean to imply that unemployment is generally harmless.

6. Hugh Folk, "The Problem of Youth Unemployment," in *The Transition from School to Work* (Princeton, N.J.: Industrial Relations Section, Princeton University, 1968), p. 84.

7. See, for example, Peter Doeringer and Michael J. Piore, *Internal Labor Markets and Manpower Analysis* (Lexington, Mass.: D. C. Heath, 1971), or Bennett Harrison *Education, Training, and the Urban Ghetto*, (Baltimore, Md.: Johns Hopkins University Press, 1972). For a critical review of the dual labor market literature see Glenn Cain, "The Challenge of Dual and Radical Theories of the Labor Market to Orthodox Theory," *Journal of Economic Literature*, 14, no. 4 (December 1976): 1215-1257.

8. Michael J. Piore, "The Dual Labor Market," in David M. Gordon, ed., *Problems in Political Economy* (Lexington, Mass.: D. C. Heath, 1971), pp. 90-94.

9. Michael J. Piore, "On the Technological Foundations of Economic Dualism," Massachusetts Institute of Technology Department of Economics Working Paper No. 110, May 1973.

10. David M. Gordon, Michael Reich, and Richard Edwards, *Labor Market Segmentation* (Lexington, Mass.: D. C. Heath, 1975), pp. xi-xxi.

11. Paul Osterman, "Reply," *Industrial and Labor Relations Review*, 30, no. 2 (January 1977): 221-224.

12. Martin Carnoy and Russell Rumberger, "Segmented Labor Markets: Some Empirical Forays" (Center for Economic Studies, Stanford University, 1975); Paul J. Andersanni, "An Empirical Analysis of Dual Labor Market" (Ph.D. Dissertation, Ohio State University, 1973).

13. Doeringer and Piore, *Internal Labor Markets.*

14. The term *successful* may be objectionable to those concerned with working conditions, occupational health and safety, alienation, and other aspects of the social relations of production. It is obvious that jobs in many of these firms have one or more of these deficiencies. I do not intend to judge whether these are "good" jobs about which young people should feel good and toward which they should be directed. I view finding one of these jobs as successful only in the context of other jobs available and in terms of pay and job security.

15. As Lester pointed out in his study of hiring in Trenton, New Jersey, "Managements with a fairly long perspective tend to consider an applicant, not in terms of his qualifications for an initial job, but for the job he (or she) is likely to hold during his working life with the firm, and to emphasize psychological traits such as cooperativeness, dependability, adaptability, and loyalty to the firm." Richard A. Lester, *Hiring Practices and Labor Competition*, (Princeton, N.J. Industrial Relations Section, Princeton University, 1954), p. 28.

16. The importance that firms assign to an applicant's trainability is the driving force behind the queue theory of income distribution. In this model firms rank applicants on the basis of their ability to learn the jobs within the firm at the lowest training costs. Lester Thurow, *Generating Inequality* (New York: Basic Books, 1975).

17. The importance of attitude indirectly supports the proposition argued by Bowles and Gintis (which in turn is based on work by Edwards) that a major function of the school system is to inculcate proper attitude in youth and that this attitude is an important determinant of success in the labor market. However, the results that I have presented here also raise a serious difficulty for this proposition. Since there tends to be a period of several years between leaving school

and entering primary firms — much of which is spent in the secondary labor market where attitude is not so important — there is some mystery about how the lessons of school are translated to the workplace. The labor market experience of youth, particularly their inability to get primary jobs without the proper attitude, seems to play at least as important a role as the schools in creating proper personality characteristics. See Samuel Bowles and Herbert Gintis, *Schooling in Capitalist America* (New York: Basic Books, 1976), and Richard C. Edwards, "Individual Traits and Organizational Identities: What Makes a 'Good' Worker?" *Journal of Human Resources*, 11, no. 1 (Winter, 1976), 51-68.

18. Lester, *Hiring Practices*, p. 53.

19. Theodore F. Malm, "Recruiting Patterns and the Functioning of Labor Markets," *Industrial and Labor Relations Review*, 7, no. 4 (July 1954): 507-525.

20. Lester, *Hiring Practices*, p. 36.

21. Lester also found that "only a very small number of managements seek to recruit production workers through the high and vocational schools. The reason many do not is because they hesitate to hire youngsters for fear they may be lacking in responsibility and dependability." Firms do not hesitate to hire clerical workers right out of high school. Ibid., p. 45.

22. For a good survey of the literature on the effectiveness of vocational education programs see Beatrice G. Reubens, "Vocational Education for All in High School," in James O'Toole, ed., *Work and the Quality of Life* (Cambridge, Mass.: MIT Press, 1974).

23. It is not unusual for employers to actively seek to enlarge their potential labor supply. For a discussion of this practice using immigration as an example see Michael J. Piore, *Birds of Passage* (New York: Cambridge University Press, 1978).

24. Hollingshead, *Elmtown's Youth*, p. 199.

25. Arthur Okun, "Upward Mobility in a High Pressure Economy, *Brookings Papers on Economic Activity*, 1973, no. 1; Wayne Vroman, "Worker Upgrading and the Business Cycle," *Brookings Papers on Economic Activity*, 1977, no. 1, pp. 229-252.

26. For a useful volume that draws together and summarizes some of the recent work in the sociological tradition see W. M. Williams, ed., *Occupational Choice* (London: George Allen and Unwin, 1974). For an exception to the generalization that the labor market tends to be ignored, see Peter M. Blau, John Gustad, Richard Jessor, Herbert Parnes, and Richard Wilcock, "Occupational Choice: A Conceptual Framework," *Industrial and Labor Relations Review*, 9, no. 4 (July 1956): 531-543. This paper includes labor market conditions as a variable but does not inquire deeper into how the labor market functions.

27. See, for example, Simon Rottenberg, "On Choice in Labor Markets," *Industrial and Labor Relations Review*, 9, no. 2 (January 1956): 183-199.

28. Gary Becker, *Human Capital*, 2nd ed. (New York: Columbia University Press, 1975), p. 16. This is the classic work on human capital theory.

29. Richard B. Freeman, *The Market for College-Trained Manpower* (Cambridge, Mass.: Harvard University Press, 1971).

30. Ibid., p. 1.

31. Sherwin Rosen, "Learning and Experience in the Labor Market," *Journal of Human Resources*, 7, no. 3 (Summer 1972): 326-342; William R. Johnson, "A Theory of Job Shopping," *Quarterly Journal of Economics*, 92, no. 2 (May 1978): 261-277.

32. Stanley Stephenson, "The Economics of Youth Job Search Behavior." *Review of Economics and Statistics*, 58, no. 1 (February 1976): 104-111.

Chapter 4

1. U.S. Department of Labor, Special Labor Force Report No. 199, "Employment and Unemployment in 1976," p. A-4.

2. See Joseph F. Kett, *Rites of Passage: Adolescence in America 1790 to the Present* (New York: Basic Books, 1977), chap. 8.

3. Ibid., p. 146.

4. Oscar Handlin and Mary Handlin, *Facing Life: Youth and the Family in American History* (Boston: Little, Brown, 1971).

5. See Stephen Thernstrom, *The Other Bostonians* (Cambridge, Mass.: Harvard University Press, 1973); Stephen Thernstrom and Peter Knights, "Men in Motion: Some Data and Speculation about Urban Population Mobility in Nineteenth-Century America, *"Journal of Interdisciplinary History,* Autumn 1970; Michael B. Katz, *The People of Hamilton Canada West* (Cambridge, Mass.: Harvard University Press, 1975).

6. Katz, *People of Hamilton Canada West,* p. 212.

7. Ibid, p. 166.

8. Ibid., p. 308.

9. By 1920 high school enrollment had increased 20-fold over the 1880 levels. In 1880, 2.5 percent of 17-year-olds were high school graduates; in 1920 the figure was 16.8 percent and in 1930, 29.0 percent. *Historical Statistics of the United States* (Washington, D.C.: U.S. Government Printing Office, 1960), Series H-223-233, p. 207.

10. The extent of "retardation" was considerable. Roughly one-third of eighth graders were "retarded" in 1910.

11. There are several sources of difficulty with the data. In 1910 the census was taken in April, while in 1920 the data were collected in January. Thus seasonality problems are introduced. More serious, in 1900 enumerators were instructed not to record as employed a youth who worked less than half of the year. This instruction was omitted in the next two censuses, and in 1930 the enumerators were instructed to record any gainful work. Thus the 1900 census probably understates the extent of youth employment that year, both in absolute terms and relative to later censuses.

12. This line of argument is valid for both men and women, but with less force for women. Throughout this period girls had a higher rate of school attendance and a lower rate of labor force participation than boys, probably due to social norms and the greater availability of home labor.

13. School enrollments were higher in urban areas, and a portion of the extended enrollments depicted in table 4.1 is due to rural to urban migration. However, even within the largest cities (controlling for location) the same pattern prevailed. In Pittsburgh, for example, the enrollment of 14-16 year olds increased from 55 percent in 1910 to 84 percent in 1930. Another example is St. Louis, where the enrollment rates of 14-16 year olds grew from 51 percent in 1910 to 70 percent in 1930. In Providence 10.6 percent of 17-year-olds were enrolled in 1880, while 53.6 percent were enrolled in 1925. Twelfth Census, 1900, vol. 1. *Population,* p. 1159; Fifteenth Census, 1930, vol. 2, *Population,* p. 1150; Selwyn K. Troen, *The Public and the Schools: Shaping the St. Louis System, 1838-1920,* (Columbia, Mo.: University of Missouri Press, 1965), p. 201. W. Norton Grubb and Marvin Lazerson, "Education and the Labor Market: Recycling the Youth Problem," paper presented at a conference on the historiography of education and work, Stanford, Calif., August 1979, p. 15.

14. Robert S. Lynd and Helen Merrell Lynd, *Middletown* (New York: Harcourt, Brace and World, 1956).

15. Ibid., p. 31.

16. Ibid., p. 30.

17. A. B. Hollingshead, *Elmtown's Youth and Elmtown Revisited* (New York: Wiley, 1975); James Coleman, *The Adolescent Society* (New York: Free Press, 1961).

18. The growth in the percentage of the cohort attending school was not due simply to an influx of middle-class youth. Rather the trend affected all groups, as it should have if the argument about the relationship of child labor and school attendance is to hold. Thus, for example, 80 percent of the 14- and 15-year-old children of native white parents attended school in 1910, compared with 74 percent of the children of foreign-born (or mixed) parents and 59 percent of foreign-born children. Yet by 1930 the figures were 90 percent, 91 percent, and 93 percent respectively. However, this does not imply equal grade attainment. See Michael R. Olneck and Marvin Lazerson, "School Achievement of Immigrant Children, 1900-1930," *History of Education Quarterly*, 14, no. 4 (Winter 1974): 455.

19. David B. Tyack, "Ways of Seeing: An Essay on the History of Compulsory Education," *Harvard Educational Review* 46, no. 3 (August 1976): 359.

20. The term *unskilled* is difficult to define. The reader who is uncomfortable with it can think of the arguments in terms of an increase in the supply of workers willing to perform the kind of work previously done by children, combined with a change in the skill mix demanded by employers.

21. David S. Landes, *The Unbound Prometheus: Technological Change and Industrial Development in Western Europe from 1750 to the Present* (Cambridge: Cambridge University Press, 1969), p. 235.

22. U.S. Department of Commerce, *Long-Term Economic Growth* (Washington, D.C., 1973), Series A163, p. 208.

23. Landes, *Unbound Prometheus*, pp. 280-282.

24. Irwin Feller, "The Draper Loom in New England Textiles, 1894-1917: A Study of the Diffusion of an Innovation," *Journal of Economic History*, 16, no. 3 (September 1966): 336.

25. Tsung-Yuen Shen, "*A Quantative Study of Production in the American Textile Industry 1840-1940*" (Ph.D. Dissertation, Yale University, 1956), p. 23.

26. Alfred Chandler, Jr., *The Visible Hand: The Rise of Modern Business Enterprise in the United States* (Cambridge, Mass.: Harvard University Press, 1977), pp. 240-286. Chandler's work is a superb history of continuous processing.

27. Peter Temin, *Iron and Steel in Nineteenth-Century America* (Cambridge, Mass.: MIT Press, 1964), p. 230; Landes, *Unbound Prometheus*, pp. 266-267.

28. Quoted in Katherine Stone, "The Origins of the Job Structure in the Steel Industry," in Richard C. Edwards, Michael Reich, and David M. Gorden, eds., *Labor Market Segmentation* (Lexington, Mass.: D. C. Heath, 1975).

29. Stanley Lebergott, *Manpower and Economic Growth* (New York: McGraw-Hill, 1964), pp. 510-511.

30. Floyd Musgrove, *Youth and the Social Order* (Bloomington, Ind.: University of Indiana Press, 1964), pp. 73-74.

31. Lebergott, *Manpower and Economic Growth*, p. 43.

32. Computed from Richard A. Easterlin, *Population, Labor Force, and Long Swings in Economic Growth* (New York: Columbia University Press, 1968), table A-3, p. 190.

33. *Immigrants in Industries*, Report of the Immigration Commission, part 23: Summary Report, Senate Document Number 633, 61st Cong., 2d sess. (Washington, D.C.: U.S. Government Printing Office, 1911). The estimates of the percentage of the labor force who

were foreign born should not be taken as precise. The report is vague about its sampling procedure, but it appears that communities were chosen nonrandomly on the basis of industry mix and presence of immigrants, and within communities families were interviewed in proportion to the ethnic mix in the industries. Thus the sample is random within communities and industries within those communites but biased with respect to communities chosen.

34. The conventional view of these immigrants is that their skill levels were considerably below those of the average native American as well as some earlier immigrant groups which often included skilled craftsmen. Thus, for example, the Immigration Commission reports that in the iron and steel industry only 51 percent of the immigrants from non-English-speaking nations spoke English. Even a recent article seeking to debunk this view showed that 59.5 percent of immigrants in 1890 were unskilled or semiskilled, compared with 44.8 percent of natives. See Peter J. Hill, "Relative Skills and Income Levels of Native and Foreign-Born Workers," *Explorations in Economic History*, 12, no. 1 (January 1975): 57. In addition, even immigrants with higher-than-average skills may have been forced into the low-skill labor market because of difficulties with English, lack of access to job contacts, and discrimination. The Immigration Commission provides strong evidence of the predominantly unskilled work performed by the immigrants. For convincing evidence that East European immigrants experienced discrimination, which in part took the form of confinement in low-skilled jobs, see Paul F. McGuldrick and Michael B. Tannen, "Did American Manufacturers Discriminate against Immigrants before 1914?" *Journal of Economic History*, 37, no. 3 (September 1977) 723-746. After immigration was closed, the next source of unskilled low-wage labor was the black population from the rural South who migrated to northern industries. The pattern of advanced capitalist economies drawing in and exploiting successive waves of unskilled migrants is described in Michael J. Piore, *Birds of Passage and Promised Lands: Long-Distance Migrants and Industrial Societies* (New York: Cambridge University Press, 1979).

35. Jeffrey G. Williamson, "The Relative Cost of American Men, Skills, and Machines: A Long View," Institute of Research on Poverty, Discussion Paper No. 289-75 (Madison, Wisc., 1975), pp. 57-58.

36. Ibid.

37. Selwyn K. Troen, "The Discovery of the Adolescent by American Educational Reformers, 1900-1920: An Economic Perspective," in Lawrence Stone, ed., *Schooling and Society*, (Baltimore, Md.: Johns Hopkins University Press, 1976), pp. 239-251.

38. U.S. Senate, *Report on the Conditions of Woman and Children Earners*, vol. 1: *The Cotton Textile Industry*, 61st Congress, 2nd Session, pp. 27-32.

39. Ibid., p. 404.

40. Ibid., p. 51.

41. Warren C. Scoville, *Revolution in Glassmaking* (Cambridge, Mass.: Harvard University Press, 1948), p. 81.

42. Quoted in Walter I. Trattner, *Crusade for Children: A History of the National Child Labor Committee and Child Labor Reform in America* (Chicago: Quadrangle Books, 1970), p. 79.

43. U.S. Congress, *Report on the Condition of Women and Child Wage Earners*, p. 165.

44. Ibid., p. 164.

45. Ibid., p. 168.

46. There were 23,000 accountants and auditors in 1900, 118,000 in 1920, and 192,000 in 1930. *Historical Statistics*, p. 75.

47. There are numerous histories describing the political and legislative history of school reformers. See, for example, Forest Chester Ensign, *Compulsory School Attendance and Child Labor* (New York: Arno, 1960), Trattner, *Crusade for Children*.

48. U.S. Commissioners Report on Education, (Washington, D.C., 1920), p. 77.

49. See, for example, Raymond E. Callahan, *Education and the Cult of Efficiency* (Chicago: University of Chicago Press, 1962).

50. Edith Abbot and Sophonisba P. Breckinridge, *Truancy and Non-Attendance in the Chicago Schools* (Chicago: University of Chicago Press, 1917), pp. 97, 122-125. The figures are from a sample of roughly 5,000 students.

51. New York City, Committee on School Inquiry, Board of Estimate and Appointment, Final Report vol. 1, 1911-1913, p. 675. It is unclear how many of these cases were repeaters. For additional discussion of truancy problems in New York City and the steps taken to force people into school see Moses Stambler, "The Effect of Compulsory Education and School Attendance on High School Attendance in New York City, 1898-1971," *History of Education Quarterly*, 8, no. 2 (Summer 1968). The Pittsburgh figures are from Ensign, *Compulsory School Attendance* p. 117.

52. David B. Tyack, *The One Best System: A History of American Urban Education* (Cambridge, Mass.: Harvard University Press, 1974), pp. 183-184. Available evidence does not indicate how much additional attendance resulted from compulsion. Some economists are inclined to argue that compulsory school laws had no effect and that they merely ratified market decisions. The leading exponents of this view are Landes and Solomon. However, their study focuses largely on the period 1880-1890, a period of nonenforcement of schooling laws. Enforcement became serious only after the turn of the century. See William Landes and Lewis Solomon, "Compulsory Schooling Legislation: An Economic Analysis of Law and Social Change in the Nineteenth Century," *Journal of Economic History* 32, no. 1 (March 1972); 54-91 for evidence that enforcement was not serious prior to 1900 see Tyack, *One Best System*, pp. 66-71. For an argument that child labor legislation reduced youth employment see Allen Sanderson, *Journal of Economic History*, 34, no. 1 (March 1974) 297-299.

53. This line of argument has reversed the emphasis normally given to the motives and actions of the reformers and has instead emphasized changes in "background" conditions that led to the reformers' success. It remains then to ask why the reformers pushed for change and why they received political support. This question, of course, has been the subject of great debate in the general literature on the progressive period and I make no claim of resolving it. It does seem appropriate to point out that middle-class parents were under considerable pressure during this period. Immigrants flooding into industry must have represented a social threat. In addition, the immigrants and the technological changes displaced craftsmen and denied their children the traditional routes for occupational success. The middle class faced the growing importance of large corporations which were reducing opportunities for self-employment and small enterprises. It may be possible to argue that as a result of these developments the middle class supported the extension of schooling as a strategy for opening channels for themselves into the new jobs created by the modern economy and as a mechanism for maintaining control over and limiting competition from the new immigrants.

54. Congressional Report on the Condition of Women and Child Wage Earners, vol. 1, pp. 17, 19, 29.

55. Trattner, *Crusade for Children*, pp. 125-127.

56. Ensign, *Compulsory School Attendance*, pp. 123-124, 132; John R. Commons et al., *History of Labor in the United States*, vol. 3 (New York: Macmillan, 1935), p. 415. The glass industry was a strong opponent of child labor legislation in 1908 yet did not oppose federal legislation in 1916. See Report of the Consumers League of Illinois, in National Child Labor Committee, *Child Labor and Social Progress* (New York, 1908), p. 125, and Trattner, *Crusade for Children*.

57. The immigration commission reported that "their numbers are so great and the influx is so continuous that even with the remarkable expansion of industry during the past few years there has been created an oversupply of unskilled labor." Immigration Commission, *Abstract of Reports*, vol. 1, p. 39.

58. They were 65 percent male; 83 percent were in this age range, and the bulk were without families. Ibid., pp. 24, 38, 59.

59. National Industrial Conference Board, *The Employment of Young Persons in the United States* (New York, 1925), p. 56.

60. Kett, *Rites of Passage*, p. 147.

61. Immigration Commission, Abstract of Report, p. 494. See also John R. Commons, *Races and Immigrants in America* (New York: Macmillan, 1907), in which he reports that "partly fear, partly hope, make the fresh immigrant the hardest if not the most intelligent worker in our industries" (p. 127).

62. For some evidence that immigrants were less likely than natives to join unions see the Immigration Commission Reports, vol. 90, *Iron and Steel Manufacturers*, p. 278.

63. Commonwealth of Massachusetts, *Final Report of the Special Commission on Stabilization of Employment* House Document No. 1200, (Boston, 1932) pp. 152-153; Paul David, *Barriers to Youth Employment* (Washington, D.C.: American Council on Education, 1942), p. 55; U.S. House of Representatives, Joint Hearings before the Committee on Education and Labor on S2475 and HR 7200 (Fair Labor Standards Acts), 75th Cong., 1st sess., 1937, p. 383.

64. Frances T. Spaulding, *High School and Life* (New York: McGraw-Hill, 1938), p. 67; Alice Channing, *Employed Boys and Girls in Rochester and Utica, New York* (Chicago: University of Chicago Libraries, 1932), p. 37.

65. David, *Barriers to Youth Employment*, p. 27.

66. Spaulding, *High School and Life*, pp. 65, 64.

67. Clare Lewis, "Some Problems in Junior Placement," *Journal of Personnel Research* 13 (August 1929): 131.

68. C. J. Ho, "Which Workers Have Good Attendance," *Journal of Personnel Research* 7 (February 1929): 387; Marion A. Bills, "Stability of Office Workers and Age at Employment," *Journal of Personnel Research* 5 (April 1927): 475-477.

69. Channing, *Employed Boys and Girls*, p. 61.

70. See, for example, Channing, *Employed Boys and Girls*.

71. Conference on the Role of College People in Industry, *Personnel* 6 (May 1929): 29-32.

72. Edward Krug, *The Shaping of the American High School*, vol. 1 (New York: Harper and Row, 1964), pp. 289-308.

73. George Counts, *Secondary Education and Industrialization* (Cambridge, Mass.: Harvard University Press, 1929), p. 13.

74. For example, the American Youth Commission's Report, *What the High School Ought to Teach* (Washington, D.C., 1940), explicitly recognized the link between labor market conditions and school enrollment and suggested various devices such as work-study arrangements.

75. Maurice B. Hexler, *Juvenile Employment and Labor Mobility in the Business Cycle* (Boston: Massachusetts Child Labor Committee, 1937); Ralph Fletcher and Mildred Fletcher, "A Statistical Analysis of Juvenile Employment in St. Louis," *Journal of the American Statistical Association*, 24 (June 1929): 174-177; Channing, *Employed Boys and Girls*.

76. Krug, *Shaping of the Modern High School*, vol. 2, p. 54.

77. Franklin Jones, "Selection for Training," *Personnel* 4 (August 1927): 11-27.

78. For a good brief historical essay on vocational education see Marvin Lazerson and W. Norton Grubb, eds., *American Education and Vocationalism* (New York: Teachers College Press), 1974. See also Lawrence A. Cremin, *The Transformation of the School* (New York: Knopf, 1961), chap. 2.

79. Layton Hawkins, Charles Prosser, and John Wright, *Development of Vocational Education* (Chicago: American Technical Society, 1951), p. 356.

80. Quoted in Krug, *Shaping of the Modern High School*, vol. 2, p. 311.

81. Beatrice Reubens, "Vocational Education for All," in James O'Toole, ed., *Work in America* (Cambridge, Mass.: MIT Press, 1974), pp. 299-337.

82. Spaulding, *High School and Life*, p. 91.

83. Howard Bell, *Matching Youth and Jobs* (Washington, D.C.: American Council on Education, 1940), p. 49.

84. Lazerson and Grubb, *American Education and Vocationalism*, p. 154.

85. Spaulding, *High School and Life*, pp. 159-173.

86. Ibid., p. 59.

87. White House Conference on Child Health and Protection, *A Report of the Subcommittee on Vocational Guidance* (New York: Century Company, 1932), pp. 46, 218.

88. Bell, *Matching Youth and Jobs*, p. 7.

89. Ibid.

90. For example, James Coleman et al., *Youth: Transition to Adulthood* (Chicago: University of Chicago Press, 1974).

91. John D. Durand, *The Labor Force in the United States, 1890-1960* (New York: Social Science Research Council, 1948), p. xiv.

92. Albert Westfield, *Getting Started: Youth in the Labor Market* (1943, reprint ed., New York: DeCapo Press, 1971), p. 31.

93. American Council on Education, *Youth and the Future*, p. 13.

94. David, *Barriers to Youth Employment*, p. 27.

95. U.S. Senate, Hearings on the American Youth Act (S1463), Subcommittee of the Committee on Education and Labor, 1938, p. 35.

96. U.S. Senate Hearings before the Committee on Education and Labor on S3658 (American Youth Act), 74th Cong. 2d sess. 1936, p. 115.

97. Ibid., p. 68.

98. Senate, Hearings on S1463, 1938, p. 188.

99. Ibid., p. 293.

100. Thacher Winslow, "Youth in Crisis," in Thacher Winslow and Frank Davidson, eds., *American Youth: An Enforced Reconnassance* (Cambridge, Mass.: Harvard University Press, 1940), p. 41.

101. Massachusetts, Commission on the Stabilization of Employment, *Final Report*, p. 32.

102. Quoted in George Phillip Rawick, "The New Deal and Youth: The Civilian Conservation Corps, the National Youth Administration, and the American Youth Congress" (Ph.D. dissertation, University of Wisconsin, 1957), p. 201.

103. Krug, *Shaping of the American High School*, vol. 2, p. 218.

104. Ibid., pp. 219, 310-313.

105. Ibid., p. 218.

106. Ibid., p. 345.

107. Ibid., p. 324.

108. Winslow, "Youth in Crisis," p. 51.

109. Trattner, *Crusade for Children,* pp. 189–90.

110. Charles F. Roos, *NRA Economic Planning* (Bloomington, Ind.: Principia Press, 1937), p. 54.

111. Ibid., p. 176.

112. Ibid., p. 455. For a considerably higher but unsupported estimate see Trattner, *Crusade for Children,* p. 192.

113. Joint hearings on the Fair Labor Standards Act (S2475, HR7200), 1937, 75th Congress, 1st Session, p. 383.

114. Rawick, *New Deal and Youth,* pp. 202–203.

115. Ibid., p. 226.

116. Senate Hearings on the American Youth Act, 1936 and 1938.

117. Senate Hearings on the American Youth Act, 1938, p. 60.

118. Sumner Slicter, *Union Policies and Industrial Management* (Washington, D.C.: Brookings Institution, 1941), p. 15.

119. Ibid., p. 36.

120. Ibid., p. 100.

121. David, *Barriers to Youth Employment.*

122. Robert Lynd and Helen Lynd, *Middletown in Transition* (New York: Harcourt, Brace and Co., 1937), p. 49.

Chapter 5

1. U.S. Bureau of Labor Statistics, *Students, Graduates, and Dropouts in the Labor Market,* Special Labor Force Report No. 200 (Washington, D.C., 1977), table P.

2. Throughout this section when I use the NLS data, I define entry as youth who reported themselves in school in 1969 but not in 1970. Thus I am really speaking of an entry year rather than a precise point of entry.

3. These data are drawn from the May and August issues of *Employment and Earnings,* Bureau of Labor Statistics, 1978.

4. U.S. Bureau of Labor Statistics, *Employment and Unemployment in 1976,* Special Labor Force Report No. 199 (Washington, D.C., 1977), table A-10.

5. In 1975, 48 percent of unemployed teenagers were unemployed 5 weeks or less, compared with 37 percent for all employed people, and 18 percent of unemployed teenagers were out of work for 15 or more weeks compared with 32 percent for the entire work force. Congressional Budget Office, *Policy Options for the Teenage Unemployment Problem* (Washington, D.C.: U.S. Government Printing Office, 1976), pp. 9–10. However, these figures may be deceptive because unemployed youth tend to leave the labor force; and thus spells without work may be longer than reported durations. For evidence that this is so, see Kim Clark and Lawrence Summers, "The Dynamics of Youth Unemployment," National Bureau of Economic Research, May 1979.

6. U.S. Bureau of Labor Statistics, Special Labor Force Report No. 200, p. A-15.

7. *Employment and Training Report of the President* (Washington, D.C.: U.S. Government Printing Office, 1977), p. 172.

8. Otherwise we would compare out-of-school 18–19-year-olds, most of whom have no college, with out-of-school 20–24-year-olds, many of whom have attended or graduated from college.

9. Actual unemployment for age group i is $U_i = \Sigma P_{ij} W_{ij}$, where P_{ij} is the fraction of the ith

in industry j and W_{ij} is the mean weeks of unemployment experienced by the group within each industry. Letting 1 refer to the younger group and 2 to the older, I have calculated $U_1 = \sum P_{2j} W_{ij}$.

10. The cells were empty in the remaining industries.

11. See, for example, Edward Kalachek, "Determinants of Teenage Employment," *Journal of Human Resources* 4, no. 1 (Winter 1969): 3-21.

12. See Peter Doeringer and Michael J. Piore, *Internal Labor Markets and Manpower Analysis*, (Lexington, MA : D. C. Heath, 1972)

13. Finis Welch, "Minimum Wage Legislation in the United States," *Economic Inquiry* 12 (September 1974): 286.

14. For a more elaborate analysis of this, see Jacob Mincer, "Unemployment Effects of Minimum Wages," *Journal of Political Economy* 84, no. 4, part 2 (August 1976): S87-S104.

15. See Harvey Lieberstein, "Allocative Efficiency vs. X-Efficiency," *American Economic Review* 56 (June 1966): 392-415. There is also a literature on the "shock" effect of unionization which argues that emergence of unions forces firms to behave more efficiently and thus the predicted effects of higher union wages on employment are confounded. Much the same argument could be applied to the minimum wage.

16. For a good review of the literature, which was helpful in organizing this summary, see Robert S. Goldfarb, "The Policy Content of Quantitative Minimum Wage Research," in *Proceeding of IRRA Winter Meetings* (San Francisco: Industrial Relations Research Institute, 1974), pp. 261-268.

17. Hyman Kaitz, "Experience of the Past: The National Minimum," in *Youth Unemployment and Minimum Wages*, U.S. Bureau of Labor Statistics Bulletin No. 1657, (Washington, D.C.: U.S. Government Printing Office, 1970), pp. 30-54; Mincer, "Unemployment Effects of Minimum Wages"; James F. Regan, "Minimum Wages and the Youth Labor Market," *Review of Economics and Statistics* 59, no. 2 (May 1977): 129-136; Welch, "Minimum Wage Legislation in the United States"; Edward M. Gramlich, *Impact of Minimum Wages on Other Wages, Employment, and Family Incomes*, Brookings Papers on Economic Activity, 1976, no. 2, pp. 409-462.

18. U.S. Senate Hearings on S1871, Subcommittee on Labor, Committee on Human Resources, 95th Cong., 1st Sess. p. 15.

19. Ibid., p. 95.

20. Martin Feldstein, *Lowering the Permanent Rate of Unemployment*, (Joint Economic Committee, U.S. Congress, September 1973) p. 22.

21. Welch, "Minimum Wage Legislation in the United States," p. 286.

22. Senate, *Hearings on S1871*.

23. Ibid., p. 26.

24. Calculated from Congressional Budget Office, *Youth Unemployment: The Outlook and Some Policy Strategies* (Washington, D.C.: U.S. Government Printing Office, 1978), table A-1.

25. The distinction between spells of unemployment and spells out of the labor force is weak for teenagers, and in the discussion of the East Boston interviews I lump them together. For example, many youth who reported no job search during the spell also reported that they took the first job they were offered. Conversely, many youth who said they looked for work during the spell could recall no specific places they looked. Time out of the labor force reduces the length of a spell of unemployment.

26. These categories were not exclusive, and some youth reported both.

27. Edward Bakke, *Citizens without Work* (New Haven, Conn.: Yale University Press, 1940).

28. Stephen Thernstrom, *The Other Bostonians* (Cambridge, Mass.: Harvard University Press, 1973), p. 233

29. This can be seen by examining the unemployment rates of 16-24 year old noncollege high school graduates ordered by year of graduation. In October, 1973 the unemployment rate of white youth who graduated before 1971 was 4.4 percent; for youth who graduated in 1971, 5.2 percent; for youth who graduated in 1972, 8.3 percent; and for those who graduated in 1973, 10.1 percent. The rates for black youths were 10.4 percent, 9.2 percent, 22.3 percent, and 28.3 percent. As is apparent older youth (the earlier graduates) have lower unemployment rates. U.S. Bureau of Labor Statistics, Special Labor Force Report No. 168, table A-10.

30. This approach is formally similar to that used by Ashenfelter in examining the long-term effects of training programs. See Orley Ashenfelter, "Estimating the Effects of Training Programs on Earnings," *Review of Economics and Statistics*, 60, no. 1 (February 1978): 47-57.

31. It is important to distinguish this model and the question it seeks to answer from the question raised in the context of search theory. In that literature analysts ask whether, *for workers who are already unemployed*, an additional week of unemployment results in higher or lower wages on the job that is subsequently found. Different theoretical answers result from different assumptions about the search behavior for workers. Here I am asking about the effects of some versus no unemployment.

32. The use of the alternative measure of unemployment — actual weeks of unemployment — does not change these conclusions. For the equations reported in panel A for coefficients are -1.520 (0.663) for 1970 and -1.006 (0.722) for 1971. For panel B they are -0.450 (0.892) for 1970 and -0.236 (1.042) for 1971. For panel C they are -2.035 (1.175) and -1.718 (1.106). The only difference is that in panel C the 1970 coefficient falls just short of 5 percent significance.

33. The auxiliary equation was estimated for 1970 and 1971 for each of the three groups (panels A, B, C). Six equations were run, and the deviation used as the dependent variable is calculated using the appropriate equation. The independent variables included age, the local unemployment rate at the beginning of the period, the change in the unemployment rate over the period, marital status at the beginning of the period, health status at the beginning of the period, score on the test of knowledge of the world of work, years of school completed, and a series of industry dummy variables for the job held at the beginning of the period.

34. In these regressions I omit youth who were unemployed at the time of the 1969 interview. These youth obviously experienced both 1968-1969 unemployment and 1969-1970 unemployment (unless they found a job the day of the interview), and hence their inclusion would bias the results in the direction of finding an effect of unemployment.

35. When actual weeks of unemployment is used instead of the dummy variable, the results are essentially identical. For panel A the coefficients are 0.321 (0.051) and 0.295 (0.049); for panel B, 0.403 (0.079) and 0.153 (0.103); for panel C, 0.262 (0.047) and 0.371 (0.079).

Chapter 6

1. Richard B. Freeman, "Changes in the Labor Market for Black Americans," *Brookings Papers on Economic Activity*, 1973, no. 1, p. 80.

2. Richard B. Freeman, "Black Economic Progress Since 1964," *Public Interest*; no. 52 (Summer 1978): 55.

3. This assumes that improvement in the treatment of blacks would not alter the earnings structure of whites. This assumption is unlikely to be true, although the direction of the effect on whites is in dispute and depends on one's theory of discrimination. For example, Becker argues that in monetary terms discrimination lowers white incomes; Bergman argues that white incomes rise as a result of discrimination; and Reich argues that white workers lose and capitalists gain from discrimination. See Gary Becker, *The Economics of Discrimination*, 2d ed., (Chicago: University of Chicago Press, 1971); Barbara Bergman, "The Effect on White

Income of Discrimination in Employment," *Journal of Political Economy)* 71 (March-April 1971): 294-313; Michael Reich, "White Gains and Losses from Racial Inequality," *Journal of Human Resources* 13 (Fall 1978): 524-544.

4. Otis Dudley Duncan, "Inheritance of Poverty or Inheritance of Race," in Daniel P. Moynihan, ed., *On Understanding Poverty* (New York: Basic Books, 1969), pp. 85-110.

5. For example, 23 percent of black families in 1964 had a single female head, while in 1975 the figure had risen to 35 percent. See Freeman, "Black Economic Progress," p. 63.

6. Most economists would accept the former view. In Title VII discrimination lawsuits the courts generally require direct proof of the relationship between education and productivity, and such proof is generally very difficult to provide.

7. U.S. Bureau of Labor Statistics, *Students, Graduates, and Dropouts in the Labor Force,* Special Labor Force Report No. 200 (Washington D.C.: U.S. Government Printing Office, 1977), pp.,7-10.

8. Congressional Budget Office, *Policy Options for the Teenage Unemployment Problem,* Background Paper No. 13, 1976, table 1, p. 84.

9. These data and those in the remainder of this paragraph are taken from F. Amacher and Richard Freeman, "Young Labor Market Entrants: An Overview of Supply and Demand, 1950-1970," mimeographed (Center for Policy Alternatives, Massachusetts Institute of Technology, 1973).

10. This led to the recent decline in the market for college graduates. See Richard B. Freeman, "Overinvestment in College Training?" Harvard Institute for Economic Research, Discussion Paper No. 371, July 1974.

11. Congressional Budget Office, *Policy Options,* p. 87.

12. Calculated from U.S. Census Bureau, 1970 Census, vol. 1, *Charateristics of the Population,* table 53.

13. Charles Silberman, "What Hit the Teenagers," *Fortune Magazine,* April 1965, quoted in Edward Kalachek, *The Youth Labor Market,* (Ann Arbor, Mich.: Institute of Labor and Industrial Relations, 1969), p. 54.

14. Kalachek, *Youth Labor Market,* p. 55.

15. In 1960 construction accounted for 5.9 percent of all jobs, in 1970, 5.4 percent. Nondurable manufacturing declined from 11.7 percent to 9.8 percent, retail employment rose from 14.8 percent to 15.0 percent. Calculated from 1970 Census, vol. 1, *Characteristics of Population,* table 235.

16. For an analysis of this framework see Lester Thurow, *Generating Inequality* (New York: Basic Books, 1976).

17. U.S. Department of Labor, *Employment and Training Report of the President, 1977* (Washington D.C.: U.S. Government Printing Office, 1978), p. 194.

18. Gath Mangum and Stephen Seniger, *Coming of Age in the Ghetto,* (Baltimore, Md.: Johns Hopkins University Press, 1978), pp. 25, 36.

19. John Kain, "Housing Segregation, Negro Employment, and Metropolitan Decentralization," *Quarterly Journal of Economics* 82 (May 1968): 175-197. For a critique see Bennett Harrison, *Urban Economic Development* (Washington, D.C.: Urban Institute, 1974).

20. Congressional Budget Office, *Youth Unemployment: The Outlook and Some Policy Strategies* (Washington, D.C.: U.S. Government Printing Office, 1978), p. 39. I characterize this as casual evidence because the data contain no controls.

21. Paul Offner and Daniel Saks, "Note," *Quarterly Journal of Economics* 85 (February 1971): 147-160. They found that black employment in a zone increases more than propor-

tionately with the fraction of the zone's residents who are blacks. The effect was strongest in youth-intensive industries—business services and wholesale and retail trade.

22. U.S. Department of Labor, *Employment and Training Report of the President, 1977,* (Washington, D.C.: Government Printing Office) p. 203.

23. Finis Welch, "Black-White Differences in Returns to Schooling," *American Economic Review* 63 (December 1973): 893–907.

24. Robert Flanagan, "On the Stability of the Racial Unemployment Differential," *American Economic Review* 66 (May 1976): 302–308.

25. Michael J. Piore, *Birds of Passage: Long-Distance Migrants and Industrial Society* (New York: Cambridge University Press, 1979).

26. The classic study of labor force participation is William Bowen and Thomas Finnegan, *The Economics of Labor Force Participation* (Princeton, N.J.: Princeton University Press, 1969). Other studies are reviewed in Arnold Katz, "State Minimum Wages and Labor Markets for Youth," mimeographed (University of Pittsburgh, 1972). Not surprisingly, given this analysis, there is little consistency among the studies with respect to signs and magnitudes of parameters, and many studies get surprising results that have to be explained in an ad hoc way. Youth labor supply is a very slippery concept. Examples of studies of school enrollment are Linda Nasif Edwards, "The Economics of Schooling Decisions, Teenage Enrollment Rates," *Journal of Human Resources* 10, no. 2 (Spring 1975): 155–173; and Robert I. Lerman, "Some Determinants of Youth School Activity," *Journal of Human Resources* 7, no. 3 (Summer 1972): 367–379. Examples of labor demand studies are Edward Kalachek, "Determinants of Teenage Employment," *Journal of Human Resources* 4, no. 1 (Winter 1969): 2–21; Stanley Friedlander, *Unemployment in the Urban Core* (New York: Praeger, 1972).

27. Arnold Katz, "Teenage Employment Effects of State Minimum Wages," *Journal of Human Resources* 8, no. 2 (Spring 1973): 250–256.

28. The SMSAs included are New York, Los Angeles, Chicago, Philadelphia, Detroit, San Francisco, Washington, Boston, Pittsburgh, St. Louis, Baltimore, Cleveland, Houston, Newark, Minneapolis, Dallas, Seattle, Milwaukee, Atlanta, Cincinnati, Paterson, San Diego, Buffalo, Miami, Kansas City, Denver, San Bernardino, Indianapolis, New Orleans, Tampa, Phoenix, Columbus, Rochester, San Antonio, Dayton, Louisville, Sacramento, Memphis, Forth Worth, Birmingham, Toledo, Norfolk, Akron, Hartford, Oklahoma City, Gary, Fort Lauderdale, Jersey City, Greensboro, Nashville, Omaha, Youngstown, Jacksonville, Richmond, Wilmington. These SMSAs account for 81 percent of black 16–19 year olds living in urbanized areas in 1970.

29. Most of the 1960 data were generously provided by Arnold Katz. Several variables were omitted because of the expense involved in collecting the data. The comparisons between the 1970 and 1960 equations remain valid when the 1960 equations are compared with 1970 equations using only the 1960 variables.

30. The Becker discrimination model predicts that the demand curve for black labor in the presence of discrimination is less elastic than the white model with respect to wages (for a demonstration see Freeman, *Changes in the Labor Market for Black Americans,* pp. 92–93). However this model is not well suited for this analysis. First, it is a full-employment model and hence does not consider the implications of unemployment. Second, as Flanagan has demonstrated, the model's predictions with respect to the relationship between relative employment and relative wages of blacks and whites are inaccurate (Robert Flanagan, "Racial Wage Discrimination and Employment Segregation," *Journal of Human Resources* (Fall 1973): 456–471). Recent studies have found that the minimum wage has a larger disemployment effect for blacks than for whites (Jacob Mincer, "Unemployment Effects of Minimum Wages," *Journal of Political Economy* 84 (August 1976): S87–S104; James Ragan, Jr., "Minimum Wages and the Youth Labor Market," *Review of Economics and Statistics* 59 (May 1977): 129–136), and if the coverage rate is roughly equal for the two races, then this implies a more elastic demand curve for black labor. A rationing model of employment im-

plies a more elastic demand curve for blacks. Imagine that whites are allocated (perhaps because of superior contacts or strong employer preferences) a larger share of the SMSAs youth jobs than are blacks. Then if the remaining jobs (firms) have demand curves of equal wage elasticity for blacks and whites, the overall wage elasticity will appear larger for blacks.

31. Recall that the definition of the variable differs for men and women.

32. Michael Borus, Frank Mott and Gilbert Westel, "Counting Youth: A Comparison of the Labor Force Statistics in the Current Population Surveys and the National Longitudinal Surveys," in Robert Taggert and Naomi Berger Davidson, eds., *Employment Statistics and Youth* (Washington, D.C.: U.S. Government Printing Office, 1978), pp. 15-34.

33. See Edwards, "Economics of Schooling Decisions," A measurement error for this variable is that it measures family income in the SMSA, but some of the 16-19-year-old enrolled youth are in college and have families who reside elsewhere. This will bias the coefficient to zero.

34. These negative wage effects were also observed by Bowen and Finnegan although they used a different wage variable. They attribute the effect to problems in measuring labor supply. In addition, many youth are "target" earners; that is, they work to earn money for recreational purposes, and thus high wages may reduce labor participation. See William G. Bowen and T. Aldrich Finegan, *The Economics of Labor Force Participation,* (Princeton, N.J.: Princeton University Press), 1969.

35. Susan Fields, "A Comparison of Intercity Differences in the Labor Force Participation Rates of Married Women in 1970 with 1940, 1950, and 1960," *Journal of Human Resources* 11, no. 4 (Fall 1976): 568-577.

36. For example, D. Mortensen, "Job Search, the Duration of Unemployment, and the Phillips Curve," *American Economic Review* 60 (December 1960): 847-862; or S. A. Lippman and J. F. McCall, "The Economics of Job Search: A Survey," *Economic Inquiry* 14 (June-September 1967): 155-189, 347-368.

37. Stephen Marston, "The Impact of Unemployment Insurance on Job Search," *Brookings Papers on Economic Activity* 1975, no. 1, pp. 13-60.

38. The NLS data, for reasons not yet understood, report unemployment rates below those reported by the monthly census and hence may seem a poor data source for examining unemployment. However, the racial ratios are very similar to those in the census. For example, the October 1970 Current Population Survey reported racial ratios of 1.84 for out-of-school 18-19-year-old males and 1.65 for 22-25-year-olds. The NLS ratios for the same period were 1.88 and 1.66 respectively.

39. No observation of a spell is included if it occurred while the youth was in school. However, because observations are pooled, some youths in the sample were in school during some portion of the period.

40. Every spell that occurred any time between the 1969 and 1971 interviews is included, except that spells in progress at the time of the 1971 interview are excluded because information on their length is unavailable. Thus the measure employed here seems to be the closest possible approximation of the theoretically appropriate variable. There is still some bias since a very long spell, say one that began at the time of the 1969 interview and was still in progress at the time of the 1971 interview, would be excluded. However, the length of the sample period (over two years) makes this bias of little practical importance since there is plenty of opportunity to capture long spells.

41. See Martin Feldstein, "The Importance of Temporary Layoffs: An Empirical Analysis," *Brookings Papers on Economic Activity,* 1975, no. 3, pp. 735-745. In the entire sample there were only 68 affirmative responses in the 1969-1970 period to the question "Did you experience a spell of unemployment while holding this job?"

42. In these definitions the term *year* should be understood to refer to the interview period, either 1969-1970 or 1970-1971. When a variable is described as measured at the beginning of

the year, this means at the time of the 1969 interview if the spell occurred during 1969-1970 and at the time of the 1970 interview if the spell was in the 1970-1971 period.

43. The variable is defined analogously to that employed in Ronald Ehrenberg and Ronald Oaxaca, "Unemployment Insurance, Duration of Unemployment, and Subsequent Wage Gain," *American Economic Review* 66 (December 1966): 754-766.

44. These results as well as later ones are limited to youth out of school and not in the entry period.

45. A spurious positive correlation between duration and benefits is caused by the fact that the NLS data do not tell whether a worker is covered, only whether he received benefits. Most states have waiting periods, and thus a minimum spell length is required for even a covered worker to receive benefits.

46. In cross-sectional data the level variable may capture long-run equilibrium behavior. This is because of the very high correlation over time of an area's unemployment rate. Thus in this equation the level unemployment rate may serve as a proxy for structural characteristics of the local economy. Since high unemployment areas also tend to have high hourly wages, the welfare interpretation is ambiguous.

47. The formula is the same as that used in the earlier decomposition of wages.

48. The auxiliary equation was

$\ln(\text{hourly wage}) = \beta_o + \beta_1 \text{EDUCATION} + \beta_2 \text{KWW} + \beta_3 \text{TENURE} + \beta_4 \text{UNION} + \beta_5 \text{TENURE}^2 + \beta_6 \text{EXXP} + \beta_7 \text{EXXP}^2 + \beta_8 \text{MAR} + e$

49. The incidence of multiple quits or layoffs during one year is very low. During 1969-1970 only 1.2 percent of whites and 0.7 percent of blacks experienced more than one layoff, for quits the figures are 1.1 percent and 1.4 percent.

50. The logit functional form is convenient because it constrains predicted values to a (0,1) interval, an essential characteristic if the equation is to have a probability interpretation.

51. Ordinary least-squares estimates of linear probability models produce equivalent results. For example, black values substituted into the white quit equation produce a predicted quit rate of 0.049.

52. Phyllis Wallace, *Pathways to Work* (Lexington, Mass.: D. C. Heath, 1975).

53. An overly high reservation wage might occur because blacks, perhaps due to inadequate information, overvalue their potential earnings. Another possibility is that blacks, perhaps due to changing attitudes, are refusing to take jobs that offer wages below those that comparable whites would earn. This shift in the supply curve could also explain the equalization of earnings found in earnings equations since these are actually reduced forms of supply and demand equations. In fact according to most studies young people take the first job offered. However, the reservation wage mechanism might operate through patterns of search. If youth have information about the characteristics of firms, they may search only among firms whose entry wage is equal to or better than their reservation wage.

54. The positive, though insignificant, sign on the coefficients is contrary to that predicted by theory. Evidently, for this sample, duration has no effect on reservation wage. When the system was estimated using time not working (duration of unemployment plus time out of the labor force) the coefficient was 2.8 with a standard error of 3.7 for blacks, -4.6 with a standard error of 7.8 for whites.

55. Stanley P. Stephenson Jr., "The Economics of Youth Job Search Behavior," *Review of Economics and Statistics*, 58, no. 1, (February, 1976), p. 108.

56. This predicted value is below the mean in table 6.15 because the table included multiple quits while the dependent variable here is simply dichotomous.

57. Duncan prestige scores are a standard way of scaling occupations. They are based on a weighted combination of the mean education and income of each occupation. See Otis

Dudley Duncan, "A Socioeconomic Index for All Occupations," in Albert J. Reiss, ed., *Occupations and Social Status* (New York: Free Press, 1961).

58. Leonard Goodwin, "The Social Psychology of Poor Youth as Related to Employment," mimeographed (Worchester Polytechnic Institute, August 1979).

59. Mark Granovetter, *Getting a Job* (Cambridge, Mass.: Harvard University Press, 1975).

60. Melvin Lurie and Elton Rayack, "Racial Differences In Migration and Job Search: A Case Study," *Southern Economic Journal* 33, no. 1 (July 1966) 81-95. One study that failed to find a racial difference in job finding is Michael D. Orstein, *Entry into the American Labor Force* (New York: Academic Press, 1976), p. 54.

61. Direct contact was employed by 24.9 percent of the blacks and 22.8 percent of the whites. Newspaper ads were employed by 24.9 percent of the blacks and 22.8 percent of the whites.

62. Paul Bullock, *Aspiration vs. Opportunity, "Careers" in the Inner City* (Ann Arbor, Mich.: Institute of Labor and Industrial Relations, 1973), p. 99.

Chapter 7

1. Child labor legislation seems even today to reduce youth employment, although the effect is not large. See Daniel J. B. Mitchell and John Clapp, "The Effects of Child Labor Laws on Youth Employment," Working Paper No. 8, Institute of Industrial Relations, UCLA, December 1977.

2. Erik Erickson, *Identity, Youth and Crisis* (New York: Norton, 1968), p. 156.

3. *Fortune*, January, 1974.

4. In January 1973, 36.0 percent of those 18-19-year-old men who were working and not in school had the same occupation one year earlier. In January 1966 the comparable figure was 32.9 percent. For women the figures are 31.3 percent and 32.4 percent. By this admittedly crude measure job turnover shows no secular increase. U.S. Department of Labor, Special Labor Force Reports No. 84 and No. 176, *Occupational Mobility of Workers*, (Washington, D.C.: Government Printing Office), 1967, 1975.

5. In 1974, while the U.S. unemployment rate for teenagers was 16.0 percent, the unemployment rate for West Germany was 1.8 percent, for Great Britain 4.2 percent, for Japan 2.6 percent, and for Sweden 6.8 percent. The rates in Canada and Italy approached U.S. levels. See Beatrice Reubens, "Foreign and American Experience with the Youth Transition," paper prepared for the National Commission for Manpower Policy, March 1976, p. 7.

6. The ratio in the United States was 4.5, in West Germany 4.0, in Great Britain 2.2, in Japan 2.1, in Sweden 4.1, in Canada 3.3, and in Italy 7.2. Ibid.

7. Joan Maizels, *Adolescent Needs and the Transition from School to Work* (London: Athlore Press, 1970), pp. 112-113, 119.

8. In Leicester, England, 54 percent of male entrants were employed in firms with less than 100 employees compared with 34 percent for all males. E. Teresa Keil et al., "The Entry of School Leavers into Employment," *British Journal of Industrial Relations*, 1, (1963): 409.

9. Paul E. Willis, *Learning to Labor: How Working Class Kids Get Working Class Jobs* (London: Saxon House, 1977), p. 39.

10. Ronald Dore, *British Factory, Japanese Factory* (London: George Allen and Uhwin, 1973), p. 54.

11. Ibid, p. 32.

12. Ibid, p. 61; Beatrice Reubens, *Bridges to Work* (Montclair: N.J.: Allanheld Osmun, 1977), pp. 45, 115. Obviously the labor market stages are not replicated in all times and cultures. It can be interesting and amusing, however, to see that they have parallels in other times and places. In *Growing Up in New Guinea* (New York: Ribbon Books, 1930) Margaret

Mead describes how adolescents of the Manus tribe, who lived in the Admiralty Islands, became adults. The Manus culture was similar in some respects to ours: "To the arts of leisure, conversation, story telling, music and dancing . . . they gave scant recognition. . . . The ideal Manus man has no leisure; he is ever up and about his business turning five strings of shell money into ten. . . . [their religion] is very similar to our historical Puritan ideal, demanding from men industry, prudence, thrift and abstinence from worldly pleasures, with the promise that God will prosper the virtuous man" (p.9). However, the children are removed from these concerns. Throughout childhood they lived in a society of their own, a world in which adult social and political relations were excluded. When a young boy entered adolescence—between the ages of 12 and 16—a puberty ceremony was held but nothing much changed. He returned to his play group, though perhaps in a new leadership role. Gradually, the young men's activities changed. However, they did not fully enter the society. Rather, they engaged in war games, attacking neighboring villages, taking captives, and chasing after the young women of their village. (After white men appeared on the scene, young men at this stage often went to work for several years in white settlements and then returned to the village.) Young men settled down suddenly with marriage. When their (arranged) marriages came to pass, they suddenly found themselves deep in debt to the adults who had paid for the marriage dowries and exchanges. They settled down quickly, abandoning their peer groups and their youthful activities, and becoming serious, hardworking Manus adults.

13. Paul David, *Barriers to Youth Employment* (Washington, D.C.: American Council on Education, 1942); Howard Bell, *Matching Youth and Jobs* (Washington, D.C.: American Council on Education, 1940).

14. These observations are based on a two year study of youth programs in two Prime Sponsors, Boston and Cambridge, and are reported more fully in Paul Osterman "The Politics and Economics of CETA Youth Programs," mimeographed, Boston University Economics Department, January, 1980. There is, of course, no guarantee that these Prime Sponsors accurately represent events nationally but considerable anecdotal evidence suggests that they do.

15. See Charles Perry, Benard Anderson, Richard Rowan, and Herbert Northrup, *The Impact of Government Manpower Programs*, (Philadelphia, Pa.: University of Pennsylvania Press), 1975, p. 187.

Index

Abbot, Edith, 60
Ability, and hiring practices, 26. *See also* Hiring practices
Absences, and age, 64
Adolescence, 51. *See also* Youth
 and economy, 150
 employers' attitudes toward, 64
 institutionalized dependency of, 53
 among Manus, 187-188n12
Aetna Insurance Company, 64
Affirmative action, 114
AFL (American Federation of Labor), 72-73
Age
 and annual weeks of unemployment, 6, 7
 and hiring practices, 69-70
 and industrial distribution, 34, 35
 and instability, 11
 and job classification, 31
 and moratorium period, 172n4
 and quit rates, 85-86, 136
 and stability, 12, 13
 and unemployment, 65
 and wages, 6, 7, 8
 and youth unemployment, 87-88
Agriculture
 black youth employed in, 9, 35
 and unemployment, 79
 white youth employed in, 8, 35
 youth employment in, 36
Aliens, illegal, as competition in youth labor force, 111
Amendment, child labor, 71-72
American Youth Act, proposed, 72, 73
American Youth Commission, 73
Anderson, H. Dewey, 16
Apprenticeships, union limits on, 1, 73
Atlanta school system, 67
Attitude, 172-173n17
 and hiring practices, 26, 27
 toward unemployment, 87
Auto service operations, 25
Availability, of youth jobs, 110

Baby boom
 economic consequences of, 151
 and employment-to-population ratios, 104-105
Back-to-school drives, 70, 71
Bakers, 24
Banking, pre-World War II youth employment in, 63
Becker, Gary, 39
Becker discrimination model, 184n30
Behavior
 of black youth, 112-114

effect of age on, 8
 stable, 12 (*see also* Stability)
 of youth in labor market, 16-19, 85-86
Bell, Howard, 153
Black adults, 22
 and discouraged worker effect, 126
 employment-to-population ratio for, 102
 quit rates for, 134
 unemployment among, 76, 147-148
Black labor, demand curve for, 184n30
Black youth
 characteristics of, 112-114
 earnings equations for, 145
 employers' screening of, 102
 groups competing with, 111, 118, 119, 120, 151, 154
 high aspirations of, 142
 hourly wages for, 6, 7
 impact of early instability on, 12, 13
 industrial distribution of, 35
 industrial mobility of, 14
 job-seeking techniques of, 143-144
 and layoff rates, 136, 137-138
 and minimum wage, 82
 and occupation desired at age 30, 143
 program policy for, 158
 quit rates for, 137-138, 141
 school enrollment rates for, 105-107
 stability rates for, 10
 and structural change in local economics 110-112
 unemployment among, 3, 155
  annual weeks of, 6, 7
  consequences of early, 97
  distribution of weeks of, 156-157
  high, 75, 98
  rate of, 1
 and wage elasticity, 118, 119, 120, 123
Boredom, attitude of youth toward, 87, 97
Boston, interviews conducted in, 15
Boy Scouts, 51
Britain, unemployment statistics for, 86, 151
Building industries, pre-World War II youth employment in, 63. *See also* Construction
Bullock, Paul, 144
Business cycle, impact on youth labor market, 33
Business services
 black youth employed in, 9
 and unemployment, 79
 white youth employed in, 8

California, occupational mobility in, 16
Capital theory, human, 2, 6, 38, 39, 66, 135

Index

Career lines, 29, 30
Career patterns, 8
  and lack of planning, 17
  stability of, 9
  of workers, 40
Carter administration, 159
Census data
  SMSA, 114-115
  sources of, 148-149
CETA system, 158, 159
Child labor, 51, 53
  in glass industry, 58
  and industrial transformation, 61
  national legislation on, 60
  persistence of, 63
  and school enrollment, 54
  Supreme Court on, 71
Children's Bureau, 60, 72
Chow test, 131
Civilian Conservation Corps (CCC), 72
Civil rights movement, impact of, 113
Class, reproduction of, 38
Cleaning firms, and job classification, 30
Codes, NRA, 72
Coleman, James, 54
Commons, John R., 61
Communication industry, pre-World War II youth employment in, 63
Communities, 15
Competition, in youth labor market, 118, 119, 120, 147
Construction industry
  black youth employed in, 9, 35
  and unemployment, 79
  white youth employment in, 8, 35
  youth employment in, 6, 36
Contacts
  access to, 42, 43
  role of, 143
Continuous-processing techniques, 55-56
Convenience stores, and minimum wage, 85
Counts, George, 67
Crime rates, 145
Current Population Survey, 83, 107

Data, for empirical analysis, 114-115
David, Paul, 153
Davidson, Percy, 16
Day care, 155
Decision making vs. labor market structure, 43
Demand
  for black labor, 113
  for cheap boy laborers, 52
  for child labor, 59
  and quit rates, 136

and unemployment rates, 154
in youth labor market, 33, 78-80
Dependency, institutionalized, 53
Depression
  and effect on youth labor market, 150
  and seniority agreements, 73
  youth employment during, 70-72, 87
Developed countries, teenage unemployment in, 152
Discouraged worker effect, 126
Discrimination, occupational
  and black youth unemployment, 113
  and hiring practices, 139
  and immigrant labor, 176n34
  and layoff rates, 134
  measurement of, 147
  and policy planning, 159
  and quit rates, 135-136
  shift in, 114
  and tight labor markets, 155
  in wage elasticity, 118, 119, 120
  and white income, 182n3
  and women, 5
Disemployment effect, of minimum wage, 84
Domestic service, pre-World War II youth employment in, 63
Dore, Ronald, 152
Draper loom, 55
Dual labor market theory, 22-23
Duncan prestige scores, 142, 143, 186-187n57

Earnings equations, 145
East Boston, interviews conducted in, 15
Econometrics, in youth labor market, 115
Education. *See also* Enrollments; Schooling; Vocational education
  and child labor, 54
  compulsory, 51, 53, 59-60, 61, 67, 177n52
  and extension of length of schooling, 53
  impact of, 66
  increasing important role of, 65-66
  and industrial distribution, 34, 35
  vs. labor market entrance, 69
  and quit rates, 136
EEOC. *See* Equal Employment Opportunity Commission
Eighteen-year-olds. *See also* Youth
  attitudes toward, 17
  in wholesale and retail trade, 78
Elmtown's Youth, 33, 54
Employers, attitudes toward adolescents, 64. *See also* Hiring practices
Employment. *See also* Labor market; Work

Index

central-city vs. suburb, 111-112
full, 34
minimum age for, 72
part-time, 65, 76, 83
problems associated with, 19
secondary, 24
summer, 65
wage elasticity of, 118
Employment certificates, 67
Employment model, 116-122, 123
duration of unemployment in, 128-133
individual behavior in, 126-128
industrial structure variable in, 121-122
labor supply in, 122
spells of unemployment in, 133-138
suburbanization variable in, 121
Employment-to-population ratios, 102-104
for black youth, 105
black vs. white, 146
and regional shifts, 109
and school enrollments, 106-107, 108-109
Enclosure, 69-74
Enrollment effect, and unemployment, 146
Enrollment rates
and estimation techniques, 125
high school, 174n9
increase in, 174n13
Ensign, Forest, 61
Entertainment industry
black youth employed in, 9, 35
and unemployment, 79
white youth employed in, 8, 35
youth employed in, 36
Entry into labor market, and job shifts, 77
Equal Employment Opportunity Commission (EEOC), 159
Erikson, Erik, 150
Estimation techniques, of employment model, 116-118
Experience, previous, and hiring practices, 27. *See also* Hiring practices

Fair Labor Standards Act, 72, 80
Families
black, 101
and job seeking, 17, 18-19, 143-144
small operations of, 24-25
Federal programs
CETA system, 158, 159
for summer jobs, 77
Feldstein, Martin, 84
Field, Susan, 126
Finance
black youth employed in, 9
and unemployment, 79

white youth employed in, 8
Firing practices, and behavior of youth, 85
Firms
interest in vocational programs of, 29
interviews conducted in, 15
and job-finding techniques, 31
and minimum wage, 81
primary, 25-29
characteristics of jobs in, 32
hiring practices of, 25-29, 33
secondary, 24, 32
small vs. large, 25
Flanagan, Robert, 113
"Floundering period," 16
Folk, Hugh, 20
Fortune magazine, 151
Freeman, Richard, 39, 40
French-Canadians, 67
Friends, role in job-seeking, 17, 143-144

Gas stations, 24
George-Dean Act, 68
Gillette Company, and job classification, 30
Glass industry
impact of technological change in, 57
youth employment in, 58
Gramlich, Edward M., 82, 83
Great Britain, unemployment statistics for, 86, 151
Great Depression. *See* Depression

Hall, G. Stanley, 51
"Hanging out," 17
High school graduates. *See also* Youth
employment for, 3
unemployment rates for, 5
High schools
enrollment increases in, 71, 174n9
evolution of, 54
growth in numbers of, 53
vocational vs. general, 28
Hillman, Sidney, 70
Hiring practices
and age, 69
and behavior of youth, 85
and black youths, 102
and demand for youth labor, 78-79
and discrimination, 139
and moratorium period, 150
pre-World War II, 64
of primary firms, 25-29, 33
and racial differentials, 114
in San Francisco, 27
Hollingshead, A. B., 16
Hortatory programs, 159

Index

Hotel industry, pre-World War II youth employment in, 63
Human capital theory, 2, 6, 38, 39
  function of education in, 66
  and quit equations, 135

"Identification problem," 19
Immigrants
  employers' attitudes toward, 62
  in labor force, 55, 59, 175-176n33
  as labor source, 61-62
Incentives
  financial, 159
  standard economic, 38
Industrialized countries, teenage unemployment in, 152
Industrial revolution, second, 55, 58
Industry. *See also specific industry*
  and black youth, 9
  excluded from minimum wage coverage, 80-81
  impact of education on, 66
  predicted unemployment in, 79
  and white youth, 8
  and youth employment, 6
Instability. *See also* Stability
  and age, 11
  and hiring practices of primary firms, 27
Insurance companies
  and job classification, 30
  pre-World War II youth employment in, 63
Interviews, 15
  conduct of, 160-169

Japan, entry into labor market in, 152-153
Job(s)
  classifying, 29-33
  current, 20-22
  definition of, 171n4
  evaluation of, 172n14
  first, 20-22
  initial vs. current, 44-50
  primary, 22
  primary vs. secondary, 31, 32
  problems associated with, 19
  secondary, 22, 23
  suburbanization of, 111, 112, 118-119, 147
  "youth," 22
  "youth" vs. career, 20
Job change. *See also* Mobility
  and career patterns, 10
  and human capital theory, 39
  and settling down, 19
  and stability, 9
  and wage increases, 6
Job-finding techniques, 31, 42
  and role of contacts, 143-146
Job shifts, and entry into labor market, 77
Job-shopping model, 41
Johnson, William, 41
Johnson, Lyndon B., administration, 159
Juvenile court system, 51

Kain, John, 111, 112
Kaitz, Hyman, 82
Kalechek, Edward, 110
Katz, Arnold, 115, 121, 149
Katz, Michael B., 52
Kett, Joseph, 62

Labor, unskilled
  changing demand for, 55-56
  unskilled vs. educated, 59
Labor force
  immigrants in, 59
  tenuous attachment of youths to, 51
Labor market. *See also* Youth labor market
  craft, 30
  immigrants and, 55
  internal, and job classification, 29-30
  male vs. female, 5
  pre-World War II, 62, 65
  and stability measure, 10
Landes, David, 55
Lateness, and age, 64
Laundry services
  and minimum wage, 85
  pre-World War II youth employment in, 63
Layoffs
  annual rate for, 80
  as causes of unemployment, 77
  and racial differentials, 134, 135, 137-138
  and wage increases, 6
Learning model, for occupational choice, 41
Legislation
  compulsory education, 59-60
  youth, 71
Leisure vs. labor market entrance, 69
Lester, Richard A., 27
Lurie, Melvin, 144
Lynd, Helen Merrell, 53, 73
Lynd, Robert S., 53, 73

Macy's Department Store, 57, 64
Malm, Theodore F., 27
Management, hiring practices of, 27. *See also* Hiring practices

Index

Manpower policy, 160
Manpower program staff
  attitudes toward youth of, 17
  interviews with, 15
Manufacturing
  black youth employed in, 9, 35
  pre-World War II youth employed in, 63
  and unemployment, 79
  white youth employed in, 8, 35
  youth employed in, 6, 36
Marginality, of youth labor market, 5, 77 96, 150
Market. *See also* Labor market
  primary vs. secondary, 22, 23
  and racial differentials, 114
Market for College-Trained Manpower, 39
Market theory, dual labor, 22
Marriage, and settling-down stage, 18
Marshall, Ray, 84
Marshall Fields, 57
Massachusetts Commission on the Stabilization of Employment, 70
Maturity, 5
  and hiring practices, 26
  and previous experience, 28
Mead, Margaret, 187-188n12
Meany, George, 84
Men
  employment-to-population ratio for, 102
  and minimum wage, 83
  and racial competition, 119
  unemployment among, 76, 147-148
  and wage elasticities, 123
Middletown, 53
Middletown in Transition, 73
Migrants, employers' attitudes toward, 62
Mincer, Jacob, 82
Minimum wage, 24, 80-85
  dual, 84
  exemptions to, 159
  greatest effects of, 81
  purpose of, 84
Mining
  black youth employed in, 9, 35
  pre-World War II youth employment in, 63
  and unemployment, 79
  white youth employed in, 8, 35
  youth employed in, 36
Minorities, in primary jobs, 23
Mobility, industrial, 12-14
Mobility, occupational
  in California, 16
  and choice, 41
  of immigrants, 62
  during moratorium period, 20

Model of youth labor market, 115-116
  See also Employment model
"Mom and pop" stores, 24
Moratorium period, 16, 17
  and age, 172n4
  causes of, 150
  characteristics of, 152
  continued, 19
  and hiring practices, 33
  jobs held during, 20
  and primary jobs, 25
  and secondary jobs, 23-24
  and small family operations, 25
  transition from, 153-154
  and unemployment, 18
"More Machinists for Massachusetts" campaign, 29
Musgrove, Floyd, 56

National Alliance of Businessmen's JOBS program, 159
National Commission on Employment Statistics, 86
National Education Association, 72-73
National Industrial Conference Board, 62
National Longitudinal Survey of Young Men (NLS), 5, 76, 129, 132, 171n1
National Recovery Act (NRA), 72
National Youth Act, 70
National Youth Administration (NYA), 72-73
Neighborhood Youth Corp programs, War on Poverty, 158
Networks. *See also* Families; Friends
  and job recruiting, 19
  and job seeking, 17
New Deal, and youth unemployment, 153
New England, child labor in, 57, 61
Newsstands, 24
Nineteen-year-olds, in wholesale and retail trade, 78. *See also* Youth
NLS. *See* National Longitudinal Survey of Young Men

Occupation, desired at age 30, 142-143. *See also* Job
Occupational choice, 37-43
  economic theories of, 38
  and human capital theory, 39
  learning model for, 41
  and utility function, 40
Office of Federal Contract Compliance (OFCCP), 159
Offner, Paul, 112

Okun, Arthur, 34
Opportunity, and settling down, 19
Owens and Libby glass factories, 58

Parking lot operators, and minimum wage, 85
Parnes, Herbert, 171n1
Pay level, and job classification, 29
Peer pressures, and settling down stage, 18
Pennsylvania Child Labor Association, 61
Personal services. *See also* Services
　black youth employed in, 9
　and unemployment, 79
　white youth employed in, 8
Personnel systems, 30. *See also* Hiring practices
Piore, Michael J., 22, 113
Placement counseling, 67, 68
Polaroid Corporation, and job classification, 30
Politics, and child labor laws, 60-61
Private Sector Initiative Program, 159
Probability, of stability, 11
Probationary period, 26
Professional services
　black youth employed in, 9
　pre-World War II youth employment in, 63
　and unemployment, 79
　white youth employed in, 8
Programs
　federal, 77, 158, 159
　hortatory, 159
　for unemployed youth, 69, 158
Progression paths, 29-30. *See also* Career patterns
Promotions, and wage increases, 6
Public administration
　black youth employed in, 9, 35
　and unemployment, 79
　youth employed in, 36
　white youth employed in, 8, 35
Public services, pre-World War II youth employment in, 63

Questionnaire, 15, 161-170
Queue theory, of income distribution, 172n16
Quits, 78
　and age of youth, 85-86
　as causes of unemployment, 77
　as measure of career patterns, 8-9
　racial differentials for, 134, 135, 137-138
　reasons for, 141-142

Race. *See also* Black youth

and duration of unemployment, 128-138
and effects of unemployment, 94-96
and industrial distribution, 35-37
and industrial mobility, 14
and labor supply, 122
and layoff rates, 134-135
and occupational outcomes, 3
and quit rates, 134-135
and stability, 12, 13
and structural change in local economics, 110-112
and youth unemployment, 99-105
Rayack, Elton, 144
Real estate, pre-World War II youth employment in, 63
Recreation, pre-World War II youth employment in, 63
Recruiting, 173n21. *See also* Hiring practices
Reform, labor, 177n53
Regan, James F., 82, 83
Regional shifts, impact of, 108-109
Reliability, and hiring practices, 26
Relief programs, youth, 72
Reservation wages, 53, 139, 140, 146, 186n53
Residence, and unemployment, 111-112
Restaurant help, 25
Restaurants, and minimum wage, 85
Retail trade
　black youth employed in, 9, 35
　impact of technological change in, 57
　and job classification, 30
　and minimum wage, 85
　pre-World War II youth employment in, 63
　and unemployment, 79
　white youth employed in, 8, 35
　youth employed in, 6, 36, 78
Roosevelt, Franklin D., 68
Rosen, Sherwin, 41
Roxbury, interviews conducted in, 15

Saks, Daniel, 112
San Francisco, hiring in, 27
School(s)
　black enrollments in, 105-110
　and black unemployment, 101
　custodial function of, 70, 71
　intervention in labor market of, 67-69
　work-related services of, 67
Schooling. *See also* Education
　as custodial device, 66
　prolonging of, 74
　role of, 65-66
　unemployment and, 76-78

Index   195

School officials, interviews with, 15
"School-to-work transition," 5, 154
Search theory, and quit equations, 135
Security firms, and job classification, 30
Segmentation, in labor market, 23
Segregation, occupational, and women, 5.
    See also Discrimination
Semi-autonomy, stage of, 52
Seniority systems, and youth labor demand, 80
Services
    black youths in, 35
    white youths in, 35
    youth employment in, 36
Settling-down stage, 16
    characteristics of, 18
    and lack of opportunity, 19
    opposition to, 19
    and primary jobs, 25
Seventeen-year-olds, attitudes toward, 17.
    See also Youth
Shifts. See Job shifts
Silberman, Charles, 110
Skills, See also Training
    acquisition of, 32-33
    industry-specific general, 28
Slicter, Sumner, 73
Smith-Hughes Act, 68
Social stratification, 38
South
    black migration from, 105, 108
    child labor in, 61
Spanish-speaking people, 22, 24
Stability, job
    and age, 10
    and family networks, 18-19
    and hiring practices of primary firms, 27
    impact of prior instability on, 11, 12, 13
    index of, 9
    and job classification, 29
    and moratorium period, 16
    and previous experience, 28
    probability of, 11
Standard Metropolitan Statistical Area
    (SMSA), census data from, 115, 184n28
Steel industry, technological innovation in, 56
Stephenson, Stanley P., 139
Subeconomy, 144
Suburbanization, of jobs, 110, 111, 112, 118-119, 147
Summer, unemployment during, 77
Supply, labor, 122-126
    changing conditions of, 56
    and quit rates, 136
    in youth market, 33

Supreme Court, on child labor laws, 71
Swift Meat Company, 67

Technological innovation
    and demand for unskilled labor, 56
    firm-specific, 27
    in glass industry, 58-59
    and labor force, 55
    and unskilled labor, 110
    and youth employment, 57
Teenagers. See also Youth
    consequences of unemployment for, 91
    and minimum wage, 82-83
Tenure, and quit rates, 136
Textile industry
    child labor in, 61
    technological innovation in, 55, 57
Thernstrom, Stephen, 87
Title VII race discrimination lawsuits, 139
Toll collectors, 19
"Trainability," and hiring practices, 27, 172n16
Training, on-the-job, 32
    and minimum wage, 84
    in primary firms, 26
    and secondary firms, 24
    subsidized, 159
Transiency rate, among youth, 52
Transportation industry
    black youth employed in, 9
    pre-World War II youth employment in, 63
    and unemployment, 79
    white youth employment in, 8
Troen, Selwyn K., 57
Truancy programs, 60, 177n51
Tyack, David B., 54, 60

Unemployment. See also Youth unemployment
    adult, 87
    adult vs. youth, 75-76
    analysis for determining effect of, 92-96
    annual weeks of, 6, 7
    and behavior of youth, 85-86
    distribution of weeks of, 156-157
    effect of age on, 8
    effect of early, 90, 93-95
    elasticity of, 37
    among high school graduates, 3
    impact on wage rates, 88-92
    and minimum wage, 81
    policy planning for, 157-160
    and quit behavior, 138, 141-142
    regressions for, 37, 76, 128-133
    and residence, 111

Unemployment (continued)
  and schooling, 76-78
  in school vs. out of school, 95
  spells of, 133-138, 156, 185n40
  welfare interpretation of, 18
  and work adjustment, 16-17
Unemployment duration, 128-133
  decomposition of, 134
  estimation techniques for, 128-133
  racial differentials for, 138
  regression analysis of, 132
  and reservation wages, 139
Unemployment insurance, 133
Unemployment rates
  by age, 65
  black, 113
  black vs. white, 147
  and business cycle, 34
  "evening out," 84
  among high school graduates, 5
  in other countries, 151
  racial ratios for, 185n38
  and schooling, 124-126
  for teenagers, 1
  youth, 3
Unionization
  as measure of youth labor demand, 80
  "shock" effect of, 181n15
Union leaders
  on youth employment, 70, 71
  and youth programs, 73
Unions
  apprenticeship programs of, 1
  breaking, 62
Urbanization, and enrollment rates, 124
Urbanization index, 126

Vocational education
  federal support for, 68
  ineffectiveness of, 67, 68
Vocational programs, 28
Vroom, Wayne, 34

Wage gap, 98-105
Wages
  and age, 6, 7
  for black vs. white youth, 98
  impact of unemployment on, 88-92
  increase in, 6
  market-clearing, 81
  minimum, 80-85
  and quits, 136, 142
  racial differentials for, 99-101
  reservation, 139, 140, 146, 186n53
  and youth employment, 78

and youth labor demand, 80
Walk-ins, 24
Wallace, Phyllis, 139
War on Poverty Neighborhood Youth Corp programs, 158
Welch, Finis, 82
White adults
  discouraged worker effect for, 126
  employment-to-population ratio for, 102
  quit rates for, 134
  unemployment rates for, 76, 147-148
White youth
  competing with blacks, 111
  earning equations for, 145
  hourly wages for, 6, 7
  impact of early instability on, 11, 13
  industrial distribution of, 35
  industrial mobility of, 14
  job-seeking techniques of, 143-144
  layoff rates for, 137-138
  and minimum wage, 82
  and occupation desired at age 30, 145
  quit rates for, 137-138
  school enrollment rates for, 105-107
  stability rates for, 10
  and wage elasticity, 118, 119, 120, 123
  unemployment among
    annual weeks of, 6, 7
    distribution of weeks of, 156-157
    high rate for, 75
Wholesale trade
  black youth employed in, 9, 35
  pre-World War II youth employment in, 63
  and unemployment, 79
  white youth employed in, 8, 35
  youth employed in, 6, 36, 78
Williams, Senator, 85
Willis, Paul, 152
Women
  black vs. white, 124
  in competition with black men, 121
  as competition in youth labor force, 111
  employment-to-population ratio for, 102
  in labor market, 5
  and minimum wage, 83
  older, 22
  and racial competition, 119
  unemployment among, 76
  unemployment rates for, 147-148
  and wage elasticities, 123
Worcester
  "More Machinists for Massachusetts" campaign in, 29
  interviews conducted in, 15
Work. *See also* Employment

Index 197

adjustment to, 16
"off the books," 25
problems associated with, 19
"under the table," 25
Workers
  career patterns of, 40
  in primary jobs, 23
  unskilled, 175n20
  youth as marginal, 52
Work histories, 16-17, 40-41, 44-50
Work orientation, black vs. white, 114
Work programs, youth, 69, 77, 158, 159
Work shifts, organized to attract youth, 24
World War I, and wages, 57
World War II, and wages, 57

YMCAs, 51
Youth. *See also* Black youth; White youth
  behavior in labor market, 16-19, 85-86
  changing dependence on, 56
  consequences of unemployment for, 91
  "enclosure" of, 69-74
  groups competing with, 110
  high unemployment rate for, 75
  impact of unemployment on, 89
  industry distribution of, 34, 35, 78
  job-finding techniques of, 31
  pre-World War II employment of, 63
  restrictions on, 73-74
  in secondary jobs, 23-24
  work adjustment of, 16-17
Youth culture, 2
Youth Employment and Demonstration Projects Act, 1
Youth-intensive sectors, and black unemployment, 147
Youth labor market, 2
  behavior of youth in, 16-19
  black males in, 119
  comparisons with adult, 75-76
  competition in, 118, 119, 120, 121
  demand in, 78, 154
  econometric efforts directed toward, 115
  employment model for, 116-122
  estimation techniques for, 125
  impact of business cycle on, 33-37
  intervention of schools in, 67-69
  job classification in, 29-33
  jobs available in, 20-25
  labor force participation in, 124
  marginality of, 77, 96, 150
  minimum wage in, 80-85
  model for, 115 (*see also* Employment model)
  during the period 1920-1941, 62-65
  occupational choice in, 37-43
  primary firms in, 25-29
  racial differentials in, 146-149
  secondary firms in, 24-25
  at turn of century, 52
Youth unemployment
  and age, 87-88
  black, 98 (*see also* Black youth)
  causes of, 1, 75
  characteristics of, 89
  consequences of, 86-96
  high rate of, 75, 96, 153
  and minimum wage, 83
  nature of, 86-96
  racial differentials in, 98-105
Youth workers, interviews with, 15